Michał Kalecki: An Intellectual Biography. Vol. 1

Palgrave Studies in the History of Economic Thought Series

This series publishes contributions by leading scholars, illuminating key events, theories and individuals that have had a lasting impact on the development of modern-day economics. The topics covered include the development of economies, institutions, theories and key individuals.

Titles include:

Jan Toporowski
MICHAŁ KALECKI: AN INTELLECTUAL BIOGRAPHY: Volume 1: Rendezvous in Cambridge 1899–1939

Forthcoming titles include:

Timothy Shenk
MAURICE DOBB: Political Economist

Riccardo Bellofiore, Ewa Karwowski and Jan Toporowski (*editors*)
THE LEGACY OF ROSA LUXEMBURG, OSKAR LANGE AND MICHAŁ KALECKI: Volume 1 of Essays in Honour of Tadeusz Kowalik

Riccardo Bellofiore, Ewa Karwowski and Jan Toporowski (*editors*)
ECONOMIC CRISIS AND POLITICAL ECONOMY: Volume 2 of Essays in Honour of Tadeusz Kowalik

The full list of titles available is on the website:
www.palgrave.com/economics

Palgrave Studies in the History of Economic Thought Series
Series Standing Order ISBN 978 1–137–35018–3
(*outside North America only*)

You can receive future titles in this series as they are published by placing a standing order. Please contact your bookseller or, in case of difficulty, write to us at the address below with your name and address, the title of the series and the ISBN quoted above.

Customer Services Department, Macmillan Distribution Ltd, Houndmills, Basingstoke, Hampshire RG21 6XS, England

---

Michał Kalecki: An Intellectual Biography

Volume I, Rendezvous in Cambridge 1899–1939

Jan Toporowski
School of Oriental and African Studies, University of London

palgrave
macmillan

Softcover reprint of the hardcover 1st edition 2013 978-0-230-21186-5

First published 2013 by
PALGRAVE MACMILLAN

Palgrave Macmillan in the UK is an imprint of Macmillan Publishers Limited, registered in England, company number 785998, of Houndmills, Basingstoke, Hampshire RG21 6XS.

Palgrave Macmillan in the US is a division of St Martin's Press LLC, 175 Fifth Avenue, New York, NY 10010.

Palgrave Macmillan is the global academic imprint of the above companies and has companies and representatives throughout the world.

Palgrave® and Macmillan® are registered trademarks in the United States, the United Kingdom, Europe and other countries

ISBN 978-1-349-30322-9　　ISBN 978-1-137-31539-7 (eBook)
DOI 10.1057/9781137315397

This book is printed on paper suitable for recycling and made from fully managed and sustained forest sources. Logging, pulping and manufacturing processes are expected to conform to the environmental regulations of the country of origin.

A catalogue record for this book is available from the British Library.

A catalog record for this book is available from the Library of Congress.

To Adela Kalecka, whose contributions cannot be adequately recorded in these pages

The same orders of succession, which to one set of men seem quite according to the natural course of things, and such as require no intermediate events to join them, shall to another appear altogether incoherent and disjointed, unless some such events be supposed.

Adam Smith, *The Principles Which Lead and Direct Philosophical Enquiries as Illustrated by the History of Astronomy*

Contents

Preface and Acknowledgements

This volume brings to an initial conclusion a project that commenced nearly a quarter of a century ago. In 1989, in a hotel room in Budapest, where we were attending a conference in honour of Nicholas Kaldor, I was approached by Geoffrey Harcourt and Peter Kriesler to collaborate in a biography of Michał Kalecki, in which I was to be co-author with Peter Kriesler and Bruce McFarlane. We interviewed a number of individuals who had known and worked with Kalecki, including his widow, Adela Kalecka, David Worswick, Brian Tew and Eprime Eshag. Peter Kriesler and I undertook a memorable visit to Warsaw to undertake interviews there. I was then able to discuss further with Peter and Bruce our plans for an audacious coup: to take Kalecki out of the shadow of Keynes and place him firmly in a critique of political economy descended from Karl Marx. However, apart from preliminary surveys of Kalecki's life and work, including my own first jejune efforts, the project foundered upon the central dilemma of any attempt at a biography of Kalecki, a dilemma arising out of the lack of evidence that he left behind of his earlier years and the influences on him. This inclines scholars to provide accounts of Kalecki's theories – a daunting task, since Kalecki himself, despite some difficulties of translation, was a writer of such lapidary clarity that his explanations can rarely be improved upon. Nevertheless, by expanding upon Kalecki's connections with other theorists – principally John Maynard Keynes – writers such as Malcolm Sawyer and the editor of Kalecki's *Collected Writings*, Jerzy Osiatyński, have provided us with outstanding accounts of Kalecki's work.[1]

Their accounts of Kalecki followed what in many respects has become a classic work on Kalecki, George R. Feiwel's *The Intellectual Capital of Michał Kalecki*, where the author's scholarship is darkly flavoured with the disappointments of Kalecki's latter years. The books of Sawyer, Osiatyński and Feiwel came out before Oxford University Press made available to English-language readers the *Collected Works*, which bring together Kalecki's published writings and some of his correspondence in an edition that contains a mass of scholarly notes by their editor Jerzy Osiatyński. However, the English and Polish editions omit some of Kalecki's journalism and papers that Kalecki wrote in Cambridge and Oxford, as well as much of his correspondence, which has languished in private collections and archives that were not available to the editor at the time the edition was prepared. Since the publication of these *Collected Works*, Julio López and Michaël Assous have published a thoughtful book on Kalecki that adds to the literature López's own notes of Kalecki's lectures.[2]

Despite their extensive scholarship and insight into the work of Kalecki and his contemporaries, these books do not amount to an intellectual biography in the sense of providing an account of the origin and evolution of Kalecki's ideas. At best, in the editorial notes by Jerzy Osiatyński, the substance of such an intellectual biography is provided without its structure or analysis. The closest to such a biography may be found in the biographical essay that Tadeusz Kowalik provided for the Kalecki Festschrift.[3] Kowalik had the advantage of his own superb knowledge of twentieth-century political economy, and this makes his essay a key to understanding Kalecki. Nevertheless, as the essay challenges many interpretations of Kalecki, it will be discussed further in the forthcoming second volume of this biography.

The collaboration with Peter and Bruce fizzled out on all these issues, and my own profound ignorance, at the time, of Kalecki's economics of capitalism and post-Keynesian economic theory. Nevertheless, the publication of the Kalecki *Collected Works* provided an opportunity to overcome my own lack of knowledge. In 2002, my academic employers succumbed to financial difficulties, which they vented by releasing research-active staff from employment. Geoff Harcourt encouraged me then to undertake the intellectual biography of Kalecki, and the Leverhulme Trust provided funds for a one-year fellowship to work on this project. Further delays were caused by the need to complete existing projects (notably my book *Theories of Financial Disturbance*) and the unseemly haste with which my employment was terminated. I was fortunate to be able to secure research facilities at the School of Oriental and African Studies at the University of London. The project was further prolonged by the financial crisis that emerged in 2007. This greatly increased demands for me to lecture and write on matters of more contemporary interest than Kalecki, at a time of greatly enhanced administrative responsibilities in the School.

Among the debts incurred in writing this biography are the intellectual ones, principally to Michał Kalecki, whose ideas and ways of working had inspired me for years before that fateful afternoon in Budapest and, since that afternoon, have daunted me in this biographical endeavour. Second to him have been Jerzy Osiatyński, Malcolm Sawyer, George Feiwel, and Julio López and Michaël Assous, who have set high standards of scholarship and challenged me to think through what I can add to their learning and insights.

In addition I have more personal debts of gratitude. First and foremost among them is that to Geoff Harcourt for having initiated my interest in this biography, for encouraging it in the most tactful and helpful way over the decades since 1989 and for his scholarly and always sympathetic comments on various related and unrelated drafts. Among Kalecki's closest collaborators, two in particular deserve special mention. In the first place, his widow, Adela Kalecka, was very kind in responding with great patience to my immature enquiries and drafts. More recently Tadeusz Kowalik gave me the benefit of his immense scholarship and insight into political economy in general and into the ideas of his mentors Oskar Lange and Michał Kalecki. My greatest regret in delivering this volume to the public is that I am unable to reciprocate the kindness and generosity that were shown to me by Adela Kalecka and Tadeusz Kowalik by giving them this tribute to their integrity and loyalty to Michał Kalecki.

At an early stage in my work on this project, Peter Kreisler and Bruce McFarlane set me on my first steps towards a more comprehensive understanding of Kalecki's ideas. At this stage, too, and beyond, Victoria Chick was a crucial influence in directing my studies through Keynes and post-Keynesian economics (her guidance in my research in monetary theory remains second only to that of Kalecki). The biography has also been improved as a result of my conversations with Brian Pollitt, Robert Skidelsky, Julio López, Malcolm Sawyer, Riccardo Bellofiore, Jan Kregel, Joseph Halevi, Paul Sweezy, John Bellamy Foster, Kazimerz Łaski, Eprime Eshag, Brian Tew, Arturo O'Connell and David Worswick.

A very special contribution has been made to this biography by research students with whom I was able to discuss various points of my evolving view of Kalecki. Among those students have been Ewa Karwowski, Nina Rismal, Rob Jump, Hanna Szymborska, Jo Michell and Jago Penrose. Among them, Ewa Karwowski and Hanna Szymborska have distinguished themselves by providing much-needed editorial and research assistance. Prue Kerr, Geoff Harcourt, John King, Robert Dixon and Peter Kriesler subsequently improved various early drafts of these chapters with their comments and suggestions.

The financial support for this research has been largely inadequate. This deficiency, along with administrative burdens at the School of Oriental and African Studies, has greatly prolonged the gestation of this biography. I am therefore all the more grateful to the Leverhulme Trust, whose fellowship in 2003/4 allowed me to do much of the archival research on which this biography is based; to the Faculty of Economics and Politics at the University of Cambridge for giving me an Official Visitorship during my fellowship to facilitate archival research in Cambridge; to the archivist of the Archive Centre at King's College, Cambridge, for assistance in examining the papers of John Maynard Keynes, Joan Robinson, Austin Robinson, Richard Stone and Richard Kahn; to the archivist of Trinity College, Cambridge, for assistance with the papers of Piero Sraffa and Maurice Dobb; to the librarian of the Bodleian Library in Oxford for providing access to the archives of the Oxford Institute of Statistics; to the archivist at the Archive of the Polish Academy of Sciences, where Kalecki's papers are held; and to the librarians of the Main School of Commerce (Szkoła Główna Handlowa) in Warsaw, where Kalecki's published works are deposited. An early draft of my concluding chapter appeared in a volume edited by Philip Arestis, *Microeconomics, Macroeconomics and Economic Policy: Essays in Honour of Malcolm Sawyer*.[4]

The patience and encouragement of Ms. Taiba Batool of Palgrave is gratefully acknowledged. Finally, my most personal thanks are to Anita Prażmowska and Miriam Prażmowska-Toporowska, who have borne with fortitude the attention that I have paid over many years to a man whom they have never met, and yet they have given encouragement and advice without which this biography could never have come to print.

If this book conveys something of the vision and ideas of Michał Kalecki, the achievement is due to the above-mentioned individuals. Its errors remain the sole responsibility of the author.

1
Early Years

Michał Kalecki was born in the Polish manufacturing city of Łódź on the 22 June 1899, to Abram Kalecki, the owner of a wool-spinning mill, and his wife Klara (née Segałła).[1] Łódź at that time was a city of nearly a quarter of a million inhabitants. It had grown rapidly through the nineteenth century from a mere hamlet, with a population of 26,000 in 1860, to the second largest city in the Kingdom of Poland, as Russian Poland was called at the time, and the largest manufacturing centre of the Russian empire. The reason for its rapid growth was its strategic proximity to the main railway line from Berlin to Moscow that passed through the Polish capital, Warsaw. The opening of that railway line in the 1850s enabled the Łódź textile manufacturers to import cotton through the German port of Hamburg. The abolition of tariffs between the Polish Kingdom and the Russian Empire, following the 1830 revolution that ended the Kingdom's autonomy, had already given Polish manufacturers access to the rapidly growing markets of the Russian Empire. The abolition of serfdom in the Polish Kingdom, after the failed national uprising of 1863, 'liberated' thousands of peasants from the land, making the manufacturing centres of the Kingdom a first resort for migrant labour.

The Kalecki family had originally come as just such migrant labour from the village of Kalety, from which they took their name, in the Suwałki province in the north-east of the Kingdom, between German East Prussia and Lithuania. The Kaleckis were Jews, a traditionally urban or small-town population in Poland. Their migration to the west of the Kingdom was not just to find work and business opportunities. The tsarist authorities in the latter half of the nineteenth century followed a policy of resettling the Jewish population of the empire in Ukraine and Poland. The pressure of these migrants (distinguished by their use of the

Russian language) on the limited housing and employment possibilities in eastern Poland caused Yiddish-speaking Jews, settled in Poland for generations, to move further west, many eventually to western Europe and North America.

The Russian Empire was a confessional empire, one whose subjects were registered by religion in the first instance and by home language in the second. A separate registrar of non-Christian faiths registered the births, marriages and deaths of subjects who were not Catholic, Protestant or Orthodox. Birth certificates in the empire, even in independent Poland after 1918, before hospital births were widespread, were formal narratives reporting on community events rather than impersonal records of names and dates:

> The official of the Registry at the town Hall certifies that in the books of the Registry of non-Christian religions there is the following registration of birth No. 818/1899:
>
> It happened in Łódź on the seventeenth/twenty ninth of June [in the one] thousand eight hundred [and] ninety ninth year at 11 a.m. there arrived Abram Kalecki, thirty eight years old merchant, permanent inhabitant of the town of Łódź, accompanied by the vice rabbi Gabriel Segal and synagogical officials Moshek Kaliński thirty two years old and Vigdor Rabinowitz thirty four years old, and presented us a baby boy declaring that he was born in Łódź on the tenth/twenty second of June this year at three a.m. of his wife Shifra, née Segałła twenty six years old. To the boy was given at circumcision the name Michał. Thereafter this document was made and signed by th[os]e concerned...[2]

This official Jewishness was, however, not indicative of any observance or self-identification. With migration came assimilation. The Kalecki family did not practise any religion. Later, in a 1979 conversation with Tadeusz Kowalik and Jerzy Osiatyński, Michał Kalecki's widow, Adela Kalecka, recalled that the only remnant of their religious origins was a very good Friday dinner prepared by their excellent cook.[3] His mother, Klara, had gone further and been christened. This was the only way in which persons of Jewish origin could avoid being classified as Jews for official purposes. Adela, who was perhaps more politically militant than her husband, considered conversion as an act of 'opportunism'. Kalecki never regarded himself as Jewish but, in the 1930s, as anti-Semitism became more common in Poland, would insist on his Jewish 'nationality' in response to anti-Semitic remarks.[4] Kalecki's military service record in 1921 has him as being of 'Jewish faith' and having 'Yiddish' for his mother-tongue. But his linguistic range included then only Polish, Russian and German.[5] At home only Polish was spoken.[6]

In any case, in the bourgeois milieu of Łódź into which Kalecki had been born, national and religious differences were largely left behind in the business of making money. Łódź was a cosmopolitan centre which attracted entrepreneurs from all parts of Europe and which bred them from the representatives of the many nationalities that made up the Russian empire, who flocked to the city in search of work or business opportunities. While many languages were spoken in the city, the lingua franca was Polish, as the official language was Russian. The main industry was textiles, supplying the Russian market, which was growing apace at the turn of the century due to rising wage employment in Russia and the expansion of the Russian railway system that distributed goods from the western, industrialising, part of the empire. On the cost side, the key indicator was the German tariff on cotton, which had to be imported from Egypt and the United States principally through the port of Hamburg. Wages were kept low by the pressure of unemployment following the abolition of serfdom, which released surplus labour from Poland's rural economy. However, from the 1870s onwards, the Russian government had abandoned its previous liberal trade policies and established tariffs on industrial imports. Later these tariffs had to be paid in gold, effectively devaluing the Russian rouble, providing a protected market at home and favourable conditions for the export of Polish textiles.[7]

In this busy industrial centre, Abram Kalecki had prospered but not in any major way. At the time when his business collapsed he had a mere 45 people on his payroll.[8] The majority of the factories in Łódź were little more than workshops employing fewer than a hundred workers. But a process of mergers and takeovers and mechanisation had, by 1900, increased the number of factories which employed more than 500 workers to 24 from just 1 in 1869. By 1900 these large factories, predominantly controlled by German industrialists or descendents of German immigrants,[9] accounted for the bulk of industrial employment in Łódź. Already by 1879 the average-sized textile mill in the city employed 49 workers. By 1900 the average number of employees in such a mill had risen to 164. The largest textile firms, such as the Poznańscy, employed hundreds, even more than a thousand when business was good. In the woollen industry average employment in unincorporated businesses (i.e., businesses not registered as companies with limited liability) was just over 100. Nevertheless, Abram Kalecki made sufficient money from his business to have a house in the centre of Łódź, close to its main thoroughfare Ulica Piotrkowska. Just north of their house was the Jewish ghetto, the area to which Jews who wished to wear traditional clothes were confined. The house was also close to an area of small workshops and businesses, where the Kalecki factory was located. At the centre of that house was his ever-elegant wife, Klara. In that house Michał acquired his taste for living in large rooms.

In her 1979 interview with Tadeusz Kowalik, Adela Kalecka described her mother-in-law as 'a beautiful woman...a woman with fantasy...serious, but flirtatious'.[10] Adela Kalecki did not hide her disapproval of the woman who was to abandon Michał and her husband when Michał was still a young boy. This disapproval even extended to Klara's 'unmaternal' way of dressing. Klara came from eastern Galicia, near Lwów, in Austrian Poland. She was by Adela's account very intelligent and possessed of a flirtatious charm. She was also linguistically gifted: She spoke French, and in later years she gave English lessons to support herself.[11] Even as a young wife and mother, her priority was to cut a dash in society. There were trips to Vienna, where Michał later showed Adela the hotel where he had stayed with his mother and where she had parked him to party in the most lively capital city east of Paris.[12] At other times, Michał served as a fashion accessory for his mother, who took him to shops where she had her dresses made up. As an adult, he brought to his marriage with Adela an unlikely talent as a connoisseur of ladies' clothes.[13] Michał was even taken as a little boy to cabaret bars, where the moneyed elite of Łódź enjoyed themselves. He was spoilt by his parents, who knew that they had a lively and intelligent son. More menial care was left to nursemaids, whom the boy treated cruelly.[14]

By contrast, Kalecki's father was, by Adela's account, a 'very private man',[15] who was able to support his wife's social aspirations and their son. Adela described him as a very handsome man, very elegant, delicate and courteous to ladies. He was also a thinking individual who read widely. His social circle consisted of the educated professional men, many assimilated Jews like himself, with whom he would play bridge, a popular pastime in Polish middle-class circles.[16] Michał was brought up by governesses, who were evidently left in no doubt as to his parents' and his grandfather's (Abram's father also lived in Łódź) admiration of the young boy's precocity. Michał later admitted to his wife that he had 'terrorised' his poor governesses.[17] His earliest reading concerned natural history, with picture books of animals predominating. His earliest ambition was to be a zookeeper.

The childhood idyll was soon to end.

2
In the Crucible of the Revolution

The prosperity of Kalecki's childhood was illusory. Workers and their families had been badly affected by the protectionist trade policies of the government in Moscow and by technological progress that deskilled their work. Poverty and unemployment was endemic in Łódź. In a foretaste of what was to come, strikes and civil disturbances had broken out in 1892, culminating in anti-Semitic attacks on the Jewish population in central Łódź. Business conditions for Abram Kalecki's textile factory deteriorated in the early years of the twentieth century, soon after his son's birth. Demand for Polish products in the Russian empire stagnated. In the empire's Polish territories, the situation was exacerbated in 1903 and 1904 by poor harvests, which drove up food prices. Few in the rural economy benefited from those higher prices because a large proportion of the rural labour force was landless. Out of a total population of 11 million in the Kingdom of Poland in 1905, around 10 per cent were landless labourers and their families.[1] Another significant proportion had only small landholdings.

The result of these agricultural difficulties was an accelerated migration of labour from the villages. In towns and cities, unemployment kept wages stable in money terms but only for those in employment where working hours were not reduced. Even for those who took the same amount of money home, the rise in the price of food meant that real wages were falling. The embers of discontent among the workers were eagerly fanned by trade unions and the various left-wing political parties. The largest of the unions was the Bund, established in 1897. This organised Jewish workers but also had aims going beyond mere regulation of wages and working conditions. It had an explicitly socialist agenda. At the turn of the century Jews constituted only some 15 per cent of the population of the Kingdom of Poland. But in Łódź the proportion was nearly double that, because of migration from the poverty-stricken Jewish townships, the *shtetls* further east.

The left-wing political parties were fractious, vocal and divided among themselves, and frequently within themselves, over tactics, strategy and, above all, 'the national question'. Even before the 1905 revolution, the Polish Socialist Party (PPS) was in the process of splitting along generational and political lines. An 'older' faction, led by Józef Piłsudski, sought the overthrow of Russian domination by means of a Polish national uprising. A 'younger' faction, in which a leading figure was a Łódź teacher, Maria Koszutska, was more inclined to work with other nationalities to promote socialism in Poland. A nationalist agenda was inevitably provocative in the mixed Polish, Russian, German, Christian Orthodox, Catholic, Protestant and Jewish population of Łódź. In 1901 another socialist party, calling itself PPS-'Proletariat' and led by Ludwik Kulczycki, was established in the industrial parts of Warsaw and Łódź.[2] Much more explicitly within a Marxist tradition was the grandly named Social Democracy of the Kingdom of Poland and Lithuania, whose best-known leader was Rosa Luxemburg. SDKPiL regarded the struggle against tsarist autocracy and for a democratic republic for the whole Russian empire as its main priority. However, it was preoccupied with building a disciplined party with a subordinate trade union network.[3] The total membership of these parties was tiny, less than 10,000 in all the Polish territories of the empire in 1903–4. Significantly, they were dwarfed by the Jewish trade union, the Bund, whose membership at that time was 15,000. But parties were given a disproportionate significance by their concentration in the industrial districts of Warsaw and Łódź.[4]

The outbreak of the Russo-Japanese War in February 1904 exacerbated the economic difficulties. Higher taxes, rents and raw material costs were combined with financial restrictions. To transfer their capital abroad, private investors withdrew 30 million marks from banks in Warsaw. Similarly, foreign banks withdrew their reserves from banks in Russia.[5] This affected especially harshly the industrialised part of the Russian empire in the Polish Kingdom, where credit was most widely used. Although the state banks raised their interest rates only by 1 per cent, the rate of interest in private banks rose by 10 per cent. In the summer of 1904, industrial production in the Kingdom fell by around a third.[6] In Łódź there was a widespread feeling that orders for uniforms and equipment were not being placed with factories in Poland but were going to factories in Russia proper. At the same time, the conscription of young men to fight in eastern Russia was deeply unpopular. In the spring of 1904, the PPS started organising in secret groups of volunteers in Łódź and nearby Pabianice to carry out armed attacks on soldiers and policemen. Rising unemployment facilitated the recruitment of demonstrators against the war and against Russian autocracy. The funeral, on May 25, of a child killed by a factory caretaker, was attended by around 300 workers, who marched on the factory to confront the perpetrator of the killing. Cossack soldiers were called in to disperse the mob. Stones were thrown at them, and they replied with rifle fire. Further demonstrations were held on August 10, September 2, September 18 and October 25.[7] The frequency of these demonstrations was due to rising discontent; the heavy-handed response of the tsarist authorities to manifestations of antiwar, nationalist or socialist sentiment evoking further demonstrations to commemorate the victims of increasing repression; and divisions among protest organisers.

Other, similar demonstrations took place in Warsaw and other industrial centres. The game of cat and mouse between the authorities and the left and nationalist opposition took a new and more dangerous turn in November 1904, when the PPS decided that the moment for armed struggle had arrived. A demonstration in Warsaw on November 13 was marked by exchanges of shots between demonstrators and the military police called out to clear them. Six demonstrators were killed, and twenty-seven were injured.[8] In Łódź demonstrations continued, with the PPS urging more armed confrontations with the authorities. On January 5, the SDKPiL called its supporters in the Steinert factory out on strike. Ten days later, a demonstrator was shot dead on Ulica Piotrkowska, the main Łódź thoroughfare, near which the Kaleccy lived. A sinister aspect of the disturbances, perhaps the most lasting, was the rise of anti-Semitism in response to the activities of the Bund and the growing insecurity being felt in all classes of the population.

At the end of the year, Tsar Nicholas II appointed Sergei Witte his chief minister, with the promise of more local political autonomy to head off the discontent widespread throughout the Russian empire. But by then it was too late. Port Arthur fell to the Japanese, a major blow to the prestige and authority of the tsar and his advisers. On January 22, 1905, a large workers demonstration in St. Petersburg marched on the Winter Palace and was met by soldiers who opened fire. Hundreds of demonstrators were killed in the largest massacre of civilians by soldiers in Europe since the Paris Commune. 'Bloody Sunday' galvanised the left in Poland and shook the nationalist opposition with the prospect of social, rather than national, revolution. Increasing calls for a general strike were heard and were widely, even if only briefly, supported. The authorities responded with repressive measures that only reinforced grievances and the resulting unrest. At the beginning of February 1905, Cossack soldiers fired on a crowd in front of the Widzewska Manufaktura factory on the outskirts of Łódź. Eight people were killed, and a large number were injured.[9]

On January 27 the most important Łódź factory owners, Scheibler, Geyer, Grohman and Poznański, sent a telegram to the governor in Piotrków, the capital of the district in which Łódź was situated, requesting police and military protection from striking workers. Diplomatic representatives of the United Kingdom, France, Germany and Belgium added their requests for the tsarist authorities to secure from attack the industrial premises owned by their citizens. However, some smaller factory owners preferred to settle the difficulties with their workers without intervention from the authorities.[10]

The frequency of demonstrations and attacks on the police resulted in the declaration on February 21 of a 'state of reinforced defence' in the Kingdom. A police report complained that factory owners had effectively conceded the right to manage their own factories, under threat of strike action. Blacklists of suspected industrial agitators circulated among employers. The Łódź employers organised a lockout and brought in strike-breakers in an effort to force their workers to concede on their terms. But the lockout was withdrawn when it became apparent that the worsening of industrial relations could lead to a general strike. As a result of the wave of strikes since January, factory owners conceded pay rises of between 10 and 15 per cent, and employees working for 11 hours and longer won a reduction of one hour in their day's work. In many factories, employers conceded recognition rights to trade unions.[11]

However, the issues of local autonomy, the depressed state of the economy and the call-up for military service against Japan remained. In the wake of their industrial success in the first months of 1905, the prestige of the left-wing parties, the PPS and the SDKPiL, stood high and attracted an inflow of younger, enthusiastic members. While more moderate nationalists pressed the case for national autonomy and the rights of Polish and other non-Russian peoples, the radicals in PPS started organising fighting units to spearhead yet another national uprising. In Łódź bombs were thrown at police patrols. The SDKPiL denounced such 'vanguardist' action and prepared instead for a mass general strike. Rosa Luxemburg's leaflet '1 May, the Worker's Day' (*Święto robotnicze 1 Maja*), calling for a general strike, circulated widely in industrial districts.

Towards the end of April, in preparation for demonstrations on May 1, military patrols appeared on the streets in Łódź. Homes of known agitators were raided, and those caught were held in preventive arrest.

Army and police units were placed around the larger factories. May Day demonstrations in Łódź and Warsaw were dispersed, in the latter case with the killing and wounding of demonstrators as soldiers fired into the crowds.

The suppression of May Day demonstrations did not settle the matter. In the second half of May, the population learned with awed fascination of the defeat of the Russian Baltic Fleet at Tsushima. In Łódź the killing of a worker by Cossack soldiers inside the Grohman Grabczyński factory was followed by a large demonstration at his funeral. On May 27 the most important factory owners in the town telegraphed a request for further military assistance from the authorities. Reinforcements arrived on May 31 in the form of three infantry regiments, three hundred-man units of Cossacks and a regiment of dragoons. The town was placed under military rule, as it effectively remained until the outbreak of the First World War.

The response of the workers was to demand extended negotiating rights in factories. Strikes in the largest factories were met with lockouts. A demonstration on June 18 ended with the killing of five demonstrators when soldiers fired at the crowds. Two days later, the funeral of those killed turned into an even bigger demonstration. Many factories were strike-bound, as workers left them to join the funeral procession. The following day, two Jewish workers were to be buried, but their bodies were missing, and word spread that the bodies were being held for secret burial by the police. The gathering for what was to be their funeral ended with gunfire. Six workers were killed and many wounded.[12]

The following day factories were shut for the Catholic feast of Corpus Christi, which many of their workers celebrated by throwing stones at the soldiers patrolling the streets, who fired back, causing further casualties. In the evening barricades appeared on the streets in central Łódź. State-monopoly alcohol shops were attacked and pillaged. Forty-two barricades were erected in the centre of Łódź and in the western part of the city around the Scheibler factory. The Kalecki house was effectively besieged.

The police and army responded with brutal measures to restore control. On the evening of June 24, the tsar signed a ukase (imperial order) placing Łódź and the surrounding district under martial law. Cossack troops were sent in to restore control. The demonstrators responded by leaving their barricades unmanned and hiding snipers in the higher storeys of nearby houses. The barricades were then used to draw the soldiers into streets, where snipers could pick off the soldiers. The soldiers responded with random firing at houses and people on the streets. According to official figures, by the time the street fighting had ended on June 25, 151 civilians had been killed. In accordance with Russian bureaucratic practice, they were classified as 55 Poles, 79 Jews and 17 Germans.[13] Unofficial estimates of casualties put the number of dead at 200, with over a thousand wounded. Outrage at the suppression of the Łódź strikes spread around the Kingdom. Barricades went up in Warsaw. But the unrest there was also ruthlessly put down.

In spite of the state of martial law, a rash of strikes resumed in the summer. On August 19, the Russian government announced that a state Duma (or parliament) would be called, with members chosen by a system of indirect election. The left announced a boycott. In September, the Treaty of Portsmouth brought an end to the Russo-Japanese War, and the government could now concentrate on restoring some kind of normality to the empire. In October a general strike broke out in the Polish Kingdom. Participants in the strike included railway workers, workers in retail businesses and students, as well as the usual industrial suspects. In Łódź on October 27, 10,521 workers were on strike. Three days later, the number had risen to 62,362.[14] For nearly four weeks, the general strike continued, with over 100,000 workers stopping work at 474 factories. The authorities in the city received a delegation of business representatives requesting the extension of martial law and the punishment of factory owners who paid their workers during the strike.[15]

The response of the authorities was to declare a state of war in the whole Kingdom on November 11.[16] This allowed the military authorities in the Kingdom to execute troublemakers without trial, providing they informed the government of their action. This merely added another demand, for the removal of the state of war, to the list of popular grievances. At the request of the Governor-General, George Skalon, the state of war was brought to an end on December 1, after the collapse of the strike. However, December brought a renewed wave of agitation in sympathy with the Moscow Workers' Soviet, which put up barricades in the streets of the empire's capital. In Łódź nearly all factories closed.

Industrial unrest in Łódź continued through 1906, focusing increasingly on economic demands. Elections to the promised Duma raised the industrial temperature, because the electors, who were supposed to vote to elect worker representatives in the Duma, were to be elected in factories employing 50 or more people. This excluded the majority of the workers from the indirect election. While the left boycotted the elections, the Polish nationalist party National Democracy sought a mandate for its policy of cooperation with the tsarist authorities, and its armed militants fought with the militants of the left to try to ensure that the election took place. The National Democracy campaign took place under the protection of the military. In the end, voting took place in a city of demonstrations, armed attacks and shooting down of demonstrators. Elections could take place only in 15 to 20 factories, as opposed to the nearly 500 in the city. In June came news of a pogrom of Jews in Białystok, in eastern Poland, and in September another one in Siedlce. The Catholic press reported claims that the Białystok pogrom had been started by shots being fired on a Catholic procession.[17] Despite the weakening of the workers' position in the factories, trade unions were now legalised as part of the tsarist authorities' attempts to head off further unrest. The textile workers union (*Związek Zawodowy Robotników Przemysłu Włókienniczego*) was especially strong in Łódź. However, the National Democracy organised its own unions, and so too did Catholic activists. A particular target of their activities were industrialists who were deemed non-Polish or non-Catholic, such as Abram Kalecki. The Catholic unions were particularly strong among the largely illiterate female workforce in many textile mills. A Catholic priest in Łódź, Father Skolimowski, started a campaign against Mariavites (a splinter group from the Catholic Church with a following among the poorer sections of the population).[18] Attacks by various political groups continued into the following year, 1907, when a factory owner, Mieczysław Zilbersztejn, was assassinated. Nine of his killers were executed without trial.

In October the first summary executions without trial took place of six left-wing activists. The execution of the first five was followed by strikes throughout the city.[19]

Throughout April 1906, on average 15,000 to 18,000 workers were on strike in Łódź on any one day: on April 1 this average reached 50,000. The workers secured a rise in pay and effectively enforced a nine-hour day themselves. As industrial unrest diminished, clashes increased between armed units of the left-wing parties, the PPS and SDKPiL, and the nationalist National Democracy party, led by Roman Dmowski, who accused the left of undermining the accommodation, favourable to Polish 'national' interests, that he believed he could reach with the tsarist authorities. Armed units of the National Democracy were accused of targeting left-wing militants. At the same time, Józef Piłsudski's Revolutionary Fraction of the PPS, devoted to national insurrection, started attacks on soldiers, police and their informers in Łódź. According to official figures, 37 people were shot dead in the streets of the city in October 1906, and 29 in November 1906.[20] On December 19 an attempt was made on the life of the chief of police in Łódź, Iwan Chrzanowski.[21]

In January 1907 August Fremel, a well-known police informer was assassinated, not far from the Kalecki house.

The number of strikes fell off later in the year, in particular after October, when factory owners staged a lockout of their troublesome workers.[22] This started in April with a lockout in the largest textile mill, the Scheibler factory. This was followed by lockouts in December in the Poznanski, Heinzel and Kunitzer works.[23] The factory owners sought to restore their own right to manage work in their factories, a prerogative that had been taken over by workers councils. The standard tactic was the laying off of all workers and an invitation for them to return to work but under new regulations of work set by the employers. Altogether 24,000 workers were laid off. The largest factory owners and the Łódź Cotton Industry Association (*Związek Fabrykantów Łódzkiego Przemysłu Bawełnianego*) moved to the safety of Berlin, from where they coordinated their action. The unions and the left-wing parties sought money and international support for their resistance. Resistance lasted for 20 weeks, before hunger and desperation broke the workers' resistance.

The Kalecki factory, being one of the smaller ones in the city, might have avoided such extreme action on both sides of the class divide. But it could not avoid the desperate industrial atmosphere and the failing economic situation. In an official document listing industrial losses due to the 1905 uprising in Łódź (*Zestawienie fabryk które na skutek kryzysu zostały zamknięte, skróciły czas pracy lub zmniejszyły liczbe robotników* [A list of factories that had closed down, reduced hours of work or reduced employment as a result of the crisis]),[24] Abram Kalecki's factory is listed as a wool-spinning mill employing 45 workers. Employment was cut back by 15 workers from March 19, 1904 'as a result of lack of orders'. The result of the factory owners' action was to increase unemployment in Łódź to 20,000, and this reduced factory unrest. Łódź remained under military occupation until the outbreak of the First World War – effectively until the occupation by German troops in May 1915.

The political turbulence in Łódź can have reached Kalecki's consciousness only through its impact on his family life. His family could not withstand the pressure of economic depression and political siege, and we have little idea of how fragile may have been the marriage of Abram and Klara. On Adela Kalecka's later account, Klara abandoned the family home when little Michał was only 10. Michał was later to admit that her departure was a relief from the tension generated by the marriage.[25] Unusually, he continued living with his father. In that year Michał started school at Mieczysław Witanowski's Lycée in Łódź. The private school, founded in 1904, taught in Russian, as all schools in the Kingdom were obliged to teach.

Soon after the break-up of the family, a long electoral campaign started to elect (indirectly) members of the Fourth State Duma in 1912. In 1910 in Łódź, the leftist parties united behind a Bundist candidate. His election elicited a furious response from the National Democrats, who started a boycott of the city's Jewish businesses. Although the events of Kalecki's pre-school days occurred before the emergence of his political consciousness, they loomed large as he matured intellectually. The largest civilian uprising in Europe since the Paris Commune had surprised all parties, even the socialist ones that prided themselves on having a unique insight into working-class life. The Polish (and Russian) left did not stop arguing about the significance of the 1905 revolution, even after it had been overshadowed by the First World War and then by the February and October Revolutions in Russia. The Łódź events gave the industrial conflicts of emergent capitalism an unusually political edge, which they were never to lose, even in Kalecki's most technical economic analyses. That political edge to industrial strife appears in articles that a young Łódź teacher and political activist, Maria Koszutska, wrote in 1913.[26]

One of these articles, 'Cartels, trusts and industrial associations', pointed out that employers associations had a long history. Traditionally they had been set up to manage markets and regulate working conditions. However, the 1905 revolution in the Kingdom of Poland had transformed their activities. On the one hand they regularly petitioned the tsarist authorities to obtain their support in recovering control by the employers of their factories. From their base in Berlin, the largest cotton industry employers had successfully conducted a major industrial lockout in Łódź. On the other hand, they had arranged for 'hundreds' of children of striking workers to be transported from Łódź to Warsaw to be temporarily fostered in the capital while their parents were being brought back to work under worse conditions.[27]

A later article by Koszutska described industrial conditions in Łódź after unrest had been crushed and industry had resumed 'normal' working. Many of the factories were operating only a couple of days a week. One estimate put the number of unemployed workers at 20,000, compared with 83,000 actually employed. While other industries were recovering, the textiles industry did not, and the organisation of its employers to manage the market did not increase orders for production. Demand was depressed by poor economic conditions in Russia. Those factories that were operating had huge debts. Banks stood ready to call in those debts, and clients who sought loans were expected to provide as many as 12 guarantors. Credit conditions were further depressed by the precautionary hoarding of gold in the states bordering Turkey, where the Balkan wars had increased the prospects of territorial gain by military means. These difficulties were exacerbated by the wave of anti-Semitism that swept the Kingdom. Attempts to expel Jewish traders from Kiev and Łódź seriously disrupted their banking business; the Kiev merchants owed 30 million roubles in Moscow and 10 million in Łódź.[28]

In 1913 Abram Kalecki shut up his factory and liquidated his business; a 'victim of technical progress', as his son Michał was later to claim,[29] but a victim too of the post-1905 economic depression, in which small businesses perished alongside the jobs of factory workers. Abram Kalecki paid his debts and went to work as a bookkeeper in his brother's freight transport company.

His son's education was broken off by the outbreak of the First World War when schools were shut down. For a while Łódź was not otherwise affected by the hostilities: the main fighting occurred in the South, on the Austrian front, while the German army merely held the border, concentrating their forces on the push through the Netherlands and Belgium and into France. In May 1915 the German army advanced into the Kingdom of Poland. Being close to the border, Łódź was one of the first cities to be occupied. The German military administration of the city was devastating. Cut off from their markets in the Russian empire, the Łódź industrialists now found their industrial equipment being removed by the German military authorities, effectively to prevent competition with German industrialists. Living conditions deteriorated as food, fuel and materials were requisitioned to supply the German war effort. Politics alone were brightened up – by the prospect that the war between the powers which had partitioned Poland would now induce the formation of a new Polish state.

In 1915, the Witanowski Lycée in Łódź reopened, under the direction of its founder's wife, Anna Witanowska, and was renamed the Philological Lycée.[30] Kalecki had already shown a marked aptitude for mathematics and taken private lessons during the interruption in his school career. In 1917 he matriculated from the School with his *matura* – the precious certificate that allows entry into higher education. That year he started his studies at Warsaw Polytechnic, a venerable institution that taught applied sciences and engineering; it was on a par with the older Warsaw University, which taught only humanities, social sciences and mathematics.

Back in Łódź, the withdrawal of German forces and the February Revolution in Moscow encouraged the setting up of a Council of Workers Delegates, in which an alliance of socialist and social democratic parties ran the city. This equivalent of the Russian soviets petered out with the establishment of a Polish government, with local authorities subordinated to the central government in Warsaw.

Two years after starting his studies, Kalecki was drafted into the Polish army, then in the process of extending Poland's boundaries east into the Ukraine. At the time of his draft, he was living with his father at Cegielnialny 61, on the outskirts of Łódź, just off the main road to the neighbouring village of Rzgów. The location in the suburbs of the city reflected the decline in family fortunes from the days when they lived in grander style among the well-to-do industrialists of the city centre. From June 26, 1920, Kalecki served in the VI Signals Battalion stationed in Lwów. On January 30 in the following year, he was given 12 weeks' leave to facilitate his return to his studies. His efforts to return to his studies achieved success on medical grounds in 1921, when he was classified in the lower health category 'D' and was released from further military service with the rank of a non-commissioned officer (*starszy szeregowiec*).

Kalecki seems not have had clear ideas and commitments about his studies. On February 14, 1920, he started studying mathematics at the Philosophy Faculty of Warsaw University. In February of the following year, he broke off his studies there and transferred to the Gdańsk Polytechnic, where after two years he was awarded a study diploma (*półdyplom*) that did not yet qualify him as a graduate but accredited his successful completion of the first two years of his studies. Two years later, in 1925, when he should have been approaching his graduation, Kalecki abandoned his studies. His father had lost his job and had little prospect of finding work. His son returned to Łódź to support them both.

Despite the inconclusiveness of his studies, these were formative years for Kalecki: Between 1917 and 1922 all the armed, unarmed, industrial, social and political conspiracies that had agitated and consumed the Łódź of his childhood reached their climax with the collapse of the Russian empire, the establishment of an independent Poland and the war with the Red Army. Kalecki was too cautious or insufficiently extrovert to throw himself into political activism. But he threw himself with relish into the furious political debates. A fellow student from Gdańsk later recalled him participating enthusiastically in arguments about the Russian Revolution and taking the side of the revolutionaries. Kalecki later told Tadeusz Kowalik that in Gdańsk he had been to a political meeting addressed by Eduard Bernstein, the revisionist German Marxist, and was not impressed by his arguments. Kalecki returned to Łódź with his political education more or less complete. His most pressing concern was finding work and obtaining sufficient income. The work that he managed to find provided him with his education as an economist.

3
Economic Journalism

The Łódź to which Michał Kalecki returned in 1925 was not a buoyant or even a confident city, as it had been in the last years of the nineteenth century. The optimism that followed Polish independence had been quashed by the political instability and ineffectiveness that marked the new democracy. The domestic turmoil in Germany and Russia, which facilitated the establishment and expansion of the new Polish state, also robbed the industrialists in that state of their largest markets. With the economy in depression, the new fiscal and financial arrangements put in place by the Polish government succumbed easily to hyperinflation and growing unemployment. Kalecki joined the ranks of the many thousands of urban underemployed who got by with occasional casual and short-term jobs. He arrived to better prospects than were apparent. By the time of his return to Łódź, the economy was starting to stabilise, albeit at low levels of production and employment, as Lenin's New Economic Policy reopened the Russian market to Polish exports. Without a functioning system of international credit through which payments for trade with the Soviet Union could take place, there was a build-up of gold deposits in the Polish commercial banks in eastern Poland. The prime minister and finance minister of the time, Władysław Grabski, took advantage of this to introduce a new currency which was placed on the gold standard, establishing his lasting reputation as a monetary stabiliser.

The easiest work for a near-university graduate to obtain at this time was tutoring high school students preparing for their matriculation, or *matura*, examinations. The *matura* decided whether a student got into higher education, from which the eventual degree was the key to obtaining a white-collar job in public administration, the professions or the private sector. Well-off parents were prepared to pay for such tutoring in order to secure their fortunes with another reliable income, while the less-well-off hoped to repair their fortunes through getting a child into a good university. Kalecki taught not only mathematics but also literature and even Latin.[1] Through this teaching he was to meet his future wife.

Kalecki was not diffident in coming forward with initiatives that might secure his future. Using the knowledge that he had already gleaned about his father's business, he persuaded a local businessman to finance a business periodical devoted to the textile industry, *Konjunktura Włókiennicza* (Textile Markets).[2] A first issue came out, with articles written by Kalecki, but it failed to secure a sufficient market or financing to continue.[3] However, Kalecki had got to know a local businessman, Lauterbach, who was impressed by Kalecki's knowledge of business and financial matters and liked discussing them with him. Adela Kalecka recalled a discussion that the two men had during a visit by Edward Hilton Young, an English lawyer, financial journalist and liberal politician friend of John Maynard Keynes, to advise the Polish government on measures to stabilise the currency. Lauterbach told Kalecki that the latter's advice would have been less expensive.[4]

Lauterbach owned a credit investigation agency. For a fee, the agency would advise its customers on the creditworthiness of businesses with which a customer planned to trade. This was an important function at a time of financial and commercial instability, especially so in a city like Łódź, where the principal industrial activity of textiles was fragmented into many companies specialising in buying and selling raw and semi-finished products and eventually working up raw materials, through spinning, weaving or knitting, into finished clothing or household products; in addition, there were the usual retail and wholesale businesses of urban commercial centres. Payments between businesses (and even between retailers and wealthy individuals) were made usually by means of post-dated cheques or bills, a form of informal credit. Businesses had to know whether their customers had the funds in their bank account to pay out on bills coming due. This was a question not just of the amount of credit a business had at its disposal but also of how many bills it had outstanding. Lauterbach employed Kalecki for a brief while in making these investigations. From this very practical experience arose Kalecki's later preoccupation with firms' internal finance in his later theories of the firm and investment.

Teaching and credit investigation were the better casual employment that Kalecki was able to get. At one time he was reduced to addressing envelopes. His father was on a pension, but without a woman in the house, in those times of hard gender distinctions, they still had to eat their dinners in restaurants.[5] They moved back from their flat on the outskirts of Łódź to rooms near the railway station at Kilińskiego 88.[6] Sometime in 1927, Kalecki moved to Warsaw, where he secured casual employment designing concrete structures for civil construction projects. He obtained some of this work from the largest Polish construction firm at the time, *Polskie Towarzystwo Budowlane* (the Polish Construction Association). He shared this work with a friend, who later settled in the United States under the name of Norman Bay. Kalecki had met Bay when they were still at school in Łódź; they had shared lodgings when they were both students at the Gdańsk Polytechnic. Kalecki designed a large aircraft hangar for the company. He collaborated with the engineer Stefan Brył in the designs for the roof of the Army Museum in Warsaw (Kalecki provided the calculations) and worked on a machine factory in Toruń. Kalecki continued to work with the company up to the end of 1929.[7]

When not looking for work, Kalecki devoted himself to writing. His work, as presented by his biographers and the editors of his *Collected Works*, places at the forefront his contributions to economic theory and adds, almost as an afterthought, his journalism. While this may be appropriate for an academic reader, who wishes to start with the theories for which their author is most renowned and who is least likely to be interested in Kalecki's journalism, this is not how Kalecki's ideas developed. With Kalecki, his journalism came first, and his theoretical writings grew out of it. This chronological order has to be respected, if only because in his theoretical writings Kalecki, throughout his publishing life, tended to repeat his theories, with important modifications, rather than change the subject matter of his analysis with each new work he undertook. The result is that no single work is definitive, nor, because of the successive modifications that differentiates each work, can his collected writings be regarded as definitive, since each one contains some important revision of an earlier view. If Kalecki's ideas are to be understood in their entirety, the starting point has to be his journalism, which was informed not only by his own work experience and business researches but by his interest in politics, which was broadening out into reading in economic theory.

He had read Mikhail Tugan-Baranovsky's textbook *Osnovy politicheskoy ekonomii* (Principles of Political Economy) while still a student, around the same time as he read Lenin's famous pamphlet *Imperialism The Highest Stage of Capitalism*. Tugan-Baranovsky (1865–1919) was the author of a famous study of crises in the English economy that – despite its influence on twentieth-century business cycle theory, most notably the work of Keynes – has never been translated into English.[8] Kalecki was little influenced by the Russian's work on crises. But he did take note of Tugan-Baranovsky's interpretation of Marx's scheme of capitalist reproduction, showing how the investment and consumption goods sectors must be balanced in a capitalist economy. Tugan-Baranovsky turned this into a system in which investment drives capitalist development and the profits that capitalists earn, instead of investment being merely an outlet for capitalists' profits. For a capitalist economy to be in equilibrium, the surplus generated in the consumption goods sector must equal capitalist consumption plus the consumption of workers in the investment goods sector. From this, Tugan-Baranovsky concluded that, for capitalists to realise their profits, they would invest enough to absorb whatever they did not consume from the surplus of the consumption goods sector.

While writing his first studies of business conditions, Kalecki read some of the writings of John Hobson (1858–1940), the English liberal political economist.[9] Hobson was widely translated and read in Europe during the 1920s. This was not just on account of the recommendation that Lenin gave in his pamphlet to Hobson's most famous book on imperialism, *Imperialism A Study*. Hobson's exposés of modern capitalism, integrated by an international financial system unsettled by oversaving due to excessive inequalities of income, had a wide resonance among European peoples tormented by unemployment, inflation and financial and economic instability. In particular, Hobson identified business trusts and cartels as ways in which profits were concentrated in monopolies.[10] The study of such cartels was to be Kalecki's entrée into economics.

During this time, Kalecki struck up an acquaintance with the Polish economist and university professor Henryk Tennenbaum.[11] At a time when academics were expected to devote themselves to teaching and leisurely acculturation, Tennenbaum distinguished himself by his prolific writing and engagement in politics, supporting socialist publications, as well as contributing to discussions of economic stabilisation policy. Among the periodicals in which Kalecki published his first articles, Tennenbaum was to appear frequently as either a contributor or a member of the editorial board. He also had important political connections. Later, at a breakfast in his Warsaw flat, immediately after the German invasion, the basic outlines of the wartime Polish government in exile were agreed.

Kalecki's first published article came out in 1927. Entitled 'American-Russian Economic *Rapprochement* and Poland' (*Zbliżenie gospodarcze amerykańsko-rosyjskie a Polska*), it appeared in the business fortnightly

Przegląd Gospodarczy. This was published by the Polish Association of Industry, Mining, Trade, Industry and Finance[12] and was edited, until 1928, by Henryk Tennenbaum.[13] Appearing at the end of 1927, it noted major orders for steel products from Pittsburgh (in the USA), commercial trade credits agreed with the Soviet government and concessions for foreign direct investment in oil and metals-extractive industries in the Soviet Union. Poland was benefiting indirectly through increased orders for Polish exports. But a Łódź firm, N. Eitingen & Co., was affiliated with a New York company, Eitingen Child & Co., which imported furs from Russia and exported cotton products, in particular darning thread, produced by its Łódź affiliate. Multinational companies and international cartels already featured large in Poland's export trade.

This article was followed in the first 1928 issue of the same journal by an article entitled 'The economic consequences of British-Soviet dispute'.[14] The British-Soviet dispute in question had broken out following a police search of the Soviet trade mission in London, followed by the breaking off, by the British government, of diplomatic relations with the Soviet Union. Behind this, according to Kalecki, was the 'agitation' of Henry Deterding, the chairman of Royal Dutch/Shell which, along with the Anglo-Persian Oil Company (now British Petroleum), was trying to keep Soviet oil and oil products out of the market. A key factor was the ability of British companies to offer trade credits, and these were ensuring the continuation of trade. (Trade with other countries, including the USA and Germany, was being made for cash.) The United States was not participating in the dispute. Standard Oil of New York was selling Soviet oil, and Soviet supplies of platinum, whose market was largely supplied from Soviet sources, were being redirected from the London metals exchange to the market in New York.

In a later article (1932) in a more political journal, *Przegląd Socjalistyczny* (Socialist Review), Kalecki, writing under the pseudonym Henryk Braun, commented with relish, in 'The Fall of Deterding', on the 'financier of intervention and master of corruption'. He had 'squandered' the capital of Royal Dutch/Shell (which with its associated companies controlled 16% of world petroleum supplies) in his attempt 'to ruin the Soviet Union for the benefit of humanity and civilisation'. This included financing Hitler, who had offered to 'conquer the Soviet Union in the service of international capitalism'. With the British abandonment of the gold standard in 1931, Deterding had decided that a new era of bimetallism was about to open up, and he now directed even more capital to buying silver. However, silver prices fell, resulting in a major fall in the share price of Royal Dutch/ Shell. Kalecki reported that the company was now in negotiations with

Standard Oil and Deterding's erstwhile enemy, the Soviet Neftsyndicate, for a new division of the world petroleum market.[15]

Kalecki was drawn, or perhaps encouraged, to write about the thrusting 'entrepreneurs' of his time, in particular those who dominated the international capital market that held sway over the indebted governments and businesses of Europe. Next to Deterding was the much less flamboyant (but because of that much more effective) Ivar Kreuger. Kreuger specialised in buying up and cancelling the bonds of indebted governments in exchange for monopolies on the sale of matches. These were financed by share issues by his companies in the New York market. With the collapse of that market in 1929, Kreuger had increasing difficulty in providing the security that his bank creditors demanded and, on 12 March 1932 he shot himself through the heart in his Paris apartment.

In a note on Kreuger for the *Przegląd Socjalistyczny*, Kalecki noted the financier's heroic role in 'facilitating the international circulation of capital, which was always lagging behind the development needs of the post-war capitalist world.' However, he also pointed out Krueger's business strategy of monopolising the world match market, to the point where only the United States, France and the Soviet Union had markets beyond his control. While matches may seem an odd vehicle for the extraction of monopoly profits, Kalecki noted that match markets were relatively immune to business cycles. Kreuger's business empire was compromised, in Kalecki's view, by a loan of US$125 million, which he was obliged to give to the German Treasury at the end of 1929 in order to secure a ban on imports of matches from the Soviet Union into Germany. Nevertheless, Kalecki was clear about Kreuger's role in the evolution of capitalism: 'The functioning of capitalism depends not on the nature of individual foremen who control its mechanisms, but on the structure of those mechanisms.'[16]

Kalecki's view contrasted with that in the business press generally and in the financial markets, where it was believed that Kreuger was the victim of market pressures beyond his control. The London *Economist* reported the financier's death as 'the veritably tragic wreck of a career which in its sphere was unsurpassed by that of any individual in living memory...a force for good' crushed by the bleak circumstances of his time.[17] Even Keynes, who was willing to concede that the operators on the New York Stock Exchange possessed 'a gangster mentality',[18] saw in Kreuger a 'tragic' victim of liquidity preference: '...perhaps the greatest constructive business intelligence of his age, a man whose far-flung activities have been in the widest sense in the public interest, who had conceived it his mission in the chaos of the post-war world to furnish a channel between countries where resources were in surplus and those where they were desperately required, one who built on solid foundations...crushed between the ice-bergs of a frozen world which no individual man could thaw and restore to the warmth of normal life. The spectacle of capitalists, striving to become liquid as it is politely called, that is to say pushing their friends and colleagues into the chilly stream, to be pushed in there by some more cautious fellow from behind, is not an edifying sight.'[19] Keynes had no doubt who was to blame: 'There is nothing in the world like the cruel and cold-blooded beastliness of the American bankers.'[20]

His first articles showed Kalecki to be familiar with the business literature of London (the *Financial News, The Economist*), Berlin (*Berliner Tageblatt*), the French *Informations Financières* and Soviet sources. The articles were followed by further commentaries noting the continuing decline of British-Soviet trade. But the bulk of Kalecki's economic journalism in 1928 was concerned with conditions in particular markets and the progress of various international raw materials cartels. Typical of his market studies were a series of notes on the metals markets.[21] In these notes Kalecki discussed the growing concentration of metals extraction and processing in the main ore-exporting and -smelting centres. In particular, they note the growing influence in those markets of the Aluminium Company of America. Kalecki's studies of international cartels covered an even wider range of markets. In addition to metals, they included the rubber, linoleum, matches, coal, cotton and oil markets.

In 1929 Kalecki found additional outlets for his journalism in *Przegląd Polityczny* (The Political Review), a business weekly, and in *Przemysł i Handel* (Industry and Trade). This last was a weekly that had been established in 1920 by the Polish government in order to promote Polish industry and commerce.[22] Kalecki's articles here concerned the French petroleum policy and the international steel cartel. His contributions to this magazine included, in addition, two notable articles that indicated the extent to which his understanding of economic relations had gone beyond business intrigues to control markets. His article on the control of German industry by foreign capital[23] showed his remarkable insight into corporate finance. The bulk of the article is a translation of a report that appeared in the *Berliner Tageblatt* of a discussion on the dangers of *Überfremdung* (foreign penetration). However, Kalecki noted that behind the issue lay the difficulty in obtaining loans because of 'tightness' in global money markets (interest rates were going up in the prelude to the 1929 Crash). The high interest rates would reduce the retained net profit of German business. The issue of shares to foreign firms then allowed capital to be raised without greater indebtedness. The result was a growing penetration of German industry by American capital. However, Kalecki's conclusion was an intriguing indicator of how his ideas had matured beyond mere reportage. He pointed out that Germany's steel industry was heavily cartelised. Its monopoly profits therefore allowed German steel companies to finance themselves more with debts. In his view the *Überfremdung* campaign had a more political significance as an appeal to patriotic elements in the German government to ease its restrictions on increases in iron prices.

Przemysł i Handel also published one of Kalecki's earliest and most important papers: *W sprawie aktywizacji bilansu handlowego.*[24] Here Kalecki showed his unusual ability to illuminate how individual decisions and government policy affect the evolution of the economy as a whole, not by mere aggregation of economic units, but through their impact upon the circular flow of income. This last Kalecki summarised as a simple equation between output and expenditure. From this he derived the relation that Investment (in industrial capacity) minus Saving in the economy is equal to Exports minus Imports, plus Incomes received from abroad less Incomes paid abroad. Kalecki argued that the trade balance could be improved by either domestic production of previously imported goods or a reduction in investment, since this last usually requires the import of plant, machinery and raw materials and generates additional incomes spent on imported goods or goods that would otherwise be exported.

The fragmentary national income analysis in this paper suggests, according to the editor of Kalecki's *Collected Works*, that Kalecki at this time believed that saving determines investment. Kalecki is supposed to have changed his view by 1933.[25] However, Joan Robinson appears to have obtained a similar impression from Kalecki's work in the 1950s. In this case the ambiguity arises because the terminology used is archaic. We would nowadays view the current account balance as equal to the private sector's net acquisition of monetary and financial assets (Saving minus Investment) *plus* the government's financial surplus (Revenue minus Expenditure). This version simply represents what is called the flow of funds identity between the balances of income and saving in the private sector, the public sector and the overseas sector. Placing Kalecki's text in this context, it becomes apparent that expenditure decisions determine incomes and hence investment and import and export decisions determine the trade balance and saving rather than being determined by it.

Kalecki's economic journalism up to the eve of the 1929 Crash had given him a systematic understanding of the key decisions that drove business activity, financial balances in the economy and its unstable progress. The Crash and its catastrophic consequences, as well as his professional engagement as an economist, inspired him to present that understanding in a coherent form.

4
To Warsaw

The economic turmoil that characterised independent Poland, indeed the whole of Europe, in the 1920s was exacerbated by the 1929 Crash. The subsequent depression in the United States devastated those economies that had relied on export-led growth, underpinned by the apparent prosperity of the US economy in the first decade after the First World War, or on foreign direct investment to sustain business investment. Among the most exposed countries in Europe was Poland. Kalecki was very aware of the connection between business conditions in particular countries and international capital flows in conditions of crisis. The link between them was, not through the struggle for markets and financing 'enterprise' or trade, but through deflation and forced indebtedness.

Kalecki's understanding is very apparent in his article 'The World Financial Crisis' (*Światowy kryzys finansowy*), published in the first issue of *Przegląd Socjalistyczny*.[1] There were essentially three mechanisms suppressing international capital flows. The first occurred in the commodity-exporting countries of South America and Australia. The fall in commodity prices caused difficulties in repayments of debt principal and interest. This discouraged new capital inflows into those countries and encouraged capital outflows, forcing their governments to suspend gold convertibility. The second mechanism came into operation following the fall in commodity prices, with the decline in the prices of finished goods. This price fall marked the spread of the crisis through Europe and North America. To maintain payments on their outstanding foreign loans, firms were forced to borrow more. But the fall in prices of their output was undermining the collateral that businesses could put up against further borrowing. Furthermore, borrowing in order to buy gold and foreign currency to repay foreign debts drains the foreign reserves of local banks. The only way to check the reserve outflow was to deflate the economy, reducing investment and forcing the running down of stocks. This reduced imports until the foreign currency drain was eliminated and a trade surplus was generated, allowing credit to expand again.

Kalecki gave Germany as an extreme example of this process. Because of an excessive reliance on short-term foreign borrowing and deposit withdrawals, German banks were forced to keep very large cash reserves. Despite (or perhaps because of) an agreement with a consortium of foreign banks under which they undertook to keep their deposits in German banks, credit in other economies did not expand. Exports, hampered by tariffs, reduced activity in foreign markets. The case of Britain was different, because the country was not so much a debtor country as an intermediary in the international capital market. The suspension of gold convertibility followed by the devaluation of sterling was, like deflation in Germany, effectively restricting the domestic market. The depreciation of sterling set off a third mechanism: the remaining international banks (Kalecki still referred to 'banks of issue') operating in the gold market moved from gold and foreign exchange standards to a preference for holding only gold reserves. This caused an outflow of gold from the USA that ceased only when the French government agreed not to withdraw further deposits. But this was in return for a rise in US interest rates and conservative US lending policies.

Kalecki's conclusion was striking. Initial attempts by Montague Norman (the governor of the Bank of England) and US President Herbert Hoover to alleviate the problem of international debt were followed by the collapse of German banks in July 1931, inducing German government intervention, including nationalisation of banks, to support them. The failure of international coordination signalled, according to Kalecki, a shift from international economic diplomacy to 'bickering imperialisms'. In Germany Hitler was easily able to persuade his supporters that the crisis was the work of foreigners. By remaining on the gold standard, the French government was supporting its finance capitalists, whose assets gained relative to assets held in the financial centres of depreciating currencies. In Britain, by contrast, 'the industrialist has triumphed over the banker', and industry now dreams of 'conquering the markets of the British empire and the Far East through a depreciated currency. They will awake from those dreams when retail prices start to rise again and the struggle for wage increases rekindles.' (In fact, retail prices in Britain fell by some 10 per cent up to 1935 and did not significantly rise again until the outbreak of the Second World War.)

Despite the deepening economic crisis in Poland and the apocalyptic tone of his assessment of deflationary trends throughout the capitalist world, by the time Kalecki wrote that bleak analysis he was well settled in Warsaw and enjoying some professional stability. He stayed with a distant cousin, Herman Kalecki. A more familiar companion was Adela Szternfeld. They had met in 1926, when Kalecki had given tuition to her sister Franciszka in Łódź, after his return from his studies in Gdańsk. In her later years, Adela recalled that she would open the door to her sister's tutor. Once or twice she had to tell him that her sister was out, and Kalecki would go away. One day she told him that her sister was out, but that he could come in anyway.

The Szternfeld family were merchants who had originally lived in Sieradz, a rather more historic and picturesque town near Łódź, where Adela had been born on October 14, 1903. The family had moved to Łódź, where Adela had finished her schooling. From 1921 to 1926 she studied biology at the Jagiellonian University in Kraków. When Kalecki moved to Warsaw, they corresponded 'rather reticently', as Adela was later to recall.[2] He visited her in Łódź and even met up with her once, when she went on holiday in the mountains near Zakopane. On her return to Łódź she had to find work; she eventually obtained a job translating German sales literature for imported machinery.

Early in 1929, Adela received a letter from Kalecki to say that he had found a job for her in a Warsaw school, teaching geography, Adela's minor subject in her studies. Adela was happy to move to Warsaw. Soon after, her younger sister fell ill. Adela decided to return to Łódź in order to help her parents. When she told Kalecki of her decision, he was deeply upset. He proposed marriage and then found a rabbi to marry them in a small ceremony on June 18, 1930. Both Adela and her husband detested religion: religion was what kept Jews in ghettos and divided Jews, Catholics and followers of other religions who all nevertheless were part of the society in which they lived and worked. However, independent Poland had retained from the Russian empire the system of separate registries for different religions: There was no possibility of a civil wedding.[3] The marriage took place in working hours, and Kalecki was reluctant to ask anyone to leave work to act as witness at the ceremony. So the brother of Blanka Winawer, a recent graduate and still unemployed, witnessed the marriage.[4]

Adela Kalecka was to be her husband's lifelong companion and confidante. Although she was not an economist, he told her of his plans and the fears and insecurities that arose from the professional insecurity that plagued him virtually throughout his working life. Her accounts and notes are a record of his thoughts on his situation. She was also close to him politically. Her sister was in the Polish Communist Party, but Adela, like Kalecki, avoided party politics. This was prudent. The Polish Communist Party (*Komunistyczna Partia Polski*) had been formed at the end of 1918 by a union of the SDKPiL (Social Democracy of the Kingdom of Poland and Lithuania) and the PPS-Lewica (the Left Polish Socialist Party). The party had lost much of the limited support that it had among Polish people by siding with the Red Army in the Polish-Soviet war of 1921. Along with the mainstream Polish Socialist Party, the Polish Communists had welcomed the coup by Marshal Józef Piłsudski in May 1926 against a parliamentary democracy which was on the verge of handing over government to the nationalist party, the National Democracy (*Narodowa Demokracja*). The left was discredited and divided as Piłsudski became more authoritarian but also incorporated in his regime particular individuals with socialist sympathies, such as Eugeniusz Kwiatkowski, whose interest in Polish industrialisation was to benefit Kalecki.

Kwiatkowski, a chemical engineer, was an energetic organiser who was responsible for the construction of a large port at the coastal fishing village of Gdynia, a post-independence project to give the new Polish state its own outlet to the Baltic Sea (the traditional Polish outlet had been Gdańsk, which the Versailles settlement had established as a free city under League of Nations supervision). After the 1926 coup, Kwiatkowski was chosen by Piłsudski to be his minister of Trade and Industry. The finance minister in the last pre-coup government, the economist and National Democrat politician Władysław Grabski, had implemented a monetary reform that stabilised the currency and brought down inflation, but it left mass unemployment and a weak business sector. The majority of Polish economists blamed Poland's economic difficulties on the rise of monopolies and cartels. These made less flexible the price mechanism that, they believed, could, if allowed to work, bring the economy to a full employment equilibrium. Most economists believed that economic recovery could be brought about only by making Polish industry 'more competitive' – that is, forcing down wages and prices, or creating economic deflation. Kwiatkowski too was a deflationist. But he also believed that industry needed to be assisted and even organised by the state. In this respect he was close to Henryk Tennenbaum. His Ministry of Trade and Industry therefore engaged in a campaign against price cartels and monopolies, as well as planning industrial development culminating, later, in a Central Industrial Zone embodying state and private sector industrial cooperation. However, this cooperation required the support of Lewiatan, the Polish Association of Industry, Mining, Trade, and Finance, which had published Kalecki's first articles in its fortnightly *Przegląd Gospodarczy*. It also fitted uneasily with the campaign against price fixing. The number of registered cartels increased sharply: on 1 January 1926 there were 53 registered domestic cartels, and 8 international cartels in which Polish companies participated. Four years later, the numbers had increased to 133 domestic cartels and 48 international ones.[5]

Behind the inconsistencies in Kwiatkowski's policies were also changes in the social and political strata on which the government relied for its support. Piłsudski had taken power in May 1926 with the backing of the left, ostensibly to block the formation of a right-wing government. However, in 1928 a shift in political alliances became apparent. Piłsudski started to court wealthy industrialists and landowners. Fiscal policy shifted taxation from profits and land towards rural and urban household income.

In the middle of 1929, Kalecki's first articles appeared in the weekly magazine of the Ministry of Trade and Industry, *Przemysł i Handel* (Trade and Industry). The articles were on the European coal crisis and French petroleum policy.[6] At around the same time as Kalecki's article on the European coal crisis appeared – the coal crisis being a sharp fall in coal prices in world markets – Kalecki published a similar article, 'International Coal Competition', in a journal which had not previously carried his work, *Przegląd Polityczny* (Political Review). Despite its name, the journal was a 'periodical devoted to foreign policy', although publishing special issues on the coal and oil industries that were crucial for Poland's foreign trade. On its editorial board was the indefatigable Henryk Tennenbaum.

In his articles on the coal market Kalecki made clear that the cause of falling coal prices was, not oversupply in the market, but rather a longer-term problem of changes in technology, in particular the increased use of oil in order to generate energy. Tactfully he considered the possibility that an international coal agreement might stabilise coal prices before concluding that such a stabilisation would lead to a decline in international trade in coal as industrial coal-producing countries switched away from imported to domestically produced coal.[7]

In 1928 Kwiatkowski set up the Institute for the Study of Business Cycles and Prices (*Instytut Badań Konjunktur Gospodarczych i Cen* – IBKGiC). As indicated in Chapter 3, note 2, the Polish word *koniunktura* (in pre-war Poland it was still written in the German way: *konjunktura*) has no proper equivalent in the English language, since it suggests a temporary situation in the markets rather than the cyclical movements that are implied by the term usually used in English translation, 'business cycles'.[8] He chose as the institute's director a relatively young academic economist, Edward Lipiński, who was sent off to Harvard for a couple of months to see how Harvard Economic Society managed its business information and analysis. Lipiński was to play a key role as expert witness for the Ministry of Trade and Industry in a court case that led to the dissolution of the cement cartel.[9] A brief account is given in English of the case, in the context of the overall anticartel policy of Kwiatkowski, by a Polish banker, Roman Górecki. Inadvertently, since he was trying to show Polish economic policy at its best, Górecki also revealed the consequences of deflation on indebted farmers, the most numerous victims of the deflation, whose falling incomes increased the real value of their debts.[10] Indeed, the domestic justification for deflation was to provide relief for those indebted farmers by reducing the prices of industrial goods.

The legal standing and the subject of the institute's researches was made clear in a statement by Lipiński that led the first issue of its monthly journal, *Konjunktura Gospodarcza*:

> On 21 February this year, there appeared in the Official Gazette a decree creating the Institute for the Study of Business Cycles and Prices in the office of the Minister of Trade and Industry. The present issue is the first publication of the Institute on the subject of business cycles...In this way interested parties may obtain sufficiently early the information required to develop a view on the influences affecting the changing economic situation.[11]

In an earlier article, Lipiński had written, 'In the Polish language the study of the business cycle has two meanings: first the study of the actual possibilities of selling goods of some branch of industry at home or abroad (sale conditions in export markets); second the study of the economy as a whole in order to determine, after eliminating seasonal changes, in what stage of the economic cycle – stagnation, upswing, boom or crisis the economy is in at any given time.'[12]

In his manifesto for the institute Lipiński went on to declare that *Konjunktura Gospodarcza* would offer its Polish readers the kind of service provided by the Harvard Economic Society's *Quarterly Review of Economics and Statistics*, the monthly *London and Cambridge Economic Service*, which Keynes had helped to start in 1923 and to which he contributed up to 1930,[13] and the biennial *Voprosy Konjunktury* and monthly

Biuletień Konjuńkturnago Instituta Moskva, published in Moscow. All of these publications aimed at providing an information service that used statistics of production, trade and stocks to indicate likely movements in market prices and turnover. Although the post-war hyperinflation in Poland (and Europe generally) had abated by 1926, the war and the peace settlement of Versailles had left a legacy in Europe of debt and trade imbalances. The resulting volatility in commodity markets and manufacturing was exacerbated by the return to the gold standard in the mid-1920s (Britain in 1925, Poland in 1926). These periodicals aspired to provide a 'barometer' of business conditions.[14]

Shortly after its establishment and only weeks after the 1929 Crash, Kalecki was offered his first serious employment as an economist. From 1 December 1929 he was employed by the institute as a consultant on cartels.

5
At the Institute

Kwiatkowski's choice of Lipiński to head his institute was an inspired one. Lipiński was as energetic in economic research and theory as his patron was in industrial construction. Edward Lipiński was born in 1888 into the family of a sweet manufacturer. Orphaned at the age of 9, he had received a good education, gravitating in his later schooldays to the PPS-Lewica. Tadeusz Kowalik reports that, during the 1905–7 revolution that had so dramatically affected Kalecki's family life, Lipiński found in a Warsaw bookshop the first Polish translation of volume I of Marx's *Capital*. Unable to get beyond the first chapter, he decided to study economics, first in Leipzig, where he fell under the influence of the French anarcho-syndicalist thinker Georges Sorel, and then in Zurich. He returned to Warsaw in 1913, where he found employment in the exclusive Bank Handlowy w Warszawie.[1] However, the job lacked intellectual stimulation. In the happy phrase of Tadeusz Kowalik, 'fatigued and exhausted by incessant calculations' Lipiński resigned to take up a job as a history teacher in a secondary school.[2]

Lipiński's political activities with PPS and with a small group in Warsaw called *Plenum* gave him scope to develop his economic ideas. However, the intellectual environment among Polish economists teaching at universities was conservative and derivative. This was partly to do with Poland's distance from the main political capitals, Berlin, Moscow, Vienna and London, where arguments on political economy and method were concentrated. Partly it was also due to the neglect of Polish universities under the rule of Germany, Russia and Austria. A social factor breeding conservatism was the German system of academic hierarchy that had been established in Polish universities; it required the acquisition of successive degrees – *magister*, doctor, and a *habilitacja* – before an academic could teach and research independently. The years spent in intellectual and often personal servitude to an established professor were usually enough to purge any troublesome originality from the mind of an academic. In the medieval university in Kraków, the Jagiellonian University, established in 1364, social etiquette made it difficult for anyone who was not of gentry origin to acquire professorial status. One of the few ways for an ambitious scholar of more humble origin, say the son of a wealthy manufacturer (as Oskar Lange was), to do this was to marry his professor's daughter and in this way acquire gentry status. In addition the *numerus clausus* quotas on Jews ensured that Jewish students had to be much cleverer than their Gentile fellow students to get into university but then had even fewer possibilities of advancement. In this way, as Poland achieved its independence in 1918, a caste-like professoriate protected economics faculties in Polish universities from intellectual controversies that lacked pedigree or at least ten years of research, preferably abroad. Lively, educated minds gravitated to discussion groups, such as *Plenum*, and the movement for free universities that appeared in the main population centres.

The leading university departments of economics in independent Poland were at the universities of Poznań and Kraków and, from its incorporation in 1924 as an autonomous university, the School of Commerce in Warsaw (*Szkoła Główna Handlowa*, or SGH). Under its leading professor, Edward Taylor (despite the name, a thoroughly Polish economist), Poznań propagated the economics of the Lausanne School – the mathematical and neoclassical general equilibrium theories associated with the Lausanne economists Léon Walras and Vilfredo Pareto. In Kraków the leading professor Adam Krzyżanowski promoted the liberal market economics of English classical political economy. At SGH the mathematical economist Władysław Zawadzki, who also held a chair at the University of Wilno, adhered to the principles of the Lausanne School and later became a founder member of the Econometric Society.[3] The only competition to the liberal and mathematical thought in economics was provided by the adherents of the German historical school of economics, among whom a notable figure was the politician and agrarian economist Władysław Grabski (1874–1938) who, as minister of finance in 1924, was responsible for reducing the post-war inflation and stabilising (perhaps even equilibrating) the Polish currency.[4]

From 1923 Edward Lipiński taught business cycle theory at SGH. Later in the 1930s, he also lectured on the history of economic thought at the University of Warsaw. However, like Tennenbaum, he was not content merely to pass on to Polish students the conventional wisdom that was created abroad. Lipiński was also willing to encourage and promote new ideas incubated outside the universities, often in political controversies and by younger researchers excluded from universities by their background, lack of higher qualifications or scarcity of opportunities (the Institute for the Study of Business Cycles and Prices was the ideal vehicle for this kind of work). They included a young statistician, Jan Wiśniewski, along with Ludwik Landau, Michał Kalecki and, from 1933, Marek Breit.

Kalecki's first studies at the institute were specialist statistical researches. For example, his first article in *Konjunktura Gospodarcza* was 'Changes in the consumption of white bread and meat in Poland'.[5] It showed the predictable relationship between real income and consumption of white bread (because it is considered superior to and is more expensive than rye bread), while showing that meat consumption moved with bread consumption because they were complementary foods. His second article, 'Profit margins on sawn timber',[6] showed how timber mills tended to limit output when business was poor because of their higher labour costs compared with log producers, whose labour costs were lower but whose financial circumstances prevented them from accepting a fall in income; therefore they would sell more logs. His other articles for the institute in his first year were really statistical estimates – of prices of semi-finished investment goods, the taxes on raw material commodities (an important index of investment and consumption goods' output) and lime shipments as an estimator of construction activity. Despite his official responsibility for cartels, these publications by Kalecki showed that he was increasingly taking responsibility for the detailed statistical work that was to culminate in his collaboration with Landau in the first estimates of Polish national income.

Kalecki's study of the timber industry for the institute touched the vein of humour in him. Economists, on the whole, are not known for their humour, although the best stylists have often employed humour to reinforce the serious points they are making: Keynes mocks; Galbraith cites fatuous error masquerading as wisdom; Veblen conspicuously employs the language and terminology that businessmen and the comfortably-off use to invest their business with a higher moral and social purpose. When Kalecki, who is not known as a stylist, wanted to express humour, it was as irony or paradox, pointing out the ridiculous consequences that occur when business gets down seriously and rationally to making money. For the 'queer and perverse world in which we live'[7] ensures that rational endeavour gives rise to 'paradoxical' results.[8] Two years after his study of the timber industry appeared, he published *Rynek Drzewny* (Timber Market) in a specialist business magazine. It is a brief story in which the author describes meeting the owner of a sawmill who continues to operate his sawmill, with two shifts all year round, in the face of falling prices for cut wood. All becomes clear when the sawmill owner explains that with his brother, he owns a number of undertaking businesses in a nearby town. With the economic crisis, people are postponing their purchases of new clothes and even cutting back on food. But they cannot put off dying. Accordingly, 'when the previous owner of the sawmill went bankrupt we bought it dirt cheap and... the cheaper the wood, the better business we do' as undertakers.[9]

Another colleague at the institute with whom Kalecki collaborated was Jan Wiśniewski. Wiśniewski shared with Kalecki a professional interest in cartels: a specialist in price indices, Wiśniewski constructed and maintained an index of prices of goods produced by cartelised firms. In 1931 he wrote an article with Kalecki showing how to eliminate seasonal movements in unemployment.[10] This was unusually thorough in including in the estimate of unemployment the reduction or increase in labour hours that occurs before workers are laid off or hired.

Shortly after, Kalecki published a much more substantial article on the consequences of dumping.[11] This defined 'dumping' as the export of goods at prices below the selling prices in the domestic market. Kalecki pointed out that this would happen as a consequence of the cartelisation of the domestic market, which would raise domestic prices above the level that would clear full capacity production into the market. Dumping, therefore, he associated with not only cartelisation but also excess capacity. He argued that dumping might increase employment, but it also reduced the real income of every worker. In particular, dumping keeps capital in industries whose markets are saturated, and it is preferable all round to have the capital transferred through the capital market to industries that can obtain more profitable export or domestic markets.

Towards the end of 1931, *Konjunktura Gospodarcza* published the first article that Kalecki wrote in collaboration with Ludwik Landau. Landau (1901–44) was by training a statistician who developed into an economist in the course of working out the significance of the data on which he was working. He had worked on a major study of the structure of the Polish population in 1927, before coming to work at the institute. In his lecture commemorating Landau, on the 20th anniversary of his death, Kalecki paid tribute to the statistician on account not only of their joint work together but of the unusually tragic circumstances of his death, too. Kalecki maintained that Landau was outstanding in all four stages of statistical work: selection of the topic of research, data collection, estimation and inference. Indeed, if Landau had not been distracted by his passion for statistics, he would have made an excellent economic theorist.[12]

A distinctive feature of Landau's approach to statistics was that he did not regard his function as a statistician as being merely to draw statistical inferences from data. In his approach, statistical data emerge from a social and economic reality, and it is the function of the statistician to illuminate that reality rather than just the relative proportions of the data. The range of his interests and understanding is shown in the responsibilities he was given at the institute. Until the beginning of 1935 he was in charge of general economic research in the section, Research on Business Conditions (*Sekcja Badań Konjunktury*), that was headed by Lipiński himself. In the listing of staff in the institute published in *Konjunktura Gospodarcza* in spring of that year, Landau was promoted to head of section. According to Tadeusz Kowalik, Landau had recommended Kalecki to Lipiński for employment at the institute after reading Kalecki's article 'Business Conditions in the Textile Industry in 1927–1929' in the Ministry of Trade and Industry's weekly magazine *Przemysł I Handel*.[13] The article, appearing at the end of October 1929, included not only a very full discussion of production, prices and sales data, such as one might expect from a business analysis, but also a comparison of sales with stocks and the circulation and term of traders' bills. Kalecki used this information to show that the decline in sales was much lower than had been anticipated in the industry. Landau may have been interested in securing the employment of Kalecki at the institute because of a major study of the textile industry that was being planned there (see below).

The first joint paper of Landau and Kalecki was 'An Estimate of Investment Activity in Poland'.[14] It was typical of both authors that they start their study with a consideration of the statistical methods that may be employed in calculating an index of investment. They cite a recently published study of the German *Institut für Konjunkturforschung* (Business Cycle Institute) estimating total investment from the balance sheets of a group of representative companies. Landau and Kalecki deemed this to be inappropriate for Poland, where a much smaller proportion of businesses consists of joint stock companies publishing consistent balance sheet data. They therefore used industrial sales data to obtain an estimate of total investment activity in 1929. Without any national income estimates, the authors were unable to give any indication of the share of national income devoted to investment. However, by using data on the volume of production in particular industries, on railway shipments and so on, the authors then estimated an annual series for the volume of investment going back to 1926. They were thereby able to show that investment activity in 1929 fell around 25 per cent and, by 1931, had been reduced to approximately half of its 1928 peak. In the following year Kalecki and Landau published a revised version of their estimates, using additional data that had become newly available; it showed an even greater fall in investment activity since 1928.[15]

A significant feature of their study was the use of raw production data, with sales data being used only to obtain an estimate of the value of investment in 1929. This is a procedure which raises index number problems that statisticians worry about – namely, how would the time series estimates have been affected if the starting point of the analysis had been the value of investment in 1926 instead of 1929 – or any other year for that matter. Even more importantly, by using volume of production data for comparisons over time, the study could not provide the changes in the *value* of investment that were to be crucial for Kalecki's business cycle theory.

In the summer of 1930, Kalecki and Landau had started work on a major study of the textile trade in Poland, one that was much more substantial than the usual articles and briefs appearing in *Konjunktura Gospodarcza*. Accordingly it appeared in a series of *Prace Instytutu Badania Konjunktur Gospodarczych i Cen* (Studies of the Institute of Research on Business Cycles and Prices) edited by the institute's director, Lipiński. The study was to be based on a broad survey of businesses in the main textile centres of Łódź, Warsaw and Lwów (the present-day Ukrainian city of Lviv). However, the survey fell victim to the economic crisis that hit Polish business in 1929, as well as to the fragmented nature of the industry, whose many small manufacturers and traders had little time for filling in questionnaires. In the end, sufficient data were obtained from a rather biased and small sample (only 21 firms responded, of which only 5 were small firms with a turnover less than złoty 1.1 million (UK£25,345 or US$123,699 at that time, the equivalent of some UK£125,000 or US$618,000 today). The study noted that the share of wages in total costs was higher in Poland than in Germany, due to the lack of capital in the less industrially developed Poland and that country's lower wages. Profit margins were lower in Poland than in Germany, in large part because of the fragmentation of the business and the large number of wholesale intermediaries.[16]

A part of the study examined the financing of the businesses, which were highly dependent on credit to the value of 80 per cent of their turnover. But little of this was provided by banks. Most of the credit was provided by other traders in the business, who accepted bills in payment for goods. This contrasted with the practice in Germany, where traders usually used their own financial resources in payments between each other. The different financial practice was attributed to the effect of the 1920s hyperinflation, which forced businesses to finance trade out of current income. Interviews with experts revealed the poor financial situation of both retail and wholesale traders, which limited the possibilities of expanding trade and reduced any higher profits by high discount rates that had to be paid for by converting bills into cash. This made it much more difficult for firms to accumulate financial resources. Reference was made to the relative poverty of the Polish 'petit bourgeois' (traders) relative to their counterparts in western Europe, whose income not only allowed a higher standard of living and a bigger investment in their business but also allowed them to accumulate savings in savings banks and securities. This was advanced as a reason for the shallow markets for stocks and shares in Poland. Such a complex understanding of corporate finance and its impact on production and industrial development was typical of Kalecki.

Various other joint articles with Landau came together in their most important collaboration in 1934, their estimate of social income in Poland in 1929.[17] It is important to distinguish these estimates from the national income statistics that have been compiled since the Second World War. The latter are much more comprehensive and include foreign trade and capital movements in a way that would have been beyond the means of, as well as the data available to, Landau and his younger collaborator. Their estimates covered household incomes, consumption and investment. But the distinctive feature of their estimates, which does not appear in the modern national income statistics, was their detailed breakdown of household income and consumption by rural and urban incomes and by social class: peasant, manual, worker, white-collar and middle-class households. In the following year, 1935, Kalecki and Landau published estimates of social income in 1933.[18] Both of these were published as separate booklets by the institute rather than in its periodicals series. The two men collaborated on various indices of industrial production until Kalecki left Poland in 1936.

In 1933 the young Polish monetary economist Marek Breit joined the institute. In retrospect he is the most elusive and enigmatic figure with whom Kalecki was associated at the institute; his work shows great promise and intellectual refinement, unfulfilled because of career failure and premature death. Breit came from a Jewish family in Kraków and studied at the university there, the ancient Jagiellonian University.

In 1933 he published his most substantial work, *Stopa procentowa w Polsce,*[19] which is also the least representative of his mature views on the controversies that he took up. The book itself appears to have been written three years earlier, perhaps as a doctoral thesis. It is certainly a very thorough work of monetary analysis, steeped in German monetary theory which, at that time, offered the most sophisticated, discriminating and insightful discussion of issues relating to money, covering not only the usual questions of price inflation but also credit cycle theory.[20] At the time Breit shared the view of Stanisław Pszczółkowski, Lipiński's deputy at the institute until 1931,[21] that the credit system could be regarded as one market into which demand and supply of money were funnelled and brought into equilibrium by the rate of interest. Breit argued that economic and monetary instability arose because the rate of interest could not freely adjust the supply of credit to the demand for it. In part this was because, as Hayek had argued, governments set the rate of interest in accordance with their own financing needs rather than allow the credit market to determine the rate of interest without state interference.[22] However, Breit differed from Hayek and the other credit liberals in believing that the rate of interest could also be distorted by cartels among banks. At the time of writing his book, Breit was a thoroughgoing advocate of free enterprise and market competition.

Possibly as a result of the publication of this book, Breit was invited to work at the institute under the director of research on the money market, Wacław Skrzywan, a statistician with little interest in understanding the wider significance of the data that he was reporting. Breit's inclinations were exactly opposite to this. He sought out the shifts in private sector income and expenditure and in government fiscal and monetary policy. In one of his first articles for *Prace Instytutu Konjunktur Gospodarczych,* Breit noted the contraction of credit that set in with the financial crisis in 1930, accompanied by a rise in the liquidity of banks. He argued that these deflationary tendencies were being balanced by the 'inflationary' financing of the public sector; that is, the increase in the fiscal deficit which was absorbing the excess liquidity of the private sector.[23] In 1935 he noted that the rise in long-term lending was overwhelmingly due to lending by state-owned banks, while the private sector was engaged in reducing its borrowing.[24] In one of his articles, he discussed the view that long-term credit may create a different amount of purchasing power by comparison with short-term credit, a view he attributes to Pigou (rather than Keynes). He argued that in Poland this issue centred on whether the government should borrow short-term or long-term.[25]

Breit was also active in publishing outside the institute. Perhaps his most controversial paper (politically if not economically) was a chapter that he co-authored with Oskar Lange in 1934. The chapter appeared in a book entitled "Economy – Politics – Tactics –the Organisation of Socialism" (*Gospodarka – polityka – taktyka – organizacja socjalizmu*) published by a group of radical socialists. At least one of the co-authors, Stefan Arski, was a survivor of the Socialist Review (*Przegląd Socjalistyczny*), to which Kalecki contributed[26] and which was shut down by the authorities in 1932. Breit and Lange argued that the capitalist economy had broken down as a result of the progressive concentration and centralisation of capital, which had eliminated the normal forces of competition that would have brought market capitalism to equilibrium and growth. They noted that even the repudiation of the gold standard and fiscal inflation, as Breit called it, had failed to bring about recovery. The only way forward was socialism: nationalisation and organisation of industries into trusts, under partial workers' control, obliged to employ any worker who wanted to work in a given trust. Trusts would therefore have an incentive to keep wages low, to avoid attracting the unemployed or those who wanted better wages. Banks would be nationalised and combined into a national bank that would regulate activity in the economy by controlling the credit advanced for investment.[27] Not least among the controversial features of this paper was its rejection of the Soviet model of centralised planning, which, they argued, gave monopoly market power to workers in key industries. This made it all the more surprising when Lange made common cause with the Communists in 1944 and made the paper all the more embarrassing to Lange later, when Stalinism decreed that all deviation from the Soviet model was the work of capitalist agents.

That Breit and Kalecki never collaborated is probably a relief to connoisseurs of good Polish (and English) style. Kalecki's style was economic and ironic. Breit's was prolix and rhetorical. But their ideas were converging through their shared observation of the economic crisis unfolding around them. Breit's other major contribution to economic theory was his paper 'A contribution to the theory of the money and capital markets'. This was published as 'Ein Beitrag zur Theorie des Geld- und Kapitalmarktes' in *Zeitschrift fűr Nationalőkonomie*, edited by Oskar Morgenstern.[28] Here Breit took up the question that had been thrown up by his research at the institute: If banks were liquid and interest rates were low (the central bank discount rate in Polish banks had fallen from 8% in 1929 to 5% in 1935; in Germany from 7.1% to 4%; in the UK from 5.5% to 2%), why were companies not borrowing to expand investment and production. Breit concluded that the answer lay in the risk margin which banks charged over and above their average discount rate (or the central bank's). This is commonly known to happen in a crisis. The originality of Breit's analysis lies in his explanation of risk. He put forward the notion that the risk margin increases incrementally as more is borrowed against a given amount of a company's own financial resources or liquid assets (bank deposits and suchlike). Kalecki, struck by this analysis, transformed it into his own Principle of Increasing Risk.

Not least among Kalecki's associates at the institute was Blanka Winawer. In later years she came to be known as the secretary who translated Kalecki's first essay on the business cycle into German in order to send it to Keynes. But Blanka Winawer was much more than a secretary or an administrator. She contributed articles to *Prace Instytutu Konjunktur Gospodarczych* on Polish foreign trade – in industrial exports, for example.[29] Her formal position at the institute was secretary to Lipiński, but she and her family were close to Kalecki: Her mother translated Kalecki's first "Essay on the Theory of Business Cycles" into German so that it could be sent to Keynes, and her brother was a witness at the marriage of Michał and Adela.[30]

Kalecki's work at the institute was rewarded with additional responsibilities. Having been appointed with desk responsibilities for cartels, by 1931 he was listed in *Konjunktura Gospodarcza* as researcher on trade turnover (*referent obrotów handlu*). By the beginning of 1935, he was listed as head of research on cartels (*kierownik referatu karteli*). Despite his professional success, it took a long time for Kalecki to shake off his commitments to the construction industry. He continued to write on construction materials and design (in particular on reinforced concrete) up to 1932. His last article on the subject concerned walls in reinforced concrete frames for the fearlessly modernist journal *Cement* (Kalecki 1932d).

6
The Socialist Discussions

During Kalecki's first years at the institute the economic situation in Poland deteriorated. From its post-independence peak in 1929, national income fell by 18 per cent over the following three years. The fall in business investment was even more dramatic. In 1932, it was a mere 36 per cent of its already anaemic 1929 level.[1] Unemployment, which was in any case rising steadily through the 1920s, doubled between 1929 and 1931.[2] As economic desperation, poverty and enforced idleness increased, political tensions rose. Piłsudski's 1928 rapprochement with big business and the landed classes had been followed by a crackdown on trade union and peasant activists. His supporters took to aping the political manners of the Italian fascists, whom many of them admired. Invasions of the chamber of the Polish parliament, the Sejm, by military officers seeking to intimidate deputies, preceded key votes by Polish parliamentarians. Opposition deputies were beaten up. In response, the socialist parties formed an alliance with the peasant parties and the Christian Democrats (the *Centrolew* alliance, to indicate its centre and left-wing composition) to oppose Piłsudski's government. On 25 August 1930 Piłsudski forced the resignation of the prime minister and took over personal control of the government, dissolving the Sejm and denouncing parliamentary interference with his government. On the night of 9/10 September 1930, the leaders of *Centrolew* were arrested and interned in the fortress of Brześć. The main peasant politician, Wincenty Witos, fled across the border to Czechoslovakia.

Kalecki was never a member of any political party. But his socialist sympathies were obvious. He followed politics avidly, and Adela was a member of the Międzynarodowa Organizacja Pomocy Rewolucjonistom, commonly known as International Red Aid. This organisation had been formed in Moscow in 1922 by the Communist International to campaign for the release of Communists imprisoned by fascist governments. It had a very large Polish section and actively campaigned in support of Antonio Gramsci and, later, Polish, German and Spanish socialists.

Despite the intimidation, arrest and internment of politicians and activists of the trade unions and peasant organisations, some political discussions continued, albeit under the threat of closure of newspapers by the government. Moreover, rising unemployment among white-collar workers urged caution upon those employed directly or indirectly in public administration or services. The institute, its staff engaged, well informed and with radical sympathies, could not retain its independence as Piłsudski and his supporters extended their influence over public institutions. The case of Stanisław Pszczółkowski clearly showed the constraints under which the institute worked. Pszczółkowski was an established economist who had written extensively on monetary policy and foreign capital inflows into Poland. He had been appointed Lipiński's deputy in charge of business cycle analysis. He also worked directly with Kalecki. When Kalecki was preparing his first paper on business cycles, he discussed his ideas with Pszczółkowski. Pszczółkowski had authorised a comment to appear in the institute's *Biuletyn* indicating that the political situation, following the internment of the opposition leaders in Brześć, was damaging business confidence. He was forced to resign from the institute and left in November 1931.[3]

Shortly after Pszczółkowski's departure Kalecki published his first overtly political article. This was published in the first issue of a new monthly, *Przegląd Socjalistyczny* (Socialist Review), under the title 'Światowy kryzys finansowy' (the World Financial Crisis).[4] The readers of the monthly were thus introduced to a new writer, Henryk Braun. In view of his position at an institute of the Ministry of Trade and Industry, Kalecki continued to publish in *Przegląd Socjalistyczny* under that pseudonym until the monthly was shut down, barely a year after its first issue. In these articles Kalecki could express himself more freely on the manifestations of what he regarded as the irrationality of capitalism – that is, the way in which markets and the institutions of capitalism distort the rational production, sales and financing choices of firms, thereby exacerbating the economic crisis.

Przegląd Socjalistyczny was established by a group of socialist intellectuals and edited by Antoni Pański, a philosopher and statistician. Other active contributors included Pański's brother Jerzy, Artur Salman (who was later to be active with Oskar Lange in the Polish community in the United States during the war and returned to post-war Poland under the name Stefan Arski). Oskar Lange was later to recall that one of his first meetings with Kalecki was during the preparation of the first issue of *Przegląd Socjalistyczny*.[5] With the exception of Kalecki they were members of *Związek Niezależnej Młodzieży Socjalistycznej* (the Union of Independent Socialist Youth). This had been established in 1917 and brought together students and intellectuals in support of socialism. A leading figure was Oskar Lange. However, by 1922 the organization was starting to fragment. It discussed, sympathetically but critically, what was happening in the Soviet Union and drew much of its inspiration from the British Independent Labour Party and writers such as G. D. H. Cole and Harold Laski. The organisation managed to continue its activity into the 1930s, with bucolic summer schools (at one of which Marek Breit lectured).

Kalecki and Lange were the two Polish economists who made an impact on twentieth-century economics. In many respect their relationship was much more real than that between Keynes and Kalecki, to which Kalecki's fortunes were tied in his lifetime and beyond: Lange and Kalecki knew each other for much longer (they were born and died within years of each other). They shared a common political outlook, regarding themselves as Marxists looking forward to the overthrow of capitalism, rather than the Fabian 'Left Keynesians' like, until her later years, Joan Robinson. At the same time they both dissented in significant ways from the Marxist orthodoxy of their time. The scope of their economic interests was universal, in that they engaged in the study of capitalism, socialism and developing countries. Yet in their personalities they were very different: Lange was gregarious, urbane and educated, which made him party political (he assiduously cultivated political influence) and scholarly. As a boy he had spent some time in Graz, Austria, being treated for tuberculosis, and went on to complete two doctorates, in statistics and economics, at the ancient Jagiellonian University in Kraków. His economics thesis, on business cycles in Poland, was considered sufficiently alarming to prevent his appointment to teach economics, and he taught statistics before leaving Kraków for Warsaw. He joined the Polish Socialist Party in 1927, only to be suspended because of his strong views on 'left unity' – that is, cooperation with the Polish Communist Party. After that he joined the Union of Independent Socialist Youth. The range of Lange's scholarly interests is shown by the subject of his first published paper, which was on German settlements in medieval Poland, and his extensive writings on the history of economic thought.[6]

By contrast, Kalecki had never travelled outside Poland and had no university degree. He had a scholarly interest in mathematics, but his interest in the history of economic thought, indeed economics in general, was limited to those parts of the literature that he could use in his own work on business cycles. He did not socialise easily, and he never took his dislike of capitalism to the point of joining a political party, a commitment that he regarded as incompatible with his 'expert' status as an economist. Socialism was to be for him a reasoned choice rather than an emotional response to historic events or the social choice of his milieu.

In part because of the crisis of capitalism that appeared to have set in around the world, both Lange and Kalecki engaged with the discussions that had been set off by the publication of volumes II and III of Marx's *Capital* in 1885 and 1894, respectively. These had a major impact upon German monetary and credit cycle theory (the most advanced work in this branch of economics until the 1930s) through the work of Eugen von Bőhm-Bawerk and Rudolf Hilferding. The latter played a key, unacknowledged part in Kalecki's analysis, because it was Hilferding who first enunciated the view that capitalist firms operate and finance themselves in different ways, depending on whether they compete in markets or dominate markets as monopolies.[7] As the economic crisis unfolded, the contributions of two Marxist economists in particular came to play a central part in the economic discussions of the Polish socialists.

The first, the one to whom Kalecki felt the closest affinity, was Rosa Luxemburg. Luxemburg was originally Polish before getting involved in German politics, and the unorthodox interpretation that she gave to Marx's schemes of economic reproduction highlighted the difficulties of realising profits as the major effective constraint on capitalist development. Luxemburg argued that the constraint could be overcome by the export of capital abroad but also through building up military capacity and armaments, a seemingly prophetic anticipation of political developments in central Europe in the 1930s and one which Kalecki was to identify in US politics after the Second World War.[8] At the time when Kalecki arrived in Warsaw, an extreme interpretation of the profits realisation problem was put forward by the Polish Marxist Henryk Grossman. This reasoned that capitalism was doomed to economic collapse because of the inevitable fall and extinction of the rate of profit.[9] Grossman had left Poland for Germany after having been briefly arrested in 1924 by the Polish authorities for Communist activities.[10] In the midst of these apocalyptic discussions, Kalecki raised his voice.

The first issue of *Przegląd Socjalistyczny* contained a declaration that summarised the reasoned and undogmatic (but not pragmatic) approach to politics that Kalecki and Lange shared. The declaration stated that 'socialism requires first and foremost bold deeds, but it also requires boldness of thought. We believe that it will gather strength by looking directly at the truth and, in analysing reality, guided by common sense rather than the ideas of authorities which are often an impediment rather than an aid to understanding the way in which phenomena operate . . . our tasks are to examine critically the most important economic and social aspects of capitalist countries, to follow the development of the socialist movement . . . '.[11] The issue also contained Kalecki's first article, 'The World Financial Crisis', for the review (discussed in Chapter 4).

Kalecki's second article for *Przegląd Socjalistyczny* appeared at the beginning of 1932 under the title 'Obniżka płac w czasie kryzysu'.[12] In this article he challenged the view prevailing among employers and government officials sympathetic to them that general reductions in wages can induce an increase in employment. Kalecki pointed out that the condition for this to happen is an increase in investment; consumption itself is hardly likely to rise if wages are falling. An expansion in investment is highly unlikely in a crisis when industrial capacity is underutilised. In theory workers' consumption may be maintained if the prices of consumption goods fall. But this may take time, and in the meantime, stocks of unsold consumer goods will accumulate. The lag in price adjustment to falling wages discourages increased production and motivates employers to reduce wages still further:

> An individual entrepreneur, even if growing stocks in his warehouse become a problem for him, does not understand that a reduction in prices is the result of the previous reduction in wages. He regards the 'market' in which the reduction in prices took place as an external force independent of him. So from the fall in prices he eagerly draws the conclusion that he should reduce wages still further.

Thus, far from a new equilibrium emerging at a higher level of employment:

> [T]he stocks of unsold workers' consumer goods increase once again, prices fall again and so on. An ever greater part of social income will be tied up in stocks, the crisis will continue to deepen, and workers with their shrinking wages will be unable to take advantage of price reductions to restore their previous standard of living.

Kalecki pointed out that this is, of course, a simplified picture in portraying a society in which there are only capitalists and workers. Other, 'intermediate' social classes will experience an increase in their real incomes, and this may affect their expenditure positively. He cited in particular the retail trade business, which will hold retail prices stable but enjoy higher profit margins from falling prices at the factory gate. He also noted that the deflationary situation was characteristic of a particular phase in the business cycle when underutilised capacity in industry discourages business investment. Kalecki argued that during an economic boom, when capital equipment is fully employed, a fall in wages can increase capitalists' profits, which can be realised when capitalists place new orders for capital equipment:

> In an industrial boom, even countries with starvation wages can display sustained production increases, because profits are reinvested in industry. However, this boom has its limits, since industrial expansion is inevitably followed by crisis.[13]

In the same issue of *Przegląd Socjalistyczny* Kalecki published 'Podstawy konfliktu mandżurskiego' (Foundations of the Manchurian conflict). This presented a summary economic survey of Manchuria, an agricultural region criss-crossed by railway lines, of which the East Chinese Line through Harbin was a crucial link to the Soviet port of Vladivostok. Japanese business had already developed industrial interests in Manchuria and was frustrated that the Chinese government was expanding railway links with Beijing rather than a railway connection with the Korean port of Chongjin, which could facilitate Japanese trade with Manchuria. That in turn was crucial to satisfying Japan's requirements for food and raw materials. Kalecki pointed out:

> The development of processing industries that would enable Japan to exchange her manufactured goods in return for food and raw materials is made difficult by the chaotic nature of the world economy, which moves from an international division of labour ever close to greater self-sufficiency for each country.[14]

Demography was a key factor: Japan had a surplus population whose opportunities for migration were limited by the constraints imposed on Japanese emigration to the United States, where California had a climate congenial to Japanese settlers. Kalecki viewed these as the economic factors behind the Japanese invasion of Manchuria, itself the outcome of a political alliance between Japanese big business and the army.

The economic basis of fascism was taken up in an article that appeared in the next issue of *Przegląd Socjalistyczny*: 'Remarks on Hitlerism and "business circles"'.[15] Here Kalecki argued that the economic crisis was giving rise to hoarding of gold and foreign currencies, forgoing profit in order to maintain the value of money capital. Capitalists are also willing to forgo some of their profits in order to buy political protection. The business-friendly democratic state, in these circumstances, turns out to be inflexible, bureaucratic and all too vulnerable to democratic pressures. The Nazi Party therefore offers a way in which big business can engage in political 'private enterprise'. However, Kalecki did not regard the Nazis (not yet in government in 1932) as a creature of big business. Rather, the Nazi Party emerged from the petit bourgeois, the intelligentsia and 'semi-intelligentsia' and from among those workers who did not think in class terms. The ruined shopkeeper, according to Kalecki, blamed his fate on usurious moneylenders, Jewish bankers, war reparations and international Jewish and Marxist conspiracies. Hitlerism, according to Kalecki, opposed the dominance of finance capital.[16] But the leading industrial 'patrons' of Hitler were directors of heavy industry based in the coalfields, men whose businesses were especially badly affected by the crisis, leaving those directors in greatest need of political protection. The huge indebtedness of those industries inclined their managers to sympathy with the Nazi vilification of finance capital, in the hope that they would have privileged influence over economic policy if the Nazis came to power. Even if the Nazis did not take over the government, it was useful for the big business cartels to keep the extreme right active and threatening in order to keep the Social Democratic government of Heinrich Brüning veering towards the right in its policy in an effort to undermine support for the Nazis.

Kalecki's next article was on the war in the East.[17] Here he argued that the invasion of China by the Japanese was creating tension with the Soviet Union (over that eastern Chinese railway line whose general manager was the White Russian general Dmitrii Horvath). In terms of economic interests, the big losers were the British and, to a lesser extent, the Americans. In his mordant way, Kalecki remarked on the bombing of the defenceless Shanghai population, living mostly in wooden houses, in order to preserve the 'national dignity' of Japan. His conclusion in this matter is unusual, because it is one of the rare occasions when Kalecki quoted Marx: 'With adequate profit, capital is very bold. A certain 10% will ensure its employment anywhere; 20% will produce eagerness; 50% positive audacity; 100% will make it ready to trample on all human laws; 300% and there is no crime at which it will scruple.'[18]

The next issue of *Przegląd Socjalistyczny* featured an extensive commentary on the international financial crisis under the title 'Mr. Keynes's

Predictions'.[19] The 'predictions' referred to those made by 'J. M. Keynes, possibly the most serious bourgeois economist' in speeches in Hamburg and Cambridge, later to appear as part of a series of lectures entitled 'The World's Economic Crisis and the Way of Escape' in the *Atlantic Monthly* of May 1932.[20] Keynes's Hamburg speech was originally made on 8 January 1932. He argued that the economic and financial situation in the major capitalist countries remained critical, with stock markets falling and most banks technically insolvent, in the sense that their assets on any realistic valuation would not cover their liabilities. However, he argued that economic activity had, to some degree, stabilised: employment in the UK had not fallen for a year, and the suspension of gold convertibility by Britain and most European countries, leaving the United States and France as the only major powers on the gold standard, would strengthen the trade position of Britain and those countries that had devalued against gold. In the case of Britain, this devaluation had caused an outflow of gold from India to London, attracted by the higher price. An appeal to a Hamburg audience can be detected in Keynes's remark that France's 'creditor position is likely to be completely undermined before the end of 1932. The cessation of reparation receipts, the loss of tourist traffic, the competitive disadvantage of her export trades with non-gold countries, and the importation of a large proportion of the world's available gold will, between them, do their stuff.'[21] Keynes looked forward to the adherence of other countries to the sterling area, in particular South Africa, Germany and the central European countries and possibly the Netherlands.

Writing a few months after the original Hamburg speech, Kalecki considered that Keynes's analysis illuminated the 'purely financial' difficulties and the shifts in the balance of power among the capitalist powers. Kalecki suggested that 'despite their appearance of abstraction, Keynes's arguments are closely tied up with the actual economic structure and possibilities of the British Empire'. Kalecki detected no increase in demand in India as a result of the cheaper goods due to the devaluation of sterling and pointed out that the gold hoard flowing from India to London was itself limited (as Keynes had argued was the inflow of gold into France). The trade position of the United Kingdom would improve, in particular as a result of the 10 per cent tariff that was being introduced. But this by no means meant a global improvement in economic activity:

> [W]ill the processes discussed here lead to an improvement of the entire financial system? In particular, will Keynes's hopes that this

> improvement will also pave the way for overcoming the economic crisis be realised? Today there are still no signs that these hopes are being realised. As we have pointed out, despite attempts at an 'international' approach, Keynes really speaks as a representative of British imperialism, which at this point sees a good chance for itself. But the possibilities, which form the basis of hopes for an improvement in Britain's economic situation, themselves are the prospects for a worsening of the crisis in other countries, i.e., those countries remaining on the gold standard. Moreover, as the world crisis worsens, the British chance will turn out to be short-lived and illusory.'[22]

In the event, France held out on the gold standard until 1936, the Germans established their own monetary area and Poland joined the US dollar area.

Kalecki's next article for *Przegląd Socjalistyczny* was his portrait of the Swedish 'Match King', Ivar Kreuger (see Chapter 3). In the autumn of 1932, Kalecki returned to the questions raised in the Keynes lectures and the discussions of his socialist friends in an article entitled 'Is a "Capitalist" way out of the Crisis possible?'.[23] Earlier in 1930 and even at the beginning of 1931, many reputable economists believed that natural market mechanisms would cause the capitalist economies to recover from the deep recession that followed the 1929 Crash. The article cited G. D. H. Cole, described as 'a politically moderate professor of economics of Oxford University, observing that 'with this system no lasting improvement is possible' and John A. Hobson pointing to the need to refinance international debts and stabilise prices.

Kalecki's article is most interesting for taking issue with the view presented by the Hungarian Soviet economist Yevgeni Varga of the likely evolution of the crisis. Varga was the leading Soviet economic commentator on developments in the capitalist economies. Like many orthodox Marxian economists, Varga argued that the depression was being prolonged by the slump in wages, with a consequent reduction in total demand in the economy. However, the orthodox Marxian view was based on an idea that wages and profits are inversely related so that, at some point, wages must fall so low as to cause a revival in profits. Kalecki argued that this would not happen, or if it did, the higher profits would take the form of unsold stocks of goods, which certainly would not stimulate higher production. He identified two mechanisms that were having a positive effect in the capitalist economies. First of all, the devaluation of the currencies of the indebted countries in Europe was making it easier for their governments to manage their foreign debts.

(Kalecki referred here to the international capital flows described in his article 'Mr. Keynes's Predictions'). Those countries that had gone off the gold standard had managed to reduce considerably their imports from countries remaining on the gold standard. This was obvious in the bilateral balance of payments between Britain, which had gone off the gold standard, and France, which stayed on the gold standard. Britain's gold imports from France (along with British imports of gold from India) had allowed Britain to pay off some of its borrowing from France. Indeed, French confidence in the English capital market had strengthened sufficiently to result in an increase in capital flows from France to Britain. However, new financial difficulties were arising as old ones were being overcome, the most recent problems arising out of the Kreuger collapse. If the international financial system did not break down, then devaluations against gold could contribute to ending the financial crisis.

However, ending the financial crisis did not mean ending the crisis in the economy at large. Here the most likely possibility for improving the economic situation arose out of the tendency for investment to fall much more rapidly than consumption. This raised the prospect that at some point industrial capacity utilisation would rise and encourage investment eventually to rise. Other possibilities, such as external markets or technological innovations, were unlikely. With the conquest of the entire world by imperialism, external markets were no longer available. An alternative was a war economy boom. But this would not be endured within the present capitalist system.

Kalecki concluded with a very brief consideration of getting out of the crisis by means of public works financed by government borrowing. He thought that this might have a temporary effect. But it would be at the cost of delaying (in an unspecified way) the 'natural' regulators leading to the overcoming of the crisis. The reader wonders what those 'natural' regulators might be. The only ones discussed in the article are those associated with deflation: liquidation of commodity stocks and falling prices, leading to a cheapening of capital, bankruptcies and write-offs of the book value of capital. These, according to Kalecki, eventually reduce capital values faster than profits, at which point the rate of profit on capital starts to rise, and investment starts to become profitable. Thus, Kalecki saw the crisis, not as a 'structural crisis' of capitalism à la Grossman, but as a crisis phase of the business cycle. In that phase the key factor was not economic but a (Luxemburgist) socio-political one: the strength and political action of the working class.[24]

Kalecki followed this with his own mordant observations on another businessman, Henry Deterding, the head of Royal Dutch/Shell, who ennobled his business as anti-Soviet philanthropy and his speculations as business, and one of the financial backers of Adolf Hitler (see Chapter 3). In the next issue, the 13th of *Przegląd Socjalistyczny* in 1932, Kalecki published, under the title 'Inflation and War', yet another article summarising the dilemmas faced by those who sought to reflate the crisis-affected economies of Europe.[25] Here Kalecki distinguished between credit inflation (expanding the liquidity of the banking system) and fiscal inflation. The first could not induce an increase in investment, because businessmen do not increase investment just because more money is available: if cheaper credit is available, then they will merely borrow more to repay previously incurred and more expensive debt. The money that banks lend out will return to them as debt repayments. The other kind of inflation Kalecki called 'fiscal inflation'. He considered that this could work in a closed economy; he gave the example of the United States, where imports are very small relative to the size of the economy. Reiterating an argument he had made earlier in the article called 'A Capitalist Overcoming of the Crisis', Kalecki argued that fiscal inflation was unlikely to succeed in stimulating sustainable growth in an open economy, where it would lead to balance of payments difficulties, devaluation of the currency against other currencies, capital flight and eventually hyperinflation. The only condition under which it could work would be if all countries agreed to pursue such policies. Although Kalecki does not say so, in such a situation all countries would expand their imports, and hence trade was more likely to be balanced. But according to Kalecki, imperialist rivalry is unavoidable in capitalism and precludes such international agreement.[26]

The article is notable for revealing Kalecki's view of price inflation. He denied that it was a monetary phenomenon. Rather, it was a demand phenomenon, kept in abeyance by imperfect competition and excess capacity in industry and taking off when industrial capital is fully utilised.

Apart from a book review, Kalecki wrote one further article for *Przegląd Socjalistyczny*. This was a commentary on political developments in Germany: 'On the margin of events in Germany'.[27] The article reveals more, perhaps, about Kalecki's political outlook than it does about Germany's politics. Kalecki argued that Nazi policy was inflationary, but he thought it would take a long time for hyperinflation to revive because of the underutilisation of industrial capacity. Nevertheless, he expected the big landowners and heavy industry to benefit from inflation. Hitler would try to 'split and corrupt' Social Democratic trades unions while suppressing the German Communists with the utmost vigour. Kalecki envisaged cooperation with Hitler from 'opportunistic' elements of the political centre and the German Social Democrats. However, he thought that it would be difficult to break the resistance of the German working class, another hint at Kalecki's Luxemburgist sympathies.

Kalecki's article on the prospects for German politics appeared in the last issue of *Przegląd Socjalistyczny*. The magazine was shut down at the end of 1932 by the Polish government. Writing for the *Przegląd Socjalistyczny* under the pseudonym Henryk Braun gave Kalecki a freedom which his work would not allow in addressing a milieu that was politically congenial to him. Those dozen brief articles were also his opportunity to address the key issues of the political economy of his time: the nature of capitalist crisis and the scope and effectiveness of government economic policy in dealing with that crisis. Kalecki never wrote so candidly about politics again but proceeded to develop his economic insights. The economic analysis underlying his observations on politics and economic developments was his understanding of the business cycle as an essential feature of the capitalist economy.

7
The Enigma of the Business Cycle

The business cycle was to be the most lasting preoccupation of Michał Kalecki. In equal measure it epitomised the most obvious features of what was wrong with capitalism – instability, unemployment and poverty – and, by reason of its complexity, provided the greatest intellectual challenge to the honest and objective economic researcher.

The business cycle – that is, successive periods of economic growth and prosperity followed by periods of economic contraction and rising unemployment – is a phenomenon of industrial and post-industrial capitalism. Before the industrial revolution, periods of prosperity and economic distress had natural or political causes: disease or natural disasters, good or bad harvests, civil disorders or the extension of markets by means of an empire, such as the Roman, that could protect trade, construct roads and provide irrigation and other useful infrastructure. From the nineteenth century onwards, however, a new type of fluctuation in business activity emerged that was unrelated to natural or political factors. By the twentieth century the notion put forward by the English mathematical economist William Stanley Jevons (1835–82) that business cycles are caused by sunspots was considered an amusing eccentricity.

Nevertheless, the business cycle has remained a matter of controversy: one of those useful but unsettling questions of economics whose investigation appears to provide few answers but teaches the enquiring student a great deal about economies and how they work. Part of its enigma arises because it is not obvious whether it is real (like the output of a gold mine that may be observed, weighed and valued) or a mental construct (like geometry, causality, probability or time) that we use to apprehend reality rather than objectively a part of that reality. The business cycle certainly has much in common with 'globalisation', 'financialisation' and other synthetic concepts economists use to organise linked economic processes. But the frequent use of such terms often gives rise to what the philosopher Alfred North Whitehead called the fallacy of misplaced concreteness, as processes that are combined for the sake of convenience and summary come to be regarded as particular aspects of their combination rather than more discreet processes, and the collective category replaces the actual and specific links between the various processes that are going on to make up the perceived collective process.

Until the twentieth century, business cycle theory was an approach largely confined to continental European economic discussions. Most English-speaking economists, under the influence of Mill and the neoclassical revolution in the later part of the nineteenth century, believed in market equilibrium that was only temporarily disequilibrated by changes in the money supply[1] or changes in technology. The study of the business cycle as it developed in continental Europe was a challenge to the prevailing orthodoxy in economic theory, which was built around the idea of equilibrium between demand and supply in markets, or the general equilibrium put forward by Walras and Pareto. Viewed from the starting point of equilibrium, changes in the underlying conditions of production and distribution, conditions such as individual preferences, technology and the fiscal and monetary policy of the state, only give rise to a new equilibrium. By implication, in such an analysis economic dynamics – that is, changes in economic activity, or 'business conditions' – may be caused by any factor. This view came to be prevalent in economics in the final decades of the twentieth century with the widespread adoption of Real Business Cycle terminology. According to this, economic dynamics or changes in economic activity are merely the result of 'shocks', or shifts in underlying conditions. The clear conclusion from this is that there is no systematically recurring business cycle, merely a series of unforeseen accidents, after which equilibrium is resumed. In contrast to this the influential Austrian-American economist Joseph Schumpeter (1883–1950) emphasised the role of technological innovation in investment and business cycles.

The difficulty with these approaches is that in a diversified economy, one would expect different responses to 'shocks' by different industries, according to the nature of their exposure to the 'shock'. In other words, one would expect successive changes in equilibrium brought about in succession by shifts in different industries. This is the process that Schumpeter called 'creative destruction'; that is, a process in which some industries or firms are expanding and some are declining, both doing so continuously. As a matter of empirical observation this is not what happens in the world. The rationale for business cycle theory lies in the fact that in a boom firms and industries *in general* expand output and employment and enjoy increasing profits; this is followed by a phase in which firms and industries, with marginal exceptions, reduce their output and employment and find difficulty in selling their output profitably. For this reason Schumpeter argued that the only 'real' business cycles are long ones in which generic technological innovations affect a wide range of industries. Similarly, Hawtrey, Hayek and Keynes argued that the business cycle had to be due to monetary conditions, because these are the only conditions that affect all industries.

The notion that capitalist instability is due to shocks that cannot be anticipated with any precision (if they could be they would not be 'shocks') was contrary to the very purpose of the institute where Kalecki worked, which was, as indicated in Chapter 5, to 'obtain sufficiently early the information required to develop a view on the influences affecting the changing economic situation'. Kalecki's industrial studies made clear that what brought the business cycle into existence and keeps it going is the central economic, social and political agency of the capitalist economy: the capitalist firm. His business cycle analysis is based on the simple proposition that the expenditure of capitalist firms determines employment and the overall proportions of economic activity in the capitalist economy. The reality of the business cycle, the fluctuations in economic activity and employment, emerges because of the way in which capitalists' expenditure decisions are the key factor driving changes in economic activity.

Kalecki spent 1932 in bringing together his ideas on the business cycle. His reflections were clearly motivated by considerations of whether the Polish economy or, indeed, any other would climb out of the economic depression automatically, as maintained most notably by Schumpeter and Hayek, as well as by equilibrium theorists, all of whom believed that with sufficient price flexibility, full employment would 'naturally' be restored. Towards the end of that year he published a series of papers outlining the essential elements of his theory.

A first draft appeared in *Polska Gospodarcza* under the title 'The Business Cycle and Inflation' ('Koniunktura a inflacja'). It contains the essential elements of his theory of the capitalist economy neatly summarised. It argues that business cycles are caused by fluctuations in business investment. On the simplifying assumption that all wages are consumed and all profits are saved, the economy can be kept stable if all saving is spent on investment. If capitalists wish to invest more, 'credit inflation' is necessary; that is, firms must borrow. (Here, as was common at the time, Kalecki used 'inflation' to mean expansion of lending.) This will set off a boom, because firms as a whole will receive profits equal to their expenditure on fixed capital, those profits appearing as additional deposit balances in the system. If banks have to hold reserves, then an individual bank expanding its lending to business may find itself running out of reserves as payments are cleared, and the bank finds itself paying out more reserves as cheque settlements than it receives. However, this will not happen if there is a general increase in investment, because payments between banks will be more equal. The central bank may still raise interest rates. But, Kalecki argued, the rate of interest is not a significant influence on investment: the rate of profit is far more important.

Two arguments in the article may be noted. The first is an admission that if industry is operating at full capacity, prices of finished goods will rise in response to an increase in investment. As a consequence real wages will fall. This is the 'forced saving' that, according to Austrian business cycle theory, finances excessive investment.[2] However, Kalecki argued that with excess capacity in industry, including unemployment, such 'forced saving' was unlikely.

The other argument concerns the effect of a boom in an open economy – one with open trade with other countries. Here a boom would tend to lead to a deterioration in the foreign trade balance, as more industrial raw materials or articles of consumption or investment equipment goods are imported. The drain of gold and foreign currency reserves would tend to bring the boom to an end in either a fall in the value of the domestic currency in the foreign exchange market, even perhaps a 'run' on the central bank through an excessive demand to convert local currency into foreign currency, or hyperinflation, as occurred in Poland and Germany in the early 1920s.[3]

Even before the election of Franklin D. Roosevelt as president of the United States, Kalecki argued that business depressions could be overcome by public works. This would expose a country undertaking such works to adverse trade balances and a possible drain of gold and foreign currency reserves. However, with all countries being in economic crisis, a mechanism similar to the extension of bank credit would make it possible to avoid adverse trade effects if all countries simultaneously undertook economic reflation through public works. Alternatively, an international 'central bank' of issue could provide credit to reflating countries. But such international economic coordination, in Kalecki's view, was unlikely 'for the same reason that international disarmament cannot be achieved'. In particular he highlighted a kind of international 'liquidity preference' in which capitalists prefer to import and hold gold, foreign exchange or foreign stocks and shares, through foreign trade surpluses, rather than domestic government bonds used to finance public works. Three years later, in 1935, Kalecki was to argue that an international arms race may in fact 'force' a kind of emulatory inflation on the great powers.[4]

Kalecki concluded that the present crisis would be overcome only slowly, as industrial equipment deteriorates until a replacement boom commences. The United States could undertake 'inflationary' operations. But being a relatively closed economy, in the sense that its foreign trade constituted a small proportion of the total output of the economy, the United States was unlikely to be able to stimulate an international boom. The best that could be hoped for in Europe was that a rise in prices in stock markets would reduce the liquidity preference of business.

Kalecki returned to the issue of the financing of an economic recovery and the special position in this of the United States in an article, 'Stimulating the World Business Upswing', published early in 1933.[5] He pointed out that in the wake of Roosevelt's election, there had been some recovery in industrial production due, contrary to his earlier view, to the devaluation of the US dollar. On 6 March 1933 Roosevelt had taken the dollar off the gold standard, and the American currency had, predictably, depreciated in the weeks that followed. Kalecki argued that this had caused speculative buying of stocks of raw materials and finished goods in anticipation of an increase in prices. It was this buying which had stimulated a temporary industrial revival. But it could only be temporary, because stockpiling goods and raw materials could not be sustained, unlike public works or investment. Nor was he impressed by the 'brain trust' of businessmen and academics advising Roosevelt and their plan for public works financed by a rise in taxes. This in his view could not increase profits sufficiently to sustain a boom. Kalecki was especially critical of the economic planning that the brain trust proposed; he said it consisted essentially of forming cartels to prevent 'ruinous competition' and 'overinvestment'. In practice the cartels would 'appropriate' profits from the non-cartelised, competitive sector. Even if the whole economy was cartelised, the reduced investment would correspondingly cut down profits so that, with inflexible prices, output and employment would also suffer.

Kalecki contrasted this caution with the more sustainable German recovery financed with 'inflation' – that is, borrowing – and using export subsidies to keep the foreign trade balance from deteriorating. Japan too had managed to secure a recovery in industrial production of 30 per cent since 1931 through the inflationary financing of war production, using a 60 per cent devaluation of the yen to stimulate exports: 'by the deep devaluation of yen and the low quality of Japanese goods which makes them attractive in impoverished Europe.' Both German dumping and Japanese devaluation would reduce real wages. In his essay in the previous year for *Przegląd Socjalistyczny*, Kalecki had observed that Hitler and the Japanese government were 'betting on war and inflation', leaving an open question as to whether the Nazis could 'prevent inflation from turning into hyperinflation'.[6] It should be pointed out that Kalecki was here writing before Hitler took over the government in Germany after elections in 1933.

In 'Stimulating the World Business Upswing', Kalecki identified precisely why investment plays such a crucial part in maintaining the equilibrium of the capitalist economy:

> For existing capital equipment to be fully employed, it must be continually expanded, since then retained profits are invested. If these investments are not made, profits fall, and along with them the utilisation of existing plants.

Kalecki illustrated this with a parable that summarised his vision of capitalist dynamics:

> Let us suppose, as often happens in the United States, that two competing railway lines run between two cities. Traffic on both lines is weak. How should one deal with this situation? Paradoxically, one should build a third railway line, because then the first two lines will transport the materials and labour to build the third line. What should be done when the third railway line is built? Then one should build a fourth and a fifth. This is paradoxical because undoubtedly it would be better to undertake some other investment near the first two railway lines rather than build a third one. But it perfectly illustrates the laws of development of the capitalist economy as a whole.

In another essay published in 1932, Kalecki expanded on the question of whether cartels could stabilise the business cycle. In it he examined the influence of cartelisation on the business cycle and argued that, contrary to the widespread notion that the more stable prices that cartels administered stabilised output, in fact they made business cycles more extreme. This is so because firms in cartels operate with excess capacity, which discourages investment in a recession, while their more stable profits have their counterpart in more extreme fluctuations in the profits of competitive businesses. Those competitive businesses earn more profits and invest more in a boom but suffer disproportionate falls in profits in a recession and reduce their investment accordingly.[7]

Kalecki was not the first economist to consider the effects of cartelisation on business cycles. The Austrian Marxist Rudolf Hilferding had devoted two whole chapters to the matter in his *Finance Capital*. Hilferding had argued that the more stable profits of cartels concentrated extreme changes in profits in the competitive sector of the economy. However, writing in the first decade of the twentieth century, Hilferding believed that their conspicuous vulnerability to cyclical movements in profits would encourage greater industrial concentration in the recession, or make competitive businesses form cartels, eventually leading to greater stability in the economy.[8] Kalecki challenged this view by arguing that cartelised business, because it is subject to agreed prices or production quotas, does not invest in a more stable way than competitive businesses. But profits and investment in the competitive sector of business will fluctuate more extremely due to the existence of the cartel.[9]

Kalecki's formal, mathematical treatment of the business cycle was published in July 1933 by the Institute for the Study of Business Cycles and Prices in a booklet entitled *An Essay on the Theory of Business Cycle* (*Próba teorii koniunktury*). In his introduction, Kalecki alludes to the two direct theoretical influences on his analysis in the work of the French economist Albert Aftalion (1874–1956). At the start of his paper, Kalecki quotes two paragraphs from Aftalion's book *Les Crises périodiques de surproduction*,[10] in which Aftalion, who had been one of the first French economists to criticise the notion that free markets would always find their equilibrium, argued that business cycles are caused by excessive investment in the boom, when prices are high and rising, giving high profits and indicating the profitability of investment. Once the new investments are brought into operation, overproduction causes prices to fall and overproduction of consumer goods. Profits are reduced, discouraging investment until underproduction causes businessmen to order new equipment.

Kalecki criticised Aftalion's assumption that businessmen use their plant more or less at full capacity throughout the cycle, which generates successive ascending prices in the boom, followed by descending prices in the depression. Nevertheless, Kalecki thought that this was a minor flaw in Aftalion's argument. It is clear that a key factor in the cycle is therefore the lag between the decision to invest and the expansion of production as the new equipment becomes operational. Here Kalecki made use of a study by the Dutch economist Jan Tinbergen of the shipbuilding cycle, where orders for new ships depend upon the increase in cargoes, but additions to total shipping tonnage are delayed by an average of two years because of the lengthy construction time required for cargo ships.[11] According to the Polish economist Józef Zagórski, who was also employed at the institute, the reference to Aftalion had been put in after Stanisław Pszczółkowski (who had been sacked from the institute at the end of 1931; see Chapter 6) pointed out to Kalecki that Aftalion had already presented a similar theory.[12]

Kalecki's *Essay* contains the familiar elements of his analysis. Profits are equal to capitalists' consumption and their gross expenditure on capital equipment; that is, the production of investment goods. Investment is given as a function of the expected profitability of investment, which in turn is determined by the actual gross profitability of existing capital and the rate of interest. However, once investment exceeds the amount required as replacement of worn-out capital equipment, additions to the capital stock, or net investment, eventually reduce the gross profitability of existing capital. This then brings down the amount of investment, and the economy moves into a downturn. This is modelled using a difference equation, so that, with stable lags, the system produces a regular cycle around a constant (flat) trend.

A key relation in Kalecki's system is the one between capitalists' expenditure on consumption and investment and the profits that they earn. Here, with a simplifying assumption that workers do not save, Kalecki put forward the essential idea that became his theory of profits:

> The conclusion that the increase in capitalist consumption in turn increases their profits contradicts the common conviction that the more is consumed the less is saved. This approach, which is correct with regard to a single capitalist, does not apply to the capitalist class as a whole. If some capitalists spend money, either on investment or on consumer goods, their money passes to other capitalists in the form of profits. Investment or consumption of some capitalists creates profits for others. Capitalists as a class gain exactly as much as they invest or consume, and if – in a closed system – they ceased to construct and consume they could not make any money at all.[13]

A financial implication of this is that '[i]f during a particular period more money is spent, e.g., out of bank deposits, then pro tanto more money flows back into the banks in the form of realised profits, so that the sum of deposits remains unchanged.'[14] However, Kalecki argued that some 'credit inflation' (additional borrowing) would be necessary for two reasons: First of all, because the lag in delivery of investment goods would require additional working capital and, secondly, to finance any increases in investment and consumption.[15]

The factor, then, in causing cyclical fluctuations in the economy was the investment expenditure of capitalist firms. This in turn necessarily lagged behind investment decisions, or orders. This distinction between current investment and investment decisions is one of the fundamental differences between Kalecki's macroeconomics and that of Keynes and his followers. By assuming that investment orders are delivered in the same period, the Keynesians missed a lag that is a central element in the business cycle. Kalecki put forward a simple investment function in which investment orders are an increasing function of gross accumulation (total investment deliveries in that period) and a decreasing function of the stock of capital equipment.

Having explained the essential relationships in the analysis, Kalecki presented a second section, which he called 'Mathematical Development'. This is built around his investment function, from which he derived the conditions for regular eight- to ten-year cycles around a trend, using an equation for harmonic vibrations which can have a constant, decreasing or increasing amplitude.

The Mathematical Development section is followed by one entitled 'Applications'. Its first subsection, 'The Money Market', appeared in the French edition of the *Essay* that appeared in *Revue d'économie politique* (the French translation was done by his institute colleague, the multilingual Blanka Winawer). In this section Kalecki shows how investment essentially finances itself by demonstrating that rising investment is possible with a constant overall total balance sheet of the banking system. In part investment is financed by having businessmen transfer what Kalecki calls 'unattached deposits' – that is, bank deposits that are not designated for any particular planned expenditure – into 'investment reserve funds'. In the course of investment, the reserve funds are transferred to other capitalists, who pay the costs of producing investment goods out of the reserve funds that they receive:

> It follows that, during the rising half of the cycle, the accounts of investment reserves and money in circulation increase at the expense of 'unattached' deposits. In the second half of the cycle, opposite

> transfers take place between accounts of the consolidated balance sheet. The creation of investment reserves and money in circulation takes place here – without an increase in bank credits, just by means of a change in the composition of bank liabilities: credit inflation consists in the fact that unattached deposits are transformed into investment reserves or money in circulation.[16]

In a more sophisticated financial system, one operating with bills, bonds and stocks, Kalecki argues that the conversion of unattached deposits into investment reserves takes place through the issue, by companies intending to invest, of stocks and bonds, which are sold to holders of unattached deposits. Here the rate of interest becomes a factor; but what matters is, not the absolute rate of interest (real or nominal), but the margin between the yield on stocks and bonds and the rate of interest on bank deposits. That margin must be allowed to rise in order to persuade holders of unattached deposits to invest in bonds and stocks. At the same time, the rate on deposits will rise as banks experience the transfer of investment reserve funds between individual accounts and into money in circulation and try to attract liquidity. Kalecki's conclusion from this is striking: the rate of interest effective for business and investment purposes is endogenous to the business cycle, or as he puts it:

> Thus changes in the rate of interest are determined by the mechanism of the business cycle rather than determining it.[17]

The second 'application' is to 'Production, Prices and Wages', showing that profits and the distribution of income are not dependent upon the level of wages but 'are entirely determined by the mechanisms of the business cycle'. Through its impact upon profits, investment also determines total production and employment. Government may affect the distribution of income through its fiscal policy and may even add to profits if it runs a fiscal deficit, in which case the government becomes indebted to the capitalists whose total incomes are being increased by the deficit. The final 'application' is a discussion of the influence of cartels. Here Kalecki repeats his earlier argument about the effect of cartels on the distribution of profits between the cartelised and the competitive sectors of the economy. Cartels cannot stabilise profits and the business cycle overall; they can stabilise them only within the cartelised sector, at the expense of the competitive sector, which is then subject to more extreme fluctuations. Similarly, wage stability or increases in the cartelised sector are obtained at the expense of wages in the competitive sector.

First critical responses

Richard Goodwin was later to write that Kalecki's 'presentation of his theory to the Econometric Society in 1933, after finding little resonance in Poland, was an event of great significance, though its initial impact seems to have been negligible. Fortunately Kaldor was present'.[18]

Yet Kalecki's analysis of the business cycle made sufficient impact in Poland to generate an outraged response from orthodox Marxists in the Polish Communist Party. The standard Marxist analysis of the economic crisis emphasised an inverse relationship between wages and profits, so that if wages fell or rose, profits would rise or fall proportionately. Hence the view of the doyen of Communist economists, the Soviet Hungarian Eugene Varga, that if wages fell sufficiently, profits must eventually rise and the capitalist economy embark on a recovery.[19] One Polish Communist, the economist Aleksander Rajchman, published an article in *Kwartalnik Statystyczny* (one of the few remaining journals in Poland where Communists could publish) criticising Kalecki for attempting to subject social relationships to mathematical determinism in the guise of an ineluctable business cycle. This, in Rajchman's view, left no scope for class struggle as a determinant of economic outcomes. Rajchman then proceeded to identify inconsistencies in Kalecki's mathematics.[20]

In an article that deserves greater attention as an exposition of his methodology, Kalecki responded to Rajchman's criticism by arguing that he, Kalecki, was not trying to put forward a theory in which the economy is determined by certain mathematical relationships. He pointed out that his 'Mathematical Development' came *after* the first part of the paper and merely formalised certain relationships explained in it, where the essential features of the capitalist economy, profits and the dependence of that economy on the investment process, are defined and argued out. As usual in answering questions on his theory, Kalecki reiterated the main points of analysis and defied Rajchman to find anything controversial in the assumptions made in that analysis. He proceeded to correct Rajchman's mathematical errors.[21]

Behind Rajchman's rather intemperate criticism of Kalecki's theory was a particular vision of the capitalist economy, one shared by many Communists at that time and since. Grounding themselves in a Law of Value, in which all surplus in an economy represents working time that is not paid by the capitalist in the form of wages, Ricardian Marxists overlook that part of Marx's argument (in vol. II of *Capital*) dealing with how that surplus can be realised as money. Obviously this money profit cannot come from the money that the capitalists pay their workers. Marx showed that this money comes from the capitalists themselves when they buy consumption goods or investment goods.[22] This then led to the analyses of Rosa Luxemburg and Mikhail Tugan-Baranovsky, precursors of Kalecki, who, like him, saw the central importance of capital accumulation (or investment) to the whole process of capitalist growth and development.

At the institute, however, Kalecki's analysis was well received. The director, Edward Lipiński, arranged for Kalecki to give a lecture to the Polish Association of Economists and Statisticians.[23] Kalecki was now keen and encouraged enough to present his work internationally. Blanka Winawer's mother translated the essay into German to secure publication in the language in which the most advanced monetary and business cycle analysis was discussed. However, Hitler's appointment as chancellor brought serious German economic debates to an abrupt halt. A copy of the German translation was sent to Keynes, only to be returned with a handwritten response in the margin of the paper: 'I regret I don't read German.'[24]

At the end of September 1933, Kalecki left Poland for the first time to travel to the third European meeting of the Econometric Society, in Leyden. Here he presented a French translation of his paper, under the title 'Essai d'une théorie des mouvements cycliques construite à l'aide de la mathématique supérieure'. This was eventually published in English, in the society's journal *Econometrica*, as 'A Macrodynamic Theory of Business Cycles'.[25] At Leyden Kalecki met for the first time the senior figures of mathematical economics – Ragnar Frisch, Jan Tinbergen, Jacob Marschak – and discussed with them their work as well as his. The reports from the conference indicate differences of opinion over matters as significant as the estimated average duration of a business cycle and its dependence on the time it takes to install new capital equipment. Kalecki seems to have established a view that was distinctively different from that of most of the participants, Tinbergen in particular. While they argued, in line with the accepted theory of general equilibrium since Walras and Pareto, that prices determine production and investment choices, Kalecki argued that profits and capacity utilisation were the key determinants of those choices and the business cycle in general.[26] After his paper was published in *Econometrica*, Kalecki wrote a rejoinder to Tinbergen in which he explained that the key variable in the economy is not just the price level but the level of prices relative to wages. This determines real wages and consumption, of course. But with an elastic credit system supplying means of payment, the price level becomes endogenous to the business cycle, which remains determined by the volume of industrial production, investment in particular.[27]

To the objection of Ragnar Frisch and Harald Holme that his model assumed constant amplitude (i.e., the same difference between output in the peak of the boom and output in the trough of the recession), Kalecki gave a characteristically lapidary and philosophical response:

> Frisch and Holme object to the above assumption of constant amplitude. They are right, for it is by no means sufficient to say that an assumption is correct because it is confirmed by the conditions of real life [i.e., empirically]. It must be made clear why real life is like that, otherwise the particular predilection it shows for a constant amplitude might appear metaphysical.

Kalecki did not pretend to know why industrial fluctuations had to have a constant amplitude. But he put forward an intriguing reason why this might be so. In his model, the amplitude of the cycle depends upon a parameter relating the volume of (new) investment orders to the current output of investment goods. A smaller value of this parameter would result in damped (convergent) oscillations. A higher value of the parameter would give industrial fluctuations of increasing amplitude. Kalecki suggested that damped oscillations (a smaller volume of investment orders relative to the current output of investment) would result in businesses requiring less precautionary liquidity, so that the overall effect will be an increase in business and bank reserves. In that situation the credit system becomes more elastic in its ability to advance new credit. Therefore a given rise of prices or production is less likely to evoke an increase in the rate of interest. In turn, the greater availability of credit at the current rate of interest will tend to increase the parameter relating (new) investment orders to the current volume of investment, increasing the amplitude of the cycles. In the case of cycles with a growing amplitude, the rise in precautionary reserve requirements will tend to induce monetary tightening (a rise in the rate of interest and a reduction in the availability of credit) in response to any rise in process or production. In turn this will reduce the effect of current investment output on (new) investment orders.

In this way Kalecki put forward the credit system as a regulator of the business cycle, with what Keynes was later to call the 'precautionary demand for money' serving to keep that cycle regular.

At some time in 1933 (the key dates of Kalecki's life before the war remain vague) Kalecki's father died. The failed capitalist whose plight set Kalecki on his course to understanding capitalism never witnessed the maturity of that understanding.

8
Sweden

8.1 Challenging general equilibrium

In his debut at the Econometric Society in Leyden, Kalecki had been confronted by the view prevailing in economic theory at the time – namely, that prices determine investment and production choices that lead to a general equilibrium in which all resources are applied to useful or desired outcomes. He disposed of this notion in his paper 'Three Systems'. This paper has not been well understood. The paper is Kalecki's attempt to think through the flaws in the standard general equilibrium approach to economics. The approach regards the economy as integrated by a system of relative prices abstracted from monetary factors and considers business fluctuations as being due to some kind of natural competition in markets or responses to incorrect prices (including interest rates) brought on by changes in resources, technology or consumer preferences. Needless to say, because of the object of its analysis, this is the most 'neoclassical' of Kalecki's papers, in the sense that in it he appraises the neoclassical idea that prices and wages, rather than business investment, determine production and employment decisions. As a result of this neoclassical focus, a small but significant literature has emerged around the theme that Kalecki's paper anticipates Hicks's system of Keynesian general equilibrium, known to generations of economics students as the IS/LM system.[1]

Kalecki's 'Three Systems' paper was published in the Polish economic journal *Ekonomista*. In setting out successively four sets of assumptions, the paper has a formal character. The first are general assumptions about 'economic processes': the institutional division of society into capitalists and workers, the durability of capital equipment and the existence of a given stock of productive capital. The remaining three sets of assumptions concern economic equilibrium and its consequences. In the first of those three it is assumed that all income is spent; that is, that the amount of purchasing power in the economy remains constant. In that situation, the rate of interest is determined by a kind of 'loanable funds' equality between saving and investment. A fall in wages will therefore be followed by price changes, which will shift demand from consumption goods to investment goods, balanced by a rise in investment, keeping total output and employment more or less constant. This is the standard neoclassical equilibrium.

In the second system, Kalecki allowed the amount of money in circulation to vary. The rate of interest is now determined by the velocity of circulation of money: an increase in this turnover of money increases business requirements for cash reserves. In this situation, the same general equilibrium eventually arises. However, the monetary system creates a longer and disturbed approach to that equilibrium. Unemployment causes falling prices, output and employment in the consumption goods' industries, which then reduce investment orders. The process continues until the circulation of money has been so reduced that the fall in the rate of interest induces a resumption of investment, which eventually causes the system to go back to its full employment equilibrium. Varying the supply of credit merely obstructs the rate of interest mechanism that brings about the equilibrium. Any attempt to maintain a consistent policy of low interest rates eventually leads to price inflation.

In the third system, the assumption of constant purchasing power or demand is abandoned, under conditions of excess labour supply. Here technological innovation causes a rise in investment; this increases output, employment and profits. By contrast, increased saving causes a reduction of demand, investment and profits. In his conclusion, Kalecki pointed out that the eventual general equilibrium was conditional on a given stock of capital. Whereas in systems I and II excess supply of labour sets off mechanisms that restore full employment, in system III this is no longer the case. Once the capital stock is allowed to vary and change its structure because investment adds to productive capacity, the economy succumbs to cyclical fluctuations. 'In my opinion, these are proper business fluctuations'.[2]

In system II changes in economic activity are driven by differences between the rate of profit and the rate of interest, differences that offer the entrepreneur the possibility of making a net profit after payment of interest if the rate of interest is below the rate of profit. This was a common feature of much business cycle theory at the time. But its origin as an explanation of business fluctuations lies in the work of the great Swedish monetary economist Knut Wicksell, who was still active in the 1920s and died only in 1926. Wicksell inspired much German and Austrian monetary theory, and by the 1930s the influence of his ideas extended even to Britain.

'Three Systems' was therefore a response to those critics at Leyden who had argued that the natural state of the economy was one of general equilibrium, changes in which were caused by such 'exogenous' factors as changes in consumer tastes and preferences or in technology or in the discovery of new natural resources. In the neoclassical view departures from general equilibrium, such as involuntary unemployment, were caused by a lack of price flexibility in the system. In his paper Kalecki showed that, even in the presence of complete price flexibility, such adjustments would be prolonged by the presence of monetary factors and that once the artificial assumption that the capital stock did not change was dispensed with, such a general equilibrium was unlikely to ever come about.

The following issue of *Ekonomista* published the economist A. M. Neuman's critique of Kalecki's paper, expressing general disagreement with Kalecki's assumptions and his method of reasoning by means of successive variation of assumptions. On grounds that production in the economy uses capital and labour that may be substituted, Neuman argued that the level of employment is determined by the wage rate *relative* to the cost of capital and that, therefore, a state of unemployment would not arise if prices and wages were sufficiently flexible.[3] In his rejoinder to Neuman, Kalecki made clear that he was combining assumptions which economists commonly make with a realistic view of how the economy operates, or what he called 'economic processes'. Kalecki defended the logic of his argument.[4] But, it should be stressed, he was not defending the realism of the 'Three Systems'. The point of that paper was not to argue that any of those three systems was a realistic portrayal of how the capitalist system operates; it was to show that the arguments that economists of his time used – that price and wage flexibility, or monetary policy, could secure full employment equilibrium – would not have that effect. The evaluation of these neoclassical arguments accounts for the neoclassical flavour, unusual in Kalecki's writings, of the 'Three Systems'.

8.2 Aspects of the business cycle

Over the next couple of years, Kalecki published articles in the business press explaining aspects of his essential business cycle model. For example, in 'The fate of experiments'[5] he explained why government expenditure financed by borrowing would not restrict the financial resources available to private business – the so-called crowding-out argument used by fiscal conservatives to oppose fiscal deficits:

> [In the USA] sums previously held in private banks were spent by the government. This does not force these banks to restrict credit, however, for the money spent by the government in the final analysis falls into the hands of capitalists as profits and in this form returns to the banks.

Furthermore, government expenditure that stimulates private sector investment will generate an economic upswing that will increase tax revenue, allowing for interest payments on government debt, even its repayment. Kalecki illustrated this with the following parable that highlights the interdependence of businesses on each others' expenditure:

> A certain economic region was heavily dependent on a huge steel-mill located there. The coal for this mill as well as for the entire industry of the region was supplied by a mining company. As a result of an unfortunate accident, the mill blew up. Its owners received the insured value of the mill from the insurance company. But, since business was slack in the steel market and profits were not even enough to pay a normal return on capital, the owners decided not to rebuild the mill. The result of this was the suspension of production by plants directly connected with the mill, a big increase in unemployment, and the collapse of the industries producing consumption goods for the workers. In short the region fell into acute economic crisis. As a result, coal sales of the mining company shrank to a minimum and it was faced with bankruptcy. The mining company then negotiated a loan and rebuilt the steel mill. With weak demand in the steel market the mill was still losing money. But the mining company off-set these losses with the recovery of coal sales, not only to the steel mill, but also to all the other industrial plants in the region.[6]

For Kalecki, the government was like the mining company whose increased indebtedness could generate additional revenue and employment.

In another paper, 'The Business Cycle and Welfare',[7] he examined evidence of weak growth in consumption since the crisis reached its trough in 1932. Kalecki distinguished two kinds of industrial boom. The first was a straightforward increase in private sector investment. The second was a 'synthetic' boom set off by public works organised by the government. Kalecki emphasised that 'an increase in the consumption of the working masses is never the basis for a business upswing. The creation of purchasing power for investment purposes always lies at the heart of a business upswing.' In part this was so because, in his standard framework of analysis of a closed economy with only two classes, capitalists and workers, and with no workers' saving, increased wages would cause an increase in prices and must necessarily do so in order to make increased production profitable. In (Nazi) Germany the increased employment arose because real wages actually fell since the crisis and a 'synthetic' boom was generated, financed out of savings in state unemployment benefit as employment rose.[8] In the United States the growth of consumption was hampered by the absence of unemployment insurance. This meant the rise of indebtedness among the unemployed, so that any increase in employment had a reduced effect on consumption, because the increase in wage income was used to repay debts to retailers. Kalecki concluded that the key factors holding back economic recovery were reductions in international trade and capital circulation.

Kalecki took up the foreign trade aspects of the cycle in his paper 'The Business Cycle and the Balance of Payments'.[9] This examined how a business upswing tends to cause an increase in imports, hence a deterioration in the trade balance. In a world of free capital movements, an inflow of capital may offset the trade deficit. But otherwise, in the face of a trade deficit, the central bank may be faced with an outflow of foreign currency reserves. This could be overcome temporarily by suspending the servicing of foreign debt. Otherwise the central bank may take steps to choke off the boom by tightening monetary policy: increasing interest rates or imposing credit restrictions. Kalecki doubted that devaluation of currency would work in the face of import tariffs and protection in other countries. Furthermore, devaluation and import restrictions, to prevent the deterioration of the trade balance, would tend to reduce domestic consumption by making imported goods, or goods with an imported content, more expensive in relation to wages.

The fourth distinctive paper from this period was Kalecki's analysis of the boom in Nazi Germany: 'Stimulating the Business Upswing in Nazi Germany'.[10] He argued here that the German boom was one of rearmament rather than increased consumption by the masses. The result was an increase in profits and difficulties in the foreign trade balance. What stands out in the paper, however, is Kalecki's fine analysis of the process of 'credit inflation' by which German rearmament and public works were being financed. This was through the issue of bills which the German central bank, the Reichsbank, was discounting. Kalecki saw no difficulty in the continuation of this increasing indebtedness of central and local governments of Germany. The increase in government bills held by commercial banks was matched by an increase in deposits on the liabilities side of the banks' balance sheets, and the liquidity of the banks was maintained by the willingness of the Reichsbank to discount the bills, despite the legal limits on such discounting. Indeed, Kalecki pointed out, should the Reichsbank ever wish to desist from such discounting, the same effect could be obtained by supplying commercial banks with the liquidity to allow those commercial banks to do the discounting on the Reichsbank's behalf.

8.3 A lifeline needed and found

On 12 May 1935 the head of the Polish military and the effective head of state, Józef Piłsudski, died. While originally from the Polish Socialist Party, he had allied himself with the landowning classes and big business, a relationship strengthened with the onset of the economic crisis in 1931 and associated with attacks on trade unions and the political opposition (see Chapter 6). Shortly before he died, the constitution had been changed to limit further the prerogatives of the elected legislature. Piłsudski's successors were, with exceptions like Kwiatkowski, brutal, venal, short-sighted and histrionic, modelling themselves on the Italian Fascists and the political right in the Spanish army, where General Francisco Franco was preparing his coup to overthrow the Spanish republic. Nationalism became the pretext for increasing anti-Semitism and attacks on Jews in public institutions, in universities, in business and on the streets.[11] Since his employment depended on the patronage of Eugeniusz Kwiatkowski, who in 1935 became deputy prime minister and finance minister, Kalecki steered clear of commenting critically on the political situation in Poland. He was highly thought of for his work on business cycles and cartels, work of which Kwiatkowski approved, and had been promoted earlier in 1935 to the position of head of research on cartels (*kierownik referatu karteli*). But his left-wing views were well known, and these, as events proved, made him vulnerable.

A lifeline appeared at the end of 1935, following a recommendation by Edward Lipiński to the Rockefeller Foundation in New York that Kalecki be given a fellowship to travel abroad in order to study. Oskar Lange had been a beneficiary of the Rockefeller Fellowship Programme since the beginning of 1934 and by 1935 was working at Harvard University. Supported by a positive, if not enthusiastic, opinion in his favour from Ragnar Frisch,[12] Kalecki was awarded a fellowship, with a stipend of US$200 per month together with tuition and travel expenses. Kalecki's research was to be on 'Business cycle theory, partic[ularly] from [the] standpoint of Wicksell's money theory'.[13] The programme for his research, given in summary in Kalecki's file at the Rockefeller Archive Center, stated that Kalecki would 'visit a number of Business Cycle Institutes in various European countries'. However, 'the main part of his program' would be carried out in the Scandinavian countries, where he would work with Gunnar Myrdal in Stockholm and Ragnar Frisch in Oslo, and in England 'under the direction of Prof. J. M. Keynes' in Cambridge.[14]

In the 1930s Stockholm was known as the centre for the 'Stockholm School' of monetary analysis, although its founder, Knut Wicksell (1851–1926), never actually had an academic appointment in Stockholm – he taught at the University of Uppsala and obtained his chair in Political Economy at the University of Lund. Wicksell had spent much of the 1880s and 1890s studying monetary theory and banking. This culminated in his most important work, *Interest and Prices*. Wicksell was a neoclassical thinker, in the sense that he believed that productive capital generated its own return. He called the marginal productivity of capital the 'natural rate of interest'; this played a key part in his analysis of business cycles. A great admirer of the general equilibrium theory of Walras, Wicksell's admiration was qualified by his recognition of the existence of business cycles in the modern world (Joseph Schumpeter displayed a similar admiration for Walras, similarly contradicted by Schumpeter's own business cycle analysis). Wicksell argued that business cycles were driven by differences that arose between the natural rate of interest and the rate of interest on loans, or the money rate of interest. If the natural rate of interest exceeded the money rate of interest, entrepreneurs would borrow in order to invest, and this would set off an investment boom. This would continue in a 'cumulative process', causing successive increases in economic activity until inflation set in or banks started running out of reserves, in which case they would raise the rate of interest and eventually eliminate the profits to be made from investing in fixed capital. The reduction in investment would cause the boom to turn into a recession, in which the marginal rate of profit or the natural rate of interest would fall below the money rate of interest. The recession would continue until banks reduced the rate of interest back below the natural rate of interest.

In Wicksell, the rate of interest (natural or money) is the key determinant of the economic conjuncture, but the quantity of money and its circulation are determined by business expenditure and the credit operations of banks. This was contrary to the quantity theory of money prevalent at the time among English-speaking economists, including Keynes, according to which the quantity of money in circulation determines the price level in equilibrium, and changes in that money supply cause changes in economic activity only until such time as prices have adjusted. The publication of a German translation of *Interest and Prices* in 1898 made it a founding document of German monetary theory in the first decades of the twentieth century, influencing the great Austrian monetary theorists like Schumpeter and Friedrich von Hayek, as well as Kalecki's friend and associate Marek Breit and Kalecki himself.[15] The 1936 publication of Richard Kahn's translation of Wicksell's book extended its influence among English-speaking economists.

However, well before Kalecki arrived, the Stockholm School had found the progress of its business cycle analysis stuck in the contradiction inherent in trying to create a dynamic analysis of the business cycle within a general equilibrium framework. The Swedish economist David Davidson had challenged Wicksell over the question of whether interest rate policy should be used to stabilise current economic activity or to stabilise the market for capital: The two could not be simultaneously achieved (as Kalecki showed in his 'Three Systems' paper). During the 1920s the issue was taken up by a younger generation of economists, including Gunnar Myrdal. By the 1930s the discussion in Sweden was being reformulated in terms of uncertainty and coordination failure rather than the monetary or financial determinants of the business cycle.[16]

Before Kalecki left Warsaw he placed the management of his mother's modest financial investments in the hands of his friend Marek Breit. Klara Kalecka had remarried after the break-up of her marriage to Abram, and her second husband had been able to maintain her in the style to which she had been accustomed. However, he too had been affected by the crises that afflicted Poland after independence, and by the 1930s she was reduced to paying her way out of her savings and the foreign language tuition that she was able to give.

Kalecki arrived in Stockholm with his wife, Adela, in January 1936. The only account of his time in Sweden comes from the report that he gave to the Rockefeller Foundation on 16 November of that year. He worked on 'problems of monetary equilibrium and Wicksellian cumulative process', which he discussed with Myrdal, Bertil Ohlin, Erik

Lindahl and the Dutch economist Tjalling Koopmans. In his comment on Kalecki's report, the foundation's assistant director of social sciences, Tracy B. Kittredge noted that:

> In spite of K's shyness and difficulty of expression [at the time, apart from his native Polish, Kalecki spoke only Russian and some German – JT] he has made a uniformly favourable impression on the economists with whom he has worked. Profs. Ohlin and Myrdal have spoken very highly of the papers that he read in Stockholm and of his participation in discussions of the Economic Society there. Dr. Koopmans...feels that his scholarship is sound, that he has definite originality and is 1 of the most promising of younger economists in South-Eastern Europe.[17]

8.4 The reaction to Keynes

Kalecki started his fellowship work in Stockholm on 6 February 1936. Two days earlier Keynes had published his *General Theory of Employment Interest and Money*. Reports of its reception by Kalecki are dramatic: Joan Robinson was later to write: 'He [Kalecki] told me that he had taken a year's leave from the institute where he was working in Warsaw to write the *General Theory*. In Stockholm someone gave him Keynes's book. He began to read it – it was the book he intended to write. He thought that perhaps further on there would be something different. No, all the way it was his book. He said: "I confess, I was ill. Three days I lay in bed. Then I thought – Keynes is more known than I am. These ideas will get across much quicker with him and then we can get on to the interesting question, which is their application. Then I got up."'[18]

Much the same reaction is reported by George Shackle, who helped Kalecki with his English when Kalecki published his first book in Britain in 1939.[19] George Feiwel, basing himself on Joan Robinson's and Shackle's recollections, has it that Kalecki 'interrupted his work and left for England'.[20]

The truth may be more prosaic. According to Kalecki's own later account, given in interviews with Tadeusz Kowalik at the beginning of the 1960s, the book on which Kalecki was working at the time he decided to come to England was 'of a general nature, but particularly on the extension of the profit theory [i.e., Kalecki's view that profits depend largely on business investment – JT]. When he had already begun to dictate the book to his wife, he received news of the appearance of a book by Keynes solving certain questions in a similar way. So he gave up work on his own book and went to England'.[21] The news of Keynes's book was given Kalecki by a colleague from the institute, Józef Zagórski, who was at the time on study leave in London and heard of the publication of Keynes's book. Shortly afterwards Kalecki obtained a copy of the book.[22] If nothing else, the book and the discussion around it would have clearly indicated to him that the new theory of capitalism was emerging not in Sweden but in England. Since research in Britain was included in his programme of study under the fellowship, Kalecki and his wife moved to London at the end of March.[23]

The book on which Kalecki was supposed to have begun working in Stockholm was to appear at the end of 1936 as his paper 'A Theory of the Business Cycle' in the *Review of Economic Studies*. In it Kalecki expressed, perhaps unconsciously, the influence of Swedish business cycle ideas and his differences with them in an oft-quoted passage that concludes his paper:

> [T]he question 'What causes the periodic crises?' could be answered briefly: the fact that investment is not only produced but also producing. Investment considered as capitalist spending is the source of prosperity, and every increase of it improves business and stimulates a further rise in investment. But at the same time investment is an addition to the capital equipment, and right from birth it competes with the older generation of this equipment. The tragedy of investment is that it calls forth the crisis because it is useful.[24]

Kalecki was echoing a passage in Wicksell's *Lectures on Political Economy*, where in his discussion of the marginal productivity of capital, the Swede had argued: 'If we consider an increase...in the total capital of society...In the first instance, new capital competes with the old and thereby results, in the first place, in a rise of wages and rent, possibly without causing much change in the technical composition of the product or the magnitude of the return...The increase in wages and rent may absorb the superfluous capital, so that the latter is now just sufficient for the needs of production' (Wicksell *Lectures*, vol. 1, 148).

For Wicksell then, the income effects arising out of the addition of new capital adjust the composition of demand to maintain full utilisation of productive capacity. But those income effects would arise only if there was full employment before the increase investment took place. But since capitalist market economies normally operate with spare capacity, in the form of unemployed workers and less than full utilisation of equipment, the rise in wages and rent expected by Wicksell could not occur. Kalecki therefore came to the opposite conclusion. He had already shown in his 'Three Systems' paper that such equilibrating income changes would not arise and therefore the market capitalist system would fall into crisis due to inconsistencies between productive capacity and demand. The true significance of 'Three Systems' is as a critique of Wicksellian general equilibrium, supposedly established by price and wage flexibility.

9
London

In April 1936 Michał and Adela Kalecki arrived in London, where they rented a room in 34 Coram Street, just off Russell Square, in the Bloomsbury area. Kalecki would not have been aware at the time that Keynes was living just around the corner, in Gordon Square. It is more likely that the Kaleckis came there because another Polish economist from Lange's Union of Independent Socialist Youth, Władysław Malinowski, was already lodging there.[1] The location was convenient, too, for getting to the London School of Economics, where in addition to learning English as fast as he could, Kalecki attended the research seminar organised by Lionel Robbins. The house in Coram Street was demolished in the 1960s to make way for the imaginative scheme of social housing that is Brunswick Square today.

Lionel Robbins was at that time the head of the Economics Department at the LSE. The pre-eminence of German monetary theory at that time had convinced Robbins that the future lay in Austrian economics, a school of thought firmly rooted in the belief that free markets and flexible prices would eventually overcome any temporary disequilibrium, whether in the labour market with unemployment or in international trade. To this end, Robbins had secured the employment of Friedrich von Hayek as professor in the department. Hayek had as a research assistant a bright Hungarian, Nicholas Kaldor, who was later to describe the seminars as follows:

> Every Wednesday, he [Robbins] held a seminar lasting two hours, for which the programme was settled for many weeks in advance, and on each occasion somebody read a paper. It was unusual in general, but it was usual on this occasion, for the... other professors, readers and lecturers to attend the seminar.[2]

Kaldor went on to give a vivid picture of Kalecki arguing his case in the seminars, oblivious to any considerations of academic seniority:

> Kalecki was an active member of the seminar from the very beginning. At the outset he gave the impression of a little man with a loud and creaking voice, who spoke English completely unintelligibly. He spoke with a very strong and peculiar accent, and nobody could follow what he meant. But he persisted in making frequent interventions, and gradually the situation changed. At first, he was a source of annoyance to most people, but then we gradually learnt to respect him, including Robbins, because gradually it emerged more clearly what he said, and his contributions were always relevant and appropriate for the occasion. And so he emerged, I would say, almost as an important figure.[3]

Apart from attending the seminars, Kalecki threw himself into drafting academic papers, now in English. In a letter to George Feiwel, George Shackle revealed that Kalecki engaged Shackle to visit the room in Coram Street every few days to 'improve the English' in the papers that Kalecki was writing. Characteristically, these occasions contributed little improvement of Kalecki's written English, since Kalecki preferred to lecture Shackle on his ideas.[4] Meanwhile, one of his first tasks was to review Keynes's *General Theory* for the Polish journal *Ekonomista*. The autumn issue of the journal carried two reviews of Keynes's book. One, by Władysław Zawadzki, the conservative professor of economics at the School of Commerce (SGH) in Warsaw, was a very thorough exposition of Keynes's monetary analysis, contrasting it with his earlier ideas in the *Treatise on Money* and the *Tract on Monetary Reform*. Zawadzki regretted Keynes's etatism but comforted himself and his readers that Keynes had changed his mind at least twice before; so the *General Theory* was unlikely to be his final word on the matter[5]. The other review was by Kalecki.

9.1 Kalecki on Keynes

Kalecki's review hailed a 'turning point in the history of economics'. In a characteristically lapidary statement, Kalecki reduced the 380 or so pages of the *General Theory* to five pages, excusing himself by saying that his summary is only 'slightly different…from the original'[6]. He presented Keynes's theory as consisting of two parts. The first was the determination of output and employment ('the 'short-period equilibrium') with a given stock of productive equipment and fixed capital investment in a given period of time. The second was the determination of the level of investment. Kalecki noted Keynes's assumption of a closed economy; that is, the absence of any influence of foreign trade. He added to Keynes's assumptions an assumption that workers do not save, since workers' saving, in Kalecki's view, does not play any significant part in economic processes, and taking them into account would merely obscure Keynes's analysis.

Kalecki was rather more critical of Keynes's use of the 'wage unit' as his essential unit. Keynes justified it on the grounds that prices tend to rise and fall with wages. However, in Kalecki's view, this eliminates from Keynes's analysis one of the key factors in price movements, which were the basis of a critical weakness in that analysis.

Kalecki then proceeded to show that the short-period equilibrium output is determined by capitalists' expenditure on production (wages), their own consumption and their productive investment. The profit-maximising output of the capitalist firm is determined at the intersection, in a graph devised by Kalecki showing costs and revenue against output, of the rising marginal labour cost of production (the cost of producing the next unit of output) with the decreasing marginal revenue (the revenue obtained from the sale of the last or the next unit of output) curve or the value-added curve: output should be no higher, because then wages will exceed the revenue obtained from the last items produced and sold, and no lower, because then more profit could be obtained by expanding production. Mathematically integrating the marginal revenue curves of all capitalist firms will give the total revenue of those firms. Mathematically integrating the marginal labour cost curves of all firms will give their total labour costs. Now from the assumption that workers do not save, it follows that the sales revenue of firms from selling goods and services to workers is equal to the amount that the workers are paid. From where, therefore, does the remainder of total revenue come? In a closed economy, with no government and only two classes in society, capitalists' and workers' total income consists of profits and wages. The remaining sales revenue must therefore come from capitalists' own expenditure out of profits on their own consumption and on productive investment.

In this way, Kalecki was able to show that capitalists' income, or profits, is determined by what capitalists themselves spend on their own consumption or on investment. Whereas workers, who do not save, are limited in their expenditure by their income, capitalists are not limited by their income. They may draw on their savings or borrow. Since workers will 'passively' spend what they earn and capitalists consume what they want, the short-period equilibrium output (and with a given stock of capital equipment, the level of employment) depends on how much capitalists spend on investment. If profits are in part spent on consumption and the rest saved, it follows that the amount of saving by capitalists in a given period is determined by how much they invest. In Kalecki's words, 'investment always forces savings of the same amount'.[7] It follows that the rate of interest is not determined by the demand for and supply of capital. Equilibrium between capital 'demand' and its 'supply' exists at *every* level of the rate of interest.[8]

At this point Kalecki returned to the question of Keynes's choice of the wage unit as a unit of analysis. The wage unit, by definition, does not change if money wages change. But would a change in money wages not affect investment and therefore the short-period equilibrium? 'The most important counterargument' to the proposition that a change in money wages would not affect investment is the possibility that 'a decrease in wages raises profitability and may in this way induce a rise in the volume of investment'. Kalecki found 'insufficiently convincing' Keynes's arguments, in chapter 19 of the *General Theory*, concerning the effects of changes in money wages. Kalecki argued that it is sufficient to assume that capitalists do not *immediately* increase investment as soon as wages are reduced or decrease it if wages rise; that is, that prices adjust to lower or higher wages *before* capitalists change their investment. In that case capitalists will find that their realised profits have not changed as a result of the change in wages and therefore will not change their planned investment. If investment does not change, total output and employment stay the same. In a footnote Kalecki pointed out that he had already demonstrated the independence of output and employment from money wages in his 'Essay on Business Cycle Theory' in 1933.

Kalecki then proceeded to the second part of Keynes's analysis, the determination of the level of investment. In Keynes's analysis this is done by firms investing up to the point where the expected rate of profitability equals the rate of interest. If that rate of interest is less than the expected rate of profit, investment is supposed to rise. The increase in investment will raise the price of investment equipment, bringing down its expected profitability, until that expected profitability is equal to the rate of interest. For Kalecki this was an inadequate explanation. The capitalist entrepreneur makes his decisions on the basis of current prices. Keynes's theory therefore shows only that investment will increase or decrease according to whether the rate of interest is lower or higher than the rate of expected profitability. 'Using the terminology of Swedish economists one can say that Keynes's theory determines only the *ex post* level of investment, but it does not say anything about the *ex ante* level.'[9]

However, the change in prices and output of investment goods does not take place in isolation from the rest of the economy. Increases or decreases in investment are transmitted to the economy at large, generating boom or recession, changes in prices and output in all sectors of the economy and with them changes in expectations. Kalecki cited Keynes's remark that 'the facts of the existing situation enter, in a sense disproportionately, into the formation of our long-term expectations.'[10] These will affect business expectations and optimism about the future, which in turn will again change the difference between the expected profitability of investment and the rate of interest. '"Equilibrium", then is not reached and the growth of investment will persist (we are dealing here, as may easily be seen, with a cumulative Wicksellian process).'[11]

Kalecki attributed this failure to determine adequately the level of investment to Keynes's 'approach, which is basically static, to a matter which is, by its nature, dynamic. Keynes takes as given the state of expectations of returns and, from this, derives a certain definite level of investment, overlooking the effects that investment will, in turn, have on expectations.'[12] Kalecki's suggested solution to this failure was to separate investment *decisions* from actual investment in a given period and accept that in each period planned investment, determined by prices and expectations in that period, will be different from actual investment. As a result, in the following period a new set of prices will generate a new state of expectations and a different rate of interest. These will result in a new structure of planned investment.[13] In effect, Kalecki was arguing that the business cycle approach offered a better framework of analysis to the question of determining investment, hence national income and employment, than the static, short-period analysis of Keynes.

Keynes addressed this point in a letter to Kalecki, dated 30 March 1937. Kalecki had asked him for his (Keynes's) opinion of 'A Theory of the Business Cycle', which Kalecki had just published in the *Review of Economic Studies*. Despite the paper's title, Kalecki made clear its purpose in the first paragraph: 'The paper, in which I attempt to give an analysis of investment, is closely allied to Keynesian theory... I deal with the determinants of the rate of investment and... the results are fundamentally different from those of the Keynesian theory.'[14] Keynes said that the idea that recent price *increases* would give rise to expectations of similar price increases in the future as 'an extravagant over-emphasis of the effect of the immediate situation on long-term expectations... only if future prices are expected to rise *in the same proportion* as present prices [can you conclude] that "equilibrium is not reached and the investment continues to rise".'[15]

Keynes's *General Theory* was, in its full title, a *General Theory of Employment, Interest and Money*. Kalecki's review dealt with the first part of this theory. The significant omission from Kalecki's summary and critique of Keynes's book was any consideration of Keynes's theory of interest and money, arguably the most original part of the book. As usual, Kalecki was addressing those parts of Keynes's theory that were relevant to Kalecki's own business cycle analysis. He had already, in his first essay on business cycle theory, indicated why he might consider Keynes's monetary policy analysis less relevant. In that 1933 essay Kalecki argued that monetary policy was *endogenous* to the business cycle; that is, the business cycle determined the course of monetary policy rather than, as Keynes was suggesting, monetary policy influencing the course of the business cycle.[16] More specifically, in Kalecki's analysis entrepreneurs led rentiers, or what Marx called 'functioning capitalists' led 'money capitalists',[17] rather than the other way around, with monetary policy merely influencing the balance sheet of the banks and the rate of interest in money markets. Kalecki was shortly to develop this aspect of his critique of Keynes.

Kalecki's review of Keynes's analysis did not have much impact. The review itself was translated into Italian only in 1979 and English in 1982. It is unlikely that, save for those who had already read Kalecki's 'Essay on Business Cycle Theory', the Polish readership of *Ekonomista* would have understood the interrogation of a 'deviationist from Marshall' by a 'deviationist from Marx'.[18] Keynes's economic analysis never took root in Polish economics, as it did in the West. Keynes had scandalised Polish public opinion in 1919 with his description of Poland as 'an economic impossibility whose only industry is Jew-baiting'.[19] Under communism Keynes was considered serious but 'bourgeois'.[20] After communism Keynes's doubts about capitalism have had less appeal. However, Kalecki was not unique in putting forward these reservations about Keynes's analysis. Bertil Ohlin, whom Kalecki had met in Stockholm, made much the same points in a paper that Keynes published in the *Economic Journal* in 1937 and suggested that Kalecki might make up the deficiency in Keynes's analysis of investment.[21]

On completion in July of the academic year at the London School of Economics, the Kaleckis left London for Paris and Geneva. In Paris, Kalecki visited the Institut de Recherches Économiques et Sociales and the Conseil Économique. They then went on to Geneva, where Kalecki was able to discuss 'Keynesian theory and problems of the business cycle' with, among others, Gottfried Haberler. Haberler too had read Keynes's *General Theory* but, on reflection, was to find it considerably less original than Keynes (and Kalecki) thought it was.[22]

9.2 Meeting Keynes

Before he left for Paris, Kalecki noticed an article in the June issue of the *Economic Journal* by Joan Robinson, one of Keynes's friends and associates who had also been trained by Marshall and now taught economics at Cambridge. The article, 'Disguised Unemployment', argued that when there is a reduction in employment in normal production and the workers laid off are forced to into marginal self-employment ('selling matches in the Strand, cutting brushwood in the jungles, digging potatoes on allotments'), such low productivity is a form of disguised unemployment. In such a situation actual unemployment underestimates the true level of unemployment and should be adjusted by the change in the productivity of the labour force that has been shifted to this marginal employment. Joan Robinson argued that only in this marginal employment did Say's Law (the notion that in a market economy it is possible at all times and in all places for workers to sell their labour in the market), to whose undermining Keynes devoted much of his *General Theory*, truly apply.[23]

Kalecki wrote to Joan Robinson, and they met. He immediately impressed Robinson with his understanding of the principles of Keynesian economics. He sent her his *Econometrica* paper, the business cycle theory that he had presented in Leyden and a draft – possibly the version of his *Econometrica* paper which he was to publish in the *Review of Economic Studies* in the following year, 1937. On his return from Geneva she wrote enthusiastically to tell him of her pleasure at reading his 'advance on Keynes instead of endlessly disputing with people who have not understood the elementary points'. On her own work she remarked, 'I think you are one of the ten people in Europe who will understand what I am trying to do.'[24]

Joan Robinson was, however, less pleased by the criticisms of Keynes that Kalecki seems to have put into this early draft: '[I]t is a pity that you suggest at the beginning of your paper that you are making an attack on Keynes's system, when your real object is to fill a gap in it.'[25] Kalecki seems to have taken exception to Keynes's vague treatment of saving, which obscures the fact that if firms' investment creates income and is always equal to saving, then in effect, for firms taken together, investment finances itself. Robinson conceded that Keynes was vague on this point. But she found Kalecki's analysis troublesome, too, because Kalecki did not put forward a Marshallian equilibrium output for an individual firm, at the point where marginal cost equals marginal revenue. She sent him her paper on long-period equilibrium employment (another Marshallian concept, the long period being the state of the economy when the capital stock is allowed to vary).[26] Kalecki responded by arguing that over a historical long period, the system could be stable only if investment, capital and output all increased in constant proportions at the same rate or faster than the labour force. Otherwise the stable economic growth would break down.[27] Kalecki also seems to have been keen to show that Keynes's ideas were not so new, because he, Kalecki, had held them for a considerable period of time before Keynes wrote his book. Kaldor remarked, 'A lot of the discussion in Robbins' seminar concerned Kalecki holding a thesis, and somebody else saying that it was a view of Keynes; then Kalecki used to reply that he had held these ideas for a long time already. This emerged on repeated occasions.'[28]

His exchange with Joan Robinson was to be the beginning of a lifelong friendship in which they were to exchange insights into each other's work. Their disagreements precluded the possibility of an intellectual partnership. But their sympathies and that apparent common core of ideas with Keynes made Joan Robinson and Michał Kalecki return time and again to each other, Kalecki in particular for support in his trials to come and Robinson for confirmation that she had indeed witnessed at first hand a scientific revolution.[29]

Robinson was naturally keen to introduce Kalecki to the author of the *General Theory*. Kalecki had returned to London at the beginning of September. He then participated in a meeting of the Econometric Society that was held in Oxford, in which again discussion centred on the new theory of Keynes. With the start of the new academic year, Kalecki resumed attendance at the Robbins seminars. Joan Robinson persuaded Keynes to invite Kalecki to Cambridge to give a paper at a Monday evening meeting of the Political Economy Club at King's College. Only men were allowed to be members of the college, so she could not be a member of the club. But Robinson was allowed to attend the seminar, and she wrote afterwards to Keynes to thank him 'for being kind to my Pole' and noted, 'I think your young men are very clever.'[30]

Keynes was willing to indulge his friend Joan Robinson, and he may have appreciated having an able advocate of theories that he regarded as his own. But the two were not well matched socially, and Kalecki's English still made it difficult sometimes for his listeners to understand the finer points of his arguments. Nevertheless, Kalecki was moving into the Keynes circle.

9.3 Breaking with the Institute

A first step which inevitably increased his dependence on the goodwill of his new friends in England was Kalecki's resignation from the Institute in Warsaw in November 1936. The occasion for his resignation was an incident that illustrated the politicisation of the work of the Institute, its dependence on the patronage of Eugeniusz Kwiatkowski, by now finance minister in the Polish government led by Piłsudski's coterie of generals, and Kwiatkowski's willingness to use his patronage in pursuit of his economic policy. In the background was the reduction in the publishing activity of the Institute. Its main journal, *Koniunktura Gospodarcza*, had started out as a monthly. But by 1935 it was a quarterly publication, which rather limited its ability to provide 'sufficiently early the information required to develop a view on the influences affecting the changing economic situation'.[31]

Earlier in 1936 Kwiatkowski, who was anxious to maintain the currency board with the US dollar that fixed the exchange rate of the Polish currency at złoty 5.3 per dollar, had introduced foreign exchange controls to prevent an outflow of foreign currency from the country's banking system. *Koniunktura Gospodarcza* published a report in which the measure was described as 'mildly inflationary' in the face of the general deflation afflicting the economies of Poland and other European countries.[32] Kwiatkowski, anxious to demonstrate his credentials as a guardian of 'sound' money, demanded the dismissal from the Institute of the authors of the report, Marek Breit and Ludwik Landau, Kalecki's closest collaborators. The Institute's director, Lipiński, was torn between his loyalty to his staff and his dependence on the support of his patron. He considered resigning his position. Since he also held a chair at the main Warsaw business school, the Szkoła Główna Handlowa, resignation would not have left him unemployed or financially embarrassed. In the end he preferred to keep his own position, and he sacked Breit and Landau on 18 November 1936.[33] Landau found work later as a statistician and researcher, but Breit did not find proper employment after he lost his job at the institute.

Despite his own less secure financial position, Kalecki proved to be more principled than his director. A week after, a letter from Kalecki appeared in the daily newspapers *Robotnik* (The Worker) and *Kurier Poranny* (The Morning Courier) informing their readers that he had heard about the dismissal from the Institute of Breit and Landau and the reasons for that dismissal. 'After what has happened I do not consider it possible to remain at the Institute of Business Cycles and Prices. I have therefore asked to be relieved of my position there.'[34] His resignation, like the dismissal of his colleagues, did not create the scandal that Kalecki evidently hoped to arouse. A common view was that the Institute had got rid of 'three Jews'. But his very public resignation was inevitably going to make it more difficult, if not impossible, for Kalecki to find work again in a Poland where research was increasingly politicised. There was of course no question of him finding academic employment, since he did not even have a university degree.

Temporary support was provided at the end of 1936 by the Rockefeller Foundation. The day after Breit and Landau were dismissed, Tracy Kittredge, the assistant director of social sciences, reported to John Van Sickle, another assistant director at the foundation, that 'Prof. Hayek & N. F. Hall spoke of K's work and expressed their conviction that he had obtained the maximum of profit from his fship opportunity & that it would be of distinct importance to extend somewhat the period of his appointment.'[35] At a meeting on 18 December a five-month extension was approved, at the same rate of $200 with travel, tuition and research fees. Kalecki was to continue his studies in the theory of business cycles. But he was also to apply his studies to 'an examination of the present German economic situation' and investigate the 'influence of change of interest rates on methods of production'. The latter was a subject of particular interest to Hayek, who propounded a theory that business cycles were caused by excessive investment due to interest rates being held too low.[36]

Kalecki was to study 'mainly' at the London School of Economics for two months, before travelling to work with Ragnar Frisch in Oslo for 'about' three months.

Kalecki revealed the insecurity of his position to Joan Robinson, who responded by writing to the Rockefeller Foundation in support of an extension to Kalecki's fellowship and any employment possibilities that may have been available to him. She also persuaded her close friend and colleague at Cambridge, Richard Kahn, to take up Kalecki's case. On 4 February 1937 he wrote to Tracy Kittredge: 'I want to support (Mrs Robinson's) view that he (Kalecki) is one of the outstanding economists in the world. I do not want too much to stress my own personal opinion which is that he is the most brilliant of all the economists of his own age which I know of, for I am not going to pretend that everybody would go as far as that, but enquiries in London, Cambridge and Stockholm (e.g., from Professor Ohlin) would I feel sure meet with a satisfactory response. You know the circumstances under which Klecki [*sic*] has felt obliged to resign his job in Warsaw, though I suspect that his desire to avoid causing undue trouble on his account has resulted in the full horror of his situation being concealed from you.'

Kahn went on to make 'some diffident suggestions'. He pointed out that Kalecki had applied for an extension when he still had his job in Warsaw, so that he did not apply for a full extension. 'I wonder if it would not now be possible to give him the full extension for which he would, in fact, have applied if the interests of his own job had made it possible.' Kahn also suggested that 'Klecki' may be useful to the foundation in directing 'more organized work in fundamental economics' or in the Research Department at the League of Nations in Geneva, 'another branch of the Rockefeller Foundation's work', where Gottfried Haberler had been researching the trade cycle. 'The trade cycle is Dr. Klecki's speciality, while his knowledge of languages would serve him in good stead.' Finally he enquired 'whether there may not be Universities (e.g., in Belgium) where dr. Klecki's services would be appreciated.'[37]

Kittredge wrote back from Paris, where the Rockefeller Foundation had its European office, on 20 February to say that he had been 'fully informed of the circumstances which led Dr. Kalecki to resign his post' in Warsaw and had recently discussed the matter with Kalecki in London. 'I understand, from my conversation with Kalecki, that his situation does not present so desperate a character as you have been led to believe. There are various plans now under consideration in Poland to provide a definite position for him in Warsaw as a research associate. For the moment therefore the question of finding an occupation for him abroad does not appear to arise. Thanking you for your interest in Dr. Kalecki's work.'[38]

The record in the Rockefeller Foundation archives suggests that, at the time, the foundation was unaware that Kalecki had resigned from his position at the institute. On 19 February 1937 a meeting at the foundation was informed of a possibility that '[a]s a result of a crisis in the work of the [institute]' Kalecki 'will not return to his position in this Institute.' Lipiński appears, in the notes in the Rockefeller Foundation, as genuinely supportive of his erstwhile researcher's work. In supporting Kalecki's request for an extension of his fellowship, Lipiński had 'indicated... that another position at the School of Commerce would be available for K. in the event of his deciding not to return to the... Institute.'[39] In July 1937, when Kalecki sought a further extension of his fellowship, his 'sponsor and former Director' communicated to the foundation 'the desirability of a further exten. both because K. has made excellent use of his fship experience and a longer period abroad would enable him to round out his studies satisfactorily, and because Prof. Lipiński hopes to have the future collaboration of K. in the field of business cycle research. The next 6 mos. will, he (Lipiński) believes, reveal new possibilities in this field in Poland.'

In the event, the possibilities revealed themselves in Britain rather than in Poland.

10
From London to Cambridge

10.1 Business finance and investment

The Department of Economics at the London School of Economics had its own journal, *Economica*, which was edited by the chair of the department, Lionel Robbins. Since Kalecki was attending research seminars there and, when not attending those seminars, was drafting his own papers, it was natural that he should direct one of his first papers in English to the editors of the journal for publication. His first English paper therefore appeared in *Economica* as Kalecki's alternative explanation of Keynes's 'liquidity trap', or the failure of business to respond to a loosening of monetary conditions by borrowing more for investment. Monetary policy had been loosened in Great Britain with the departure from the gold standard in 1931, allowing the bank rate to be reduced from 3.9 per cent in 1931 to 2 per cent in 1933 (the equivalent rate in Poland had been reduced from 8.6% in 1929 to 5% by 1934). However, this had given little stimulus to business investment. In his *General Theory* Keynes had attributed this apparent unwillingness to borrow for new investment to increased 'liquidity preference' due to more pessimistic expectations among businessmen. Kalecki suggested that the problem was rooted in the structure of corporate finance.

At the heart of Kalecki's explanation was an idea that had been put forward by his friend at the Warsaw Institute, Marek Breit. In a paper which Breit had published in German in *Zeitschrift für Nationalökonomie*, with a shorter version appearing in Polish, he had argued that banks increase the interest they charge on loans in proportion to the ratio of debt to the internal funds of a company (i.e., own funds, or liquid assets). Thus, even low short-term money market interest rates may fail to stimulate investment if the 'risk margin' charged to corporate borrowers has increased, due to the large amount of borrowing, in relation to own funds, which may be drained by low profits, or else due to high borrowing having drained the equity out of the firm. In this way, credit easing may fail to evoke a boom in borrowing.[1]

Kalecki took up and extended the essential concept of financial risk that Breit had put forward. In Kalecki's version the analysis became a theory of investment and a reason why increasing the supply of credit in financial markets would not increase investment, as suggested by the conventional theory, according to which the rate of interest brings the demand for and supply of credit into equilibrium.[2] Kalecki suggested that a constant prospective return on investment is more realistic than the decreasing returns advanced in their investment theory by most economists (decreasing returns being really characteristic only of agricultural or minerals production). Given such expectations of a constant return, determined by the current return on past investment, and the current rate of interest with increasing risk margins, the amount of investment that a firm can venture is limited by the amount of its savings. Borrowing in excess of the firm's own liquid assets (we might today call it borrowing that is not 'hedged' by liquid assets) incurs a higher interest margin. A similar risk constraint would apply to funds raised from the stock market, through a rising cost of funds on bond issues. In the case of shares, existing shareholders would resist the watering down of their stock by additional stock issues and would also resist being faced with rising costs of selling more than an 'optimum size of issue'.

Kalecki's paper evoked a response from N. S. Buchanan and R. D. Calkins, who argued that Kalecki's analysis would apply only to a firm owned by a single proprietor operating with unlimited liability. This would leave out joint-stock companies, the most important business organisations in modern capitalism. The analysis could not therefore be generalised to provide an 'internal financing' constraint for the economy as a whole.[3] In his reply Kalecki argued in general terms that 'the expansion of the firm depends on its accumulation of capital out of current profits' and discussed the limitations of capital market finance.[4] Bond issues reduce the return on share capital if the investment is unsuccessful, while share issues reduce the control of the controlling shareholders. The latter may be partially overcome by a holding company structure (floating off 49% of a subsidiary). But the problem remains that, if the venture is unsuccessful, earnings per share will be reduced. Finally Kalecki suggested that portfolio diversification by rentiers will limit the amount of new shares in a company to which financial investors will be willing to subscribe. He pointed out that all of these difficulties may be overcome through the accumulation of internal savings from profits – that is, entrepreneurial capital. This provides a cushion of reserves to reduce the financial risk of capital subscribers and will even 'widen the capital market for the shares of that company since, in general, the larger a company is the more important will its role in the share market be'.[5]

Kalecki had not only provided a more general analysis of financial risk and credit market impotence. He had, as Lange was later to point out, advanced a theory of the size of the firm that depended on financial factors: '...the size of the firm is thus limited by the capital owned by the entrepreneur'.[6] In contrast, the traditional Marshallian theory of the firm that prevailed in Britain at the time argued that the size of a firm is determined by the profit-maximising *scale* of production; that is, the total industrial capacity that gives the lowest cost per unit of output. The Marshallian theory contains an element for the cost of capital but does not really consider corporate finance. Moreover, strictly speaking, it is a theory of the *scale* of production in one plant or factory rather than a theory of the firm as a corporate organisation.[7] In America the common view, following Frank Knight, was that 'entrepreneurship' or enterprise was the 'scarce' factor that caused long-run average costs to rise.

10.2 A macroeconomic approach to taxation

On 4 February 1937, Kalecki sent Keynes a new paper entitled 'The commodity tax, income tax and capital tax in the light of the Keynesian theory', with a view to its publication in the *Economic Journal*, which Keynes edited. Keynes responded with literary concerns: 'I am happy to accept the enclosed, which I find very interesting, for *The Economic Journal*. The English is not bad, and the corrections required mainly affect the order of the words. The argument would be easier for an English reader to follow if the sentences were somewhat rearranged into our more habitual order.' He asked Kalecki to make explicit 'your assumption' that capitalists consume only non-wage goods and concluded, 'I have been conscious for some time of the relevance of the theory you refer to the choice between income tax and a capital tax, but I had not worked out the conclusion as rigorously as you have done.'[8] The correspondence then extended into a discussion of Kalecki's article on the business cycle, containing his criticism of Keynes's theory of investment.[9]

The paper was published in the June 1937 issue of the *Economic Journal* under the title 'A Theory of Commodity, Income and Capital Taxation' (a certain Mr. K. M. Spang assisted Kalecki with his English).[10] Kalecki put forward typically plausible simplifications to arrive at striking conclusions: The commodity tax (Kalecki meant a sales tax) is levied on wages goods alone; income tax is levied solely on profits; and total investment in a given period is the result of investment decisions in the past, so that investment does not change immediately in response to a change in circumstances. Government expenditure is spent on the salaries of government employees and incomes for the unemployed, disabled and so on.

It is easy to show that, in this situation, an increase in commodity taxes, after prices have adjusted, has no effect on profits (equal to capitalist spending) consumption or real incomes. An income tax, levied on profits and interest, would have a stimulating effect on economic activity, depending on the elasticity of supply of wage goods (now in greater demand due to increased government payments to officials and the unemployed) and providing that capitalists did not immediately decrease their consumption or investment. Their consumption and investment decisions are central to the analysis. Here, as elsewhere, the foundation of Kalecki's analysis was his profits equation according to which, in a closed economy and with no workers saving (simplifications whose removal does not affect his fundamental conclusion), makes profits realised by capitalists as a whole equal to their total expenditure on their own consumption and investment. An essential distinction, one that differentiates his analysis from that of Keynes and the neoclassical analysis of investment, is between *actual* investment, the investment expenditure in any given period of time, and investment *decisions*. Investment *decisions* take time to implement. Those investment *decisions* will therefore be affected by prices, excess capacity, and debt considerations but not by taxes because investment (being the outcome of decisions taken in the past) cannot be reduced immediately in response to a capital tax. As long as their consumption and investment are not affected by taxes, profits after tax equal to those expenditures will continue to accrue to capitalists. However, an increase in income tax would increase the rate of interest, because of the reduced inducement to lend, and therefore might lower investment in the future.

Finally, capital taxation does not affect the inducement to invest, because it is paid regardless of income. Total profits rise by the amount of the taxation, and the total income of workers (employed and unemployed) rises, too.[11] Kalecki concluded 'that capital taxation is perhaps the best way to stimulate business and reduce unemployment. It has all the merits of financing state expenditure by borrowing, but it is distinguished from borrowing by the advantage of the state not becoming indebted. It is difficult to believe, however, that capital taxation will ever be applied for this purpose on a large scale; for it may seem to undermine the principle of private property, and therefore in this case, as in general, 'any government which had both the power and the will to remedy the major defects of the capitalist system would have the will and the power to abolish it altogether.'[12]

10.3 Microeconomic first principles

On 2 February 1937 the Rockefeller Foundation approved an extension of Kalecki's fellowship for a further six months at the same rate, $200 per month, along with travel, tuition and research expenses. Kalecki was to visit Paris for two months, and the remaining four months were to be spent in England. In the event, Kalecki left London in May to go to Oslo, where he met with Frisch and Koopmans. From there, at the beginning of July, he travelled to Paris.[13] There he met with François Perroux, Jacques Rueff and Robert Marjolin and visited the Institut National de la Statistique et des Études Économiques.

In Paris Kalecki observed the aftermath of Leon Blum's Popular Front Government. The government had fallen at the end of June 1937, in the face of opposition from a conservative French senate and the government's indecision over the French franc's adherence to the gold standard and over growing difficulties in public finances. Facing widespread industrial unrest, Blum's government had encouraged the rise of money wages, and these gave Kalecki the idea that he was to formulate on his return in a paper called 'The Lesson of the Blum Experiment'.[14] In this paper he used data on the economic changes that had taken place in France in 1936 and 1937 to investigate the effects of changes in money wages. He showed that, between April 1936 and April 1937, the cost of manual labour had risen by approximately 60 per cent. At the same time, the change in the fiscal deficit and the balance of trade was small, and there was no change in the rate of interest. In Kalecki's view this allowed the French economy to be treated as a 'closed system' for the purposes of examining the effects of a change in money wages.

By a nice coincidence, the prices of imported raw materials also rose by 60 per cent, due to the devaluation of the French franc against gold (an increase in the price of gold). The increase in wages was due to the introduction of statutory paid holidays at the end of 1936, a reduction in the working week to 40 hours without loss of pay, and a wave of strikes in the spring of 1937, which resulted in a 10 per cent wage increase. After taking into account changes in labour productivity, overall labour costs rose by three-fifths over the period. Kalecki then examined the change in prices of finished goods and found that these had increased by around 60 per cent as well.[15] However, Kalecki noted that the cost of living rose much less rapidly, so that for those who remained in employment and without reduced hours, there was a real increase in wages. The increase in money wages and prices also offset the effect on the economy of the large increase in the fiscal deficit under Blum.

Kalecki's conclusion was striking: 'our investigation may be regarded as an empirical verification of the Keynesian theory that the rise of wages in an isolated system tends to change prices in the same proportion, and not to affect the output.' A possible objection is 'the rate of interest has not increased, while "naturally" it would rise appreciably and hamper the increase in the money value of production.'[16] Kalecki seems to have had in mind here a view of the functioning of the money markets that was put forward by Keynes's opponents who were later, somewhat misleadingly, to dub this the 'Keynes effect'.[17] Kalecki dismissed this:

> I think that the rate of long-term interest – and it is this rate which is important for the investment process – is fairly insensitive to fluctuations in the demand for cash. But in any case it does not affect the argument because the Keynesian theory accounts for the depressing effect of the increase in money wages *through the channel of the rate of interest*. The fact of its remaining constant in the Blum experiment just enabled us to eliminate this channel, and thus to test the point in dispute between Mr. Keynes and the classics.

Kalecki also drew an important policy conclusion, that a much greater fiscal deficit would have stimulated an economic recovery which would have increased tax revenues. The recovery, along with a tax reform to decrease the state's dependence on indirect taxation and limit widespread evasion of taxes on incomes, would have balanced the budget in the future. However, restrictions on foreign exchange would have been necessary. 'The vulgar theory according to which the deficit – in particular when financed by the central bank – is an immediate peril to the currency is deeply rooted among French economists, bankers and rentiers. Thus, a "large-scale deficit policy" must cause a tendency towards the flight of capital, followed by a depreciation of the currency, which proves in turn the "French deficit theory" – at least for France.' Even with a deficit insufficient to generate a recovery, 'the Blum government had to face a steady pressure of capital flight which, to put it mildly, was by no means opposed by the leading financiers. Hence the vacillation of the government between a wish to stimulate the economy and a willingness to reduce the budget deficit. The result was the fall of the Blum government and the return to orthodox financial policy.'[18]

Nevertheless, on one important point 'the reality of the Blum experiment seems to disagree with the Keynesian theory.' This is that the increase in money wages has increased real wages. Kalecki pointed to important changes in purchasing power between industries, sectors and social classes during the Blum period. Thus changes in prime costs (raw materials and wages) may determine prices of finished goods. But they are also accompanied by changes in the propensity to consume and shifts in demand in different parts of the economy.

The boldness of Kalecki's conclusion and his disposal of 'external' factors (the foreign trade balance and the fiscal deficit) to arrive at 'closed economy' conclusions could not fail to arouse criticism from economists reluctant to have factors of significance to their theories 'peeled away' in such an apparently cavalier fashion. Foremost among those critics was Robert Marjolin, who Kalecki had met in Paris. Still in his mid-twenties (he was born in 1911), Marjolin had been a Rockefeller fellow from 1931 and had used his fellowship to study at Yale University, where Roosevelt's New Deal had greatly impressed him. In his paper entitled 'Reflections on the Blum Experiment', published in *Economica*, Marjolin put forward his own interpretation of the structural changes that had taken place in the French economy during the Blum administration. In the course of the paper he put forward criticisms of Kalecki's approach.[19]

Marjolin disagreed with Kalecki on three crucial points. First of all, 'the period examined by Mr. Kalecki embraces two quite distinct experiments, affecting the economic indices in quite contrary directions.' The first occurred between June and September 1936, when the French economy was dominated by an overvalued franc and rising wages, both of which adversely affected economic activity. The second experiment was between September 1936 and spring 1937, when the economy recovered rapidly due to the devaluation of the franc. 'Hence a single figure relating to the whole of the period is without significance.'[20]

Secondly, there was the issue of treating the French economy in that period as a 'closed economy'. Marjolin was willing to concede that the balance of payments deficit and the fiscal deficit offset each other, so that there was no net income impact from the two taken together. However, 'the violent movements in exchange rates and in the export of capital, the fluctuations in the various elements of the balance of payments which took place in the course of the twelve-month period considered by Mr. Kalecki' could not be ignored as influences on wages. Finally, he took issue with Kalecki's conclusion that the Blum government was too timid in its fiscal policy. Under full employment, a more expansionary fiscal policy would have resulted only in inflation, and foreign exchange controls would have required a restructuring of the institutional framework of the very internationalised French economy and capital market.[21] In a letter to Keynes, dated 29 May 1938, Kalecki indicated that he had written to Lionel Robbins, who was editing *Economica* to ask if he would publish a response to Marjolin's paper. But there seems to be no further evidence of any formal response by Kalecki.[22]

A more private criticism was addressed by an American economist, Mark Liddell Wehle, who had just published a book called *Wage Reduction in the Depression*. He sent to Keynes, in the latter's capacity of editor of the *Economic Journal*, 'a short discussion which I hope you may care to insert among the Notes in the next issue of the *Economic Journal*.'[23] A copy was included for forwarding to Kalecki. Unfortunately neither the note nor Kalecki's response to it appear to have survived. Keynes replied on 30 May to the effect that he did not think that there was a case for publishing Wehle's note. However, he had passed it on to Kalecki. In the rest of his letter, Keynes addressed what one may infer to have been an important, if not the main issue, in Wehle's note. 'Since my name is mentioned perhaps I may say that in my own view Mr. Kalecki is certainly right in converting the Budget deficit out of money terms into real terms.'[24]

Wehle responded to Keynes on the 28 June by sending him a 'corrected version' of his note, along with a copy for Kalecki. He appears to have been making a case around the link between a government's fiscal deficit and economic activity:

> In correcting the deficit figure for the rise in prices before comparing it with the rise in labour cost, Mr. Kalecki counts the same thing twice. The fact that a middleman intervenes between the labour market and the consumer does not change the effect of a wage increase on employment, nor does the presence of a number of middlemen and a complete price system make things any different from what they would be if the consumer bought the labour himself. The higher prices are merely a result of the higher wages and do not have any additional effect, so that it is not necessary to correct for them. With Mr. Kalecki's 'correction' left out, the deficit seems amply to explain the situation in France.[25]

Keynes responded, in a letter dated 11 July 1938, reiterating his view that there was insufficient interest in the controversy that Wehle was putting forward. 'Moreover, I suspect that you and Kalecki are at cross purposes... Kalecki is arguing that in fact the deficit did not become an increased proportion of the national income. You are arguing, on the other hand, that, if the deficit had been constant in terms of money, and had thereby become a smaller proportion of the national income, this would, in the circumstances, have acted as a deflationary influence, so that Kalecki's argument requires that the deficit should have increased more or less in proportion to prices and wages. But I do not imagine that he or anyone else would dispute that.'[26]

A more successful response to Kalecki's article on the 'Blum experiment' was a paper that Hans Singer sent to Keynes from Manchester on 27 March 1938.[27] The paper compared the dispersion of price changes during the Blum period in France with what he believed was a similar increase in prices in the United States during 1919–20. Singer noted that the function of prices changes is to bring markets into equilibrium, but changes in wages may induce continuing price changes around the trend of increasing wages. Keynes was initially reluctant to prolong the discussion of Kalecki's paper. However, once Singer was persuaded to make his paper rather more general, Keynes agreed to publish it.[28]

On his return to England early in September 1937, Kalecki stayed in Manchester, according to the records of the Rockefeller Foundation.[29] There he met John Jewkes, the professor of social economics at Manchester, who had recently published an important study of wages and employment in the cotton spinning industry.[30] Kalecki was now working on his own formulation of industrial pricing theory in the context of imperfect competition. This was laid out in a paper, entitled 'The determinants of the distribution of national income', that was published in the following year (1938) in *Econometrica*. It displays that genius for inspired induction that was so to frustrate his critics.

Kalecki made clear from the very start of the paper that his intention was to examine 'statistically and analytically the relative share of manual labour in national income'. National income meant total value added by private enterprises. Using data on wages and income in the UK published by Arthur Bowley and Colin Clark and in the USA by Simon Kuznets and Willford King, Kalecki showed that, over time, there was little variation in the relative share of wages in national income. To explain this, Kalecki introduced a concept that had been put forward by Abba P. Lerner, the 'degree of monopoly'.[31] Lerner was lecturing at the London School of Economics when Kalecki arrived in London in 1936.

The two men would therefore have met at Robbins's research seminars. Given that the profit of a firm, per unit of output, is more or less equal to the amount by which the price of a product exceeds its marginal cost,[32] the degree of monopoly may be measured by the ratio of that excess amount of the price to the price. Multiplying the degree of monopoly by the output of the firm gives the gross profit (including dividends and depreciation but before tax) of the firm. Summing up the profits of all firms in the economy gives the total profits in the economy.[33] It is then easy to show that, as an approximation, the relative share in national (private sector) income of capitalist income and salaries is equal to the average degree of monopoly. Kalecki went on to argue that the share of profits in national income would therefore stay more or less constant as long as the degree of monopoly stayed constant and output stayed sufficiently below the full employment of capacity to keep the marginal cost constant.

In general, Kalecki thought that over time, capitalist economies would be subject to a long-run rising degree of monopoly because of industrial concentration. However, this would be offset by 'the diminishing imperfection of the market caused by the fall of transport costs in relation to prices, the standardization of goods, the organisation of commodity exchanges etc.' However, in later capitalism, industrial concentration tends to predominate. The analysis is complicated by factors such the cost of basic raw materials – whose prices and costs are subject to decreasing returns; that is, increasing marginal costs – and the business cycle. In the case of the latter, Kalecki criticised Roy Harrod, who had argued in his book *The Trade Cycle* that more demanding consumers *increase* competition in a slump and *decrease* it in a boom.[34] In fact, cartels are created in a slump in order to 'save' profits but tend to break up in a boom 'because of improving prospects of independent activity and the emergence of outsiders'. Overall, the data showed that 'the relative share of manual labour does not change much during the business cycle'. But in fact 'the prices of basic raw materials fall in the slump and rise in the boom, as compared with wages, and this tends to raise the relative share of manual labour in the slump and reduce it in the boom. If the relative share of manual labour remains more or less constant it can be concluded that the degree of monopoly tends to increase in the depression and decline in the boom.' In other words, the stable share of manual labour wages in total income is because changes in the degree of monopoly are offset by changes in raw material prices.

The final section of the paper dealt with changes in prices and wages in, respectively, the investment and consumption goods sectors of a capitalist economy. Again using data on the U.S. and UK economies, he showed that in fact prices of consumption and investment goods tend to change over time in the same direction and proportion. As for wage rates in the two sectors, these too tended to move together. Kalecki explained in a footnote: 'Wage rates in investment goods industries might be expected to fluctuate more, due to stronger changes in employment. In fact such is not the case because trade unions are strongest in heavy industry.'

Kalecki drew a striking conclusion from this. Since the ratio of prices of investment goods relative to the prices of consumption goods 'has no marked cyclical fluctuations, changes in the ratio of the prices of investment and consumption goods may be neglected in the theory of the trade cycle.' There is an echo here of his paper 'Three Systems' and his response to his critics at Leyden, in his fundamental dissent from those equilibrium theorists, most notably the Austrians Hayek and Schumpeter, who attributed important market-equilibrating powers to changes in relative prices.[35]

However, Kalecki's analysis of the 'degree of monopoly' was far less conclusive. Peter Kriesler observed that Kalecki 'found it difficult to clarify exactly what was meant by the degree of monopoly. In addition, the aggregation from the individual firm to the economy as a whole was more complex than Kalecki had initially realized.'[36] As a factor in the determination of real wage income, Kalecki's insight is striking, because it reveals how real wages cannot be just set in the labour market in isolation from other markets. However, as was later to emerge, the degree of monopoly, as proposed by Kalecki, could be interpreted in a Marshallian way, as influenced by the elasticity of demand for output in relation to its price. Such a view would then rehabilitate Harrod's view on the degree of competition being determined by demand conditions rather than on the supply side. Kalecki's approach also involved a distinctive treatment of costs that was to poison his later research at Cambridge.

11
Seeking Work Again

11.1 Geneva and journalism

However, in the meantime, an urgent professional priority was to secure paid employment. In February 1937 the Rockefeller Foundation approved a six-month extension of Kalecki's fellowship, taking it up to the end of 1937 and thereby giving him the full two-year term of such fellowships. On 15 November, Kalecki moved from Manchester to Cambridge, where he lodged at 15 King's Parade, across the road from Cambridge's most spectacular and wealthiest college, where Keynes was a fellow and, as bursar, responsible for the management of its endowment.

A few days after his move to Cambridge, Kalecki met in London with the Rockefeller Foundation's assistant director, Tracy Kittredge. He told Kittredge that he had now been offered a six-month research appointment in Cambridge assisting in theoretical research under the direction of Joan Robinson and Dennis Robertson. Kittredge reported that Kalecki 'stated that he had no definite confirmation from Warsaw of the news that the Business Cycle Inst. had as yet resumed activities'. The institute's publications had been reduced 'to the barest minimum.' At the heart of its inactivity appeared to be a stand-off between the government and the institute's director, Lipiński, over the dismissal of Breit and Landau. 'K. understands that Lipinski has personally accepted the invitation of the gov't to resume direction of institute but that he has not yet been able to obtain the approval of the Finance Minister (Kwiatkowski) for the re-employment of Breit and Landau, whose discharge last year led to the disruption of the Inst. K. apparently has very little hope of an adequate position in Poland in the near future & is therefore looking about for a permanent position in England or elsewhere.' Kittredge suggested to Kalecki that there may be possibilities in Mexico, and Kalecki said that he would be delighted to apply 'for any appointments that may be open'.[1] The Mexican opportunity came with the setting up there of a statistical research institute which the Rockefeller Foundation was supporting.

Kalecki's move to Cambridge brought him much more directly into the orbit of Keynes's and Joan Robinson's friends. While Kalecki used his Cambridge grant to put his papers together for publication as a book, *Essays in the Theory of Economic Fluctuations,* that was to come out in 1939, his new Cambridge friends continued their campaign to find employment for Kalecki. At the centre of those efforts was undoubtedly his most dedicated supporter, Joan Robinson. Unfortunately there is little surviving evidence of her promotion of Kalecki's employment prospects, as opposed to her well-known promotion of his work. The evidence that survives of the campaign to secure an income for Kalecki is largely from the correspondence of Joan Robinson's close friend in Cambridge, Richard Kahn, who was also very close to Keynes and was, like him, a fellow at King's College. This reveals not only the high regard in which Kalecki was now held by Keynes's followers. It also shows the extent to which Kalecki's friends were now prepared to go to find him a suitable position. Kahn appears to have coordinated those efforts.

As was mentioned in Chapter 9, Richard Kahn had written to the Rockefeller Foundation in February 1937. Not long after, he appears to have written to Bertil Ohlin at the University of California in Berkeley. Ohlin wrote back on 7 May:

> I am very interested in Kalecki's plight, as I share your view that he has unusual ability. As to Haberler's work in Geneva, which is to be continued by Tinbergen with the assistance of D. H. Robertson, I presume that you have long since talked to the latter about it. This work is perhaps too statistical for Kalecki. But I shall be glad to inform Loveday[2] about my opinion concerning Kalecki, if that can be any help. I have recommended him for a job here. But I doubt if there will be any opening this autumn. Perhaps next year K might send some reprints to Prof. Robert D. Calkins, Econ. Dept. University of Calif. Berkeley, Calif.[3]
>
> Kahn communicated this to Kalecki in a letter dated 25 May 1937.

High hopes were attached to the possibilities of employment in Geneva, where the Economic Secretariat of the League of Nation was researching the impact of the Depression on various countries in the world, on trade between those countries and on the international monetary and financial system. But there was also the unnamed research institute in

Mexico, to which Kittredge had alluded. On 21 December 1937, Kahn reported to Piero Sraffa:

> I have had a talk with Kalecki about his future, and he has told me about Mexico. He does not know if the job which he is in for is to be Head of the Institute, or an underling, nor does he know what salary is offered. The Institute is not definitely a Rockefeller Institute, but Rockefeller is helping financially. K believes they are putting forward fifteen names, only one of which is his own...we can no longer regard Mexico as a foregone conclusion...K. has been told that Tinbergen is leaving Geneva; K. would obviously like the job and has, I gather, himself written to Tinbergen with that in view. He has also seen Condliffe,[4] though I do not know how far he went in making a specific suggestion to Condliffe. I am myself now writing to Meade without referring specifically to Tinbergen's departure. It is clear that there is little more that I can do in this direction until you have approached D.H.R.[5] who has much influence in these quarters and whose opinion would carry great weight. I wonder, therefore, if you could now start things rolling with a letter to D.H.R.? You could tell him that K. is now installed at your old house.[6]

Then there was the National Institute of Economic and Social Research, in which Noel Hall, the Professor of Political Economy at University College, London, was active. Kahn was still 'wondering whether something cannot be done about Hall's Institute in spite of Hall's alleged antipathy to K. The trouble at Geneva, K. believes, is that Loveday is said to dislike Jews. If we are going to allow this kind of difficulty to hamper us at every turn we shall get nowhere.'

The alternative, in Kahn's view, was the International Labour Office, also based in Geneva and perhaps more politically congenial to Kalecki: 'what about approaching the International Labour Office, which might jump at a man merely because he had been turned down by the Secretariat?'[7]

That same day Kahn wrote James Meade:

> I am writing to you about the case of M. Kalecki, a Polish economist who threw up his job in the Warsaw statistical institute owing to the Government's insistence on tampering with the tenor of their reports. Kalecki has been a Rockefeller student, but is so no longer, and is spending a few months in Cambridge. The question which very much concerns several in Cambridge, such as Sraffa, Joan

> Robinson and myself, who have an extraordinary high admiration for his qualities, is what is now to become of him. I can write further about his extreme greatness as an economist...he seems to me to be the outstanding figure of his generation. He has been travelling widely in the last year or two, and you will find that such people as Ohlin, Condliffe, and very many others, are acquainted with him...combined with his knowledge of languages...Geneva is obviously the place for him...There is also the International Labour Office as a possibility. With regard to Tinbergen's department, I should add that Kalecki, being an ex-Rockefeller student, is well-known to the Rockefeller authorities in Paris.[8]

Meade replied with a very brief letter dated 10 January 1938: 'I arrived here only on January 3rd and have been waiting to speak about it to Loveday. He tells me that there was a vacancy advertised for application last month and that if Kalecki has not applied for this there is no vacancy now available.'[9]

Kahn finally decided to approach Keynes himself. On 27 January 1938, Kahn wrote to Keynes at his country house, Tilton, summarising Kalecki's position:

> I am writing to tell you the position of Kalecki, not because I think that there is anything that you can do at the moment, but in case any inquiries reach you from the various quarters concerned. Kalecki has been in Cambridge since December, and if he does not get a job in the mean time is staying here until the summer. He has been doing some further extremely interesting work, and is now engaged in putting together his various pieces of work into a comprehensive book.[10]

Kahn went on to list the various possibilities of finding employment for Kalecki that were being followed up. All of them, he thought, were 'vague and dubious'. They were:

(a) The Mexican Government appear to be contemplating setting up a Statistical Institute, and the Rockefeller Foundation, who are no doubt contributing financially, are said to have suggested Kalecki's name for a post in this institute, together with the names of others.
(b) Haberler's successor, Tinbergen, is leaving Geneva. Kalecki has been in touch with him, and is hoping that he may be regarded as a candidate for the vacancy.

(c) Kalecki has written to Professor Hall with a view to a position in the new Bureau of Economic Research. Hall's reply was noncommittal in the extreme.

As a European I should naturally prefer (b) or (c) to (a), while as an Englishman I should prefer (c) to (b). I am confident that Kalecki would be useful to any of these institutions. Every time I meet him I become more impressed by his absolutely terrific abilities. As you are aware, some of us would regard it as a terrible blot on economics and economists if towards the end of the summer he had to return to Warsaw with the idea of picking up a living by writing newspaper articles and possibly getting some minor commercial job. That is the alternative with which he is faced.[11]

Keynes wrote back on 30 January: 'If I have any opportunity of doing anything for Kalecki, I will. It will, I should expect, be quite a time before Hall gets going with his new institution, and I should be surprised if any posts were being filled up as soon as the summer. In the longer run this would be extremely suitable for Kalecki, and at the appropriate moment I will see what I can do to persuade Hall to consider him.'

Keynes went on to express his hopes that the League of Nations would enable Kalecki to introduce some sound statistical research in Geneva: 'Mexico sounds altogether too gloomy. But it would be excellent if he could succeed to Tinbergen at Geneva. Am I right in thinking that the latter's stuff is a piece of almost incredible charlatanry? I am judging from an extract from his stuff which he has just published in Econometrica.[12] If this sort of thing is being taken seriously by the League of Nations and its highly expert advisers, it is one more real disgrace to our fraternity. If I am right in the above, it is furthermore unfortunate that a highly complimentary review of Tinbergen's work is to appear in the next Economic Journal by Phelps-Brown.'[13]

Keynes concluded: 'I am printing in the next Economic Journal an article by Kalecki of a more realistic kind than most of his previous efforts, and this may, I think, help him towards the sort of job you have in mind.'[14]

Keynes then used his London connections to promote Kalecki's case in the City as well as in financial journalism. On 18 March he wrote to Kalecki:

I have now had a reply from the British Overseas Bank. They are very sorry that they have no job to offer. But they were extremely friendly.

They had checked up on the circumstances of your resigning from your Institute, and were informed that the circumstances were such as to do you nothing but credit. They said that, if they could use their influence to help you to get any journalistic work, e.g. with the Economist, they would be glad to do so.[15]

Would you like to explore the situation with the Economist, and perhaps with the Financial Times? The difficulty about this is that one doubts whether you could accumulate anything like a living wage out of such contributions. As regards the Financial News, do you happen to know Einzig? If so, are you in good or bad relations with him?[16]

Kalecki wrote back to Keynes on 21 March. 'I quite agree that it is improbable to accumulate a living wage out of contributions to the journals and thus do not consider the affair worth trouble. I am very grateful to you for writing to the British Overseas Bank. May I ask you to convey to them my thanks for their friendliness?'[17]

Keynes passed on to Kahn a copy of Kalecki's letter with a note dated 22 March 1938: 'The above would not apply presumably to a regular job with the Economist. But is there much chance of this? Perhaps you might sound Crowther.[18] If there looked to be any chance, I would tackle Layton seriously.[19] Dudley Ward,[20] who got very favourable reports on checking up what I told him about Kalecki, said that he would gladly do anything he could with the Economist to help.'[21]

Two days later, on 24 March 1938, Kahn wrote to Crowther: 'I wonder whether you can find room in *The Economist*, either part-time or full-time and either temporarily or permanently, for a very brilliant Polish economist in whom I am interested....'

Apart from being a good statistician, he is an outstanding economist, who ought, apart from his difficulty of being a foreigner, to be given an important academic position. While he has done much on the theoretical side to improve and amplify Keynesian ideas, his interests lie mainly in the application of economic theory to actual problems. His article on Monsieur Blum...displays his ability for picking up the essential facts during a short stay for what was for him a foreign country. He has recently published a number of articles in English and he is at present finishing an English book. He both writes and talks English rather well.

Keynes knows a great deal about him and, if you tell me that there is any hope, would be prepared to give his views either to you or to

> Layton. Dudley Ward, at Keynes's instigation, has had investigated Kalecki's past at Warsaw and would, I think, be prepared to report to you very favourably on the conditions under which he left the Institute. Dudley Ward, unlike Keynes, does not know Kalecki personally, but on the basis of what he has heard about him he takes the view, I understand, that he might be useful to you.[22]

Kahn was not just interceding on Kalecki's behalf. He also enquired on behalf of an Austrian economist, Dr. H. Bab, who was then on a one-year research studentship in Cambridge. 'Being a Jew, there is nothing for him in Vienna, and if you could find some work for him, even though it was of piece-work character, you would be doing him a very great turn. While he is not of Kalecki's calibre, he is extremely presentable (unlike Kalecki, I ought to say, who is a regular Pole to look at)'.[23]

Crowther wrote back on 25 March 1938. 'I am afraid I cannot hold out any hopes of a full-time post for Kalecki at present. Our staff is so small, and the turnover is so slow, that it is very rarely that there is an opening of the sort that would be suitable for him. I feel sure, however, that there must be a number of jobs he could do for us, and I would suggest that he should come up one day and talk them over with us. Perhaps you would [like] to get in touch with me and fix a convenient time... I met Bab in Vienna some years ago, and shall be glad to see him if he turns up.'[24]

Kahn forwarded Crowther's letter on to Keynes with a note: 'Kalecki is going to see Crowther on Friday. A letter from you to Layton would, I think, be most helpful.'[25]

Accordingly, on 30 March, Keynes wrote to Layton. 'May I put in an exceptionally strong word in favour of Dr. Kalecki, who is shortly seeing Crowther with a view to the possibility of work on the Economist'

> Kalecki is, in my opinion, something of a genius. He was previously Director of economic research in the Polish Conjunktur Institute. He there obtained a Rockefeller Fellowship, and whilst he was at the London School of Economics, enjoying this Fellowship, he resigned from his post as a protest against the treatment of some of his academic colleagues there. Dudley Ward has enquired into the details and agrees with the view that the circumstances were wholly to Kalecki's credit, and you would find, I think, that Dudley would very strongly support any effort to get him useful employment.
>
> Whilst his spoken English is rather queer, his written English is excellent, and you will find a heavy article from him in the March Economic Journal. He has written many learned articles, and I think

> it is a matter of time before he will get a good academic job, but he is difficult to place, since his funny way of talking English stands in the way of lecturing or teaching, and it has to be primarily a research job that one puts him into, the sort of job which cannot be found at short notice. I agree with a good many people in Cambridge in rating his gifts very highly indeed. I think they are of the sort that would be useful to you, since, not only is he a first-class theorist, but his statistical, realistic knowledge of economic problems all through Europe is unequalled.
>
> I know that there are too many such cases. But I do put Kalecki rather extra high. I would not only be extremely grateful for anything you do for him, but I believe that your paper would also gain from it.[26]

Layton wrote back on 7 April. 'There is at present no full-time opening for Dr. Kalecki at the Economist, but we are trying him with a couple of articles. If these are what we want, we may be able to use him as a contributor and on occasional investigation. I am sorry we cannot do more.'[27] On 9 April, Keynes wrote to Kahn: 'I am a little hesitant about approaching the Financial News concerning Kalecki, for I am really not quite clear what he can do. I am sure they are full up as regards "intelligence" staff, and I do not know if he would fit in with regular routine. Anyway I think it would be better to see first of all how well he pleases the Economist. If that proves successful, it will give one more to go on.'[28]

In the end, the attempt to marry Kalecki with the organ of Manchester Liberalism appears to have failed, although there may rest in the archives of *The Economist* two articles written by Kalecki at their request. At the beginning of September 1938, Kalecki wrote to Kahn, 'I got £8 from Economist for the two articles which have not been published.'[29]

11.2 The search for academic employment

Efforts turned to finding Kalecki a position at a university. Here the possibilities were limited by his lack of fluency in English, which Keynes had already noted. Apart from private tuition in his youth, Kalecki had no teaching experience. He had no university degree: his diploma in engineering merely recorded his completion of a year of study. A further handicap, which became apparent only when he finally started teaching after he obtained a full-time academic position after the Second World

War, was his distinct lack of interest in any economic theory that was not of direct relevance to his own research. This made him incapable of lecturing any standard syllabus. He was, as Keynes had pointed out in his letter to Layton, most suited to a research post. However, with rare exceptions, British universities in the 1930s did not engage in research. In this respect, Manchester University was unusual in having an economic research centre, which had been set up in 1930. Its director was Professor John Jewkes, whom Kalecki had met in 1937, during his stay in Manchester.[30] The German refugee economist Hans Singer was already working there.

On 26 Richard Kahn sat down to a new round of letters seeking employment for Kalecki. He wrote to Jewkes to inform him that Kalecki 'is badly in need of a job. Should any vacancy in your Research Department present itself, or should you happen to hear of any suitable opening, I should feel enormously grateful if you could let me know. I think you know of the extraordinary high opinion that many of us here have of Kalecki's abilities, while I believe that you have had an opportunity of forming your own impression.'[31] Jewkes eventually wrote back, on 31 May 1938, to tell Kahn that 'I constantly have Kalecki's name in mind but, at the moment, we have no vacancy on our staff, either on the teaching side or in the Research Section. Two or three months ago I expected that we would have at least two vacancies, a consequence of some of our people going off to other universities, but it happens that they have not, at least up to the moment, obtained the appointments they were looking for. But I will indeed have the University consider Kalecki if we have to fill any vacancy this summer.'[32]

Kahn circulated Jewkes' response to Piero Sraffa and Joan Robinson. Sraffa's characteristically conspiratorial response was noted by Kahn on his copy of the letter: 'This seems an argument *against* Jewkes as referee.'[33]

That same day, Kahn wrote to Jacob Marschak, a former Menshevik from Kiev who was director of the Oxford Institute of Statistics, financed in part by the Rockefeller Foundation. 'I am not sure whether you have ever met M. Kalecki, a Polish economist who is spending some months in Cambridge, but you have no doubt read some of his articles and are aware of the extremely high reputation which he enjoys. I am wondering whether there is likely to be any opening in your Department?...Unfortunately we have no Research Department in Cambridge, and it is not therefore possible to suggest that there is a job for him here.'[34]

Again, on the same day, Kahn resumed his correspondence with James Meade.

> I have not previously replied to your letter of January 10 because I was hoping that some opening for Kalecki would show itself. That now turns out not to be the case, and the position is very gloomy. I wonder if I might ask you to let me have a little more information about the post that you say was advertised. Purely as a matter of interest, and without any reference to Kalecki, where did the advertisement appear? I try to keep my eye on openings that might be available for pupils, but I never saw any such advertisement nor did anyone else to whom I have mentioned the matter.
>
> Kalecki has been in correspondence with Tinbergen about the question of an opening in Geneva, and he was rather assuming that Tinbergen would put his name in for any position that offered itself. Is there any way of discovering whether Kalecki's name was in fact put forward for the position to which you refer? I do not know whether this position was the one which Tinbergen is himself said to be vacating or whether it is something different.
>
> [A]ny help that you can give will be enormously appreciated. I feel that it would be a shocking thing for this brilliant economist to be forced to go back to Poland and become a commercial traveller, or something similar![35]

On 27 April 1938, Marschak wrote back to Kahn. 'I don't know of any openings here at present, but that may be due to my ignorance of the internal affairs of the Colleges. Harrod might tell you more. As to the Institute, only 1½ of its researchers are paid. They are supported by a Rockefeller grant which will run for another year. The rest are voluntary workers; they usually have various scholarships which would hardly be open to people from outside and to which, besides, rather low age limits are attached. In addition, two men work under the "Economists' Research Group" (Chairman: Henderson)[36] where, again, no vacancy is expected.'[37] Marschak went on to suggest that Kalecki approach the Academic Assistance Council (Society for the Protection of Learning).[38] 'Although not technically a refugee he is, I understand, definitely a victim of certain developments in Poland.'[39] Marschak offered to write to the council.

On 9 May, James Meade wrote back from Geneva to Kahn. 'I have no idea what the job, which I mentioned to you before, was for; but I was told only that one had been advertised & that if Kalecki had not put in for it it was too late. I discover on further enquiry that it was advertised in papers other than the English papers, because Englishmen were excluded on the grounds of maintaining the balance of nationalities here... I will of course let you know at once if I hear of any suitable vacant post here. I have already trained people here well with the idea that Kalecki is available.'[40]

On 19 May, Marschak wrote again to Kahn to reassure him that Kalecki's fears – that an approach to the Society for the Protection of Learning (the former name for the Academic Assistance Council) would prejudice his position in Poland – were unjustified.[41] A few days later, Keynes sent Kahn a handwritten note to the effect that he (Keynes) had discussed Kalecki's situation with Winfield Riefler, professor of economics at the Institute of Advanced Studies in the University of Princeton and formerly at the Research and Statistics Division of the Federal Reserve Board. 'Riefler has some suggestions which... can possibly achieve what is wanted. But if they come off, they don't take effect before Oct.'[42] The suggestions concerned a possible opening at Princeton (see below).

A position seems to have been identified at the University of Wales, in Swansea. Kahn drafted out his reference: 'It is with very great confidence that I write to second Mr. M. Kalecki for the post of Assistant Lecturer in Economics at Swansea... During his stay in Cambridge students have found him extremely helpful in advising them on their work and discussing their difficulties on points both of economic theory and of statistical technique. His incisive and original mind and his enthusiasm for the subject will make him an inspiring teacher.'[43]

11.3 In succession to Walras and Pareto

Efforts to place Kalecki culminated in an imaginative attempt at the chair of economics at Lausanne. On 2 July Marschak wrote to Kahn to inform him that he had received a circular letter from Professor Guiseau, the dean of the Faculty of Law at the University of Lausanne, asking Marschak to recommend 'un jeune économiste de talent ayant le goût et le don de l'enseignement, qui soit dispose à présenter sa candidature'.[44] The position was the chair in economics at Lausanne that, over the previous six decades since its establishment, had been held by Léon Walras, Vilfredo Pareto and Pasquale Boninsegni. These men, the first two in particular, had made Lausanne famous throughout the world for its distinctive approach to economic theory. The Lausanne School of mathematical economics propounded a view of the economy as a system of general equilibrium in which flexible prices brought about optimal outcomes in consumption and investment choices.

Marschak wrote: 'I wonder whether concerted action could be taken to recommend M. Kalecki. I think this would be entirely in agreement with the traditions of the Chair, as described in the letter. By the way, all three occupiers of the Chair have been foreigners.'[45] He might have added that the first two (the most distinguished) holders of the chair were also engineers. Marschak concluded: 'Yet Kalecki's chances are, for personal reasons, small unless the Lausanne Faculty can be informed by Keynes and other authoritative persons of the outstanding merits of the candidate. I am postponing my reply to the letter until I hear your opinion.'[46]

Although Kahn's letter of response is not in his files, there is a note on Marschak's letter to indicate that Kahn replied on 5 July. However, Kahn appears to have been enthusiastic, and Marschak drew up a draft memorandum to the Law Faculty at Lausanne recommending Kalecki for the chair. On 14 July Kahn returned Marschak's draft, with minor amendments, excusing himself for leaving the matter in Marschak's hands because he (Kahn) was going abroad. 'Your memorial is intended, I imagine, for the members of the Law Faculty rather than for the economic expert, and from the point of view of the former the list of articles may not appear very impressive. Anybody who wants such particulars could always apply for them...I do not think any special reference to the Cambridge phase of K's career would be useful. Your own reference to the English school of thought is quite adequate.'[47]

As to the signatories, there seems to have been some discussion as to whether only 'authoritative persons' should sign. Kahn wrote, 'I feel very definitely that you ought to sign the memorial. I appreciate, however, your arguments, and if there were any reason why I should sign it your arguments would weigh heavily against it. You will notice that Mrs. Robinson has appended her signature to the draft. In doing so she feels that, if you were able to collect the signatures of say yourself, Keynes, Ohlin, Tinbergen, Frisch and Hayek, the addition of her own would rather spoil the effect, and in such a case she would prefer it not to appear. She signed the draft because she will shortly be going away...you are free to make modifications in the wording as well as to exclude her signature...Robertson has seen very little of K. and, as you know, he is always very cautious about attaching his name to a document. I do not therefore think that there will be very much point in approaching him.'[48]

It is not clear what happened to this audacious assault on the holy sepulchre of general equilibrium. But its putative beneficiary was unenthusiastic. At the beginning of September 1938, Kalecki wrote to Kahn from Paris. 'It is very flattering for me that the people you mention recommended me for the chair at Lausanne. It is however without practical importance since I cannot of course lecture in French.'[49]

In any case, Keynes and his friends were putting together yet another possibility, that of a position as a statistical assistant in Cambridge. However, this would require broad support from the Economics Faculty in Cambridge, including Robertson, and finance. Noel Hall was director of the National Institute for Economic and Social Research, which had a Treasury grant to support research. On the same day he wrote to Marschak (14 July 1938), Kahn reported to Keynes: 'Austin (Robinson) is approaching Hall. Even, however, if Hall proves prepared to commit himself rather deeply, we still feel that the Princeton opportunity should be exploited, as offering both more certainty and more chances of advancement in the future. I wonder if you have heard from Rieffler [*sic*]?'[50]

12
The First Synthesis of Theory

12.1 A first volume of essays

In Cambridge, from his arrival in November 1937, Kalecki made himself useful. On 27 November Richard Stone wrote to him:

> I have been reading your articles in Econometrica, The Review of Economic Studies, and the Economic Journal and should like to say how very interesting I found them... My wife and I have been asked to read a paper to the study group of the Royal Statistical Society, and have chosen the subject of the relation of income to investment. One of the aspects of this problem with which we propose to deal is the quantitative determination of the multiplier for different countries... The method which has so far proved most applicable is that of correlating time series of consumption or gross investment with gross income since figures of this sort are more generally available than those required by other method. Our slight acquaintance with Polish statistics, slight because unfortunately we cannot read the language, leads us to suppose that a similar calculation could be made for Poland... may I ask you for your help in this matter'.[1]

Kalecki wrote back on 13 December to say that he had now got the available data from Poland. 'The value of gross investment was in 1929 – 2.1 milliard zlotys while the value of total consumption except that of farm products by farmers 15.3 milliard zlotys. The indices of gross investment *in fixed capital* and consumption (in the above meaning) both *in real terms* are as follows (1929 = 100)[2]:

	1927	1928	1929	1930	1931	1932	1933	1934	1935	1936
Investment	89	109	100	71	50	36	37	42	50	61
Consumption	90	97	100	94	91	84	81	82	83	85

Two days later, Stone replied to thank Kalecki 'for going to so much trouble on my behalf. I have made a very elementary analysis with your figures...On plotting consumption against income and joining the two points together I found that they formed an ellipse rotating in a counter-clockwise direction, showing that consumption tended to lag behind income'.[3]

However, Kalecki's grant was to support him in putting his essays together for publications as a book. He spent the first half of 1938 in Cambridge working on the essays. A publisher was found, George Allen and Unwin, a firm which was well known for the quality and range of its economics catalogue. This included the first English translation of volume one of Marx's *Capital*, as well as a number of John Hobson's books, including his most famous one, *Imperialism, A Study*. George Allen and Unwin was also publishing edited volumes on problems in the international monetary and financial system. Kalecki's book came out in 1939 with the title *Essays in the Theory of Economic Fluctuations* and a pink dust jacket that announced: 'This book presents a synthesis of three important currents in the modern economic thought: the doctrine of Imperfect Competition, the Keynesian Theory, and the ideas of the Swedish School.'[4] The title itself was not incidental. It echoed the blurb which Keynes had written for his own *General Theory* and which, with characteristic modesty, declared the significance of his book as 'a general assault on the adequacy of the existing orthodox economic theory as a means for handling the problems of fluctuations in employment, trade cycles and the like.'

Kalecki constructed the book around the three key papers he had published since coming to England. These were 'The Distribution of National Income', published in April 1938 in *Econometrica* as 'The Determinants of the Distribution of National Income'; 'The Principle of Increasing Risk', published in *Economica* in 1937 (see Chapter 10); and 'A Theory of the Business Cycle', which had come out in the *Review of Economic Studies* (see Chapter 9). Kalecki now added to these three other essays. The first, entitled 'Investment and Income', aimed to 'clear up some questions arising out of the Keynesian theory of the multiplier'. Kalecki started by explaining that the equality between saving and investment is not a tautology, since it arises out of the exchange equation in the markets for consumption goods and investment goods. He wanted to show how an increase in investment would give rise to a corresponding increase in saving. To do this Kalecki argued that, in a closed economy with no government, the surplus produced in the consumption goods sector had to equal the consumption of workers and capitalists in the investment goods sector. The rest of their (capitalists' and workers') income – that is, their saving – must therefore equal the total spending of capitalists on investment.

At this point Kalecki made an intriguing detour into the history of political economy to link Marx's analysis with that of Keynes. Having laid out the equations for the equality of saving and investment in the two sectors of the economy, Kalecki went on:

> It may be interesting to notice that the above equations are contained in the famous Marxian scheme of 'extended reproduction'.[5] Marx even considers the question of how to provide 'means' for increased expenditure on investment. It must be added here that the problems discussed here are treated by Marx from a rather special point of view. He is interested in finding out...the pace of investment...which is necessary in order to secure a steady expansion of output...He does not pay attention to the problem of what happens if investment is inadequate to secure the moving equilibrium [in both sectors], and therefore does not approach the idea of the key position of investment in the determination of the level of output and employment.
>
> Exactly the reverse attitude is represented by one of his eminent pupils, Rosa Luxemburg. In her *Akkumulation des Kapitals* she stressed the point that, if capitalists are saving, their profits can be 'realized' only if a corresponding amount is spent by them on investment. She, however, considered impossible the persistence of net investment (at least in the long run) in a closed capitalist economy;...it is only the existence of exports to the non-capitalist countries which allows for the expansion of the capitalist system. The theory cannot be accepted as a whole, but the necessity of covering the 'gap of saving' by home investment or exports was outlined by her perhaps more clearly than anywhere else before the publication of Mr. Keynes' *General Theory*.[6]

In an open economy with government, saving was equal to investment, plus the fiscal deficit, plus the balance of 'foreign countries' expenditure'; that is, the foreign sector balance. Kalecki went on to deliver a subtle criticism of the Keynesian multiplier by arguing that the impact of an increase in investment upon consumption was not so much differentiated by income as by social class: Consumption out of profits tended not to change in response to a change in profits, while manual workers' consumption tended to change with income. There were therefore complex changes in the distribution of income over the trade cycle, so that this distribution could not be taken as a given in the analysis.

Kalecki's second original essay in this collection was 'Money and Real Wages'. This analysed some of the points which he had discussed in his essay on the Blum experiment (see Chapter 10). Central to this was the idea that changes in money wages would be offset by changes in prices, so that real wages do not actually change very much. He concluded that real wages have no positive or negative correlation with employment, because of imperfect competition and the constant average costs that prevail in business. Nevertheless, a cut in wages raises the degree of monopoly, reducing real wages and therefore tending to reduce employment. This may be offset if there is a redistribution of income towards managers who may increase their consumption as a result. A reduction in money wages also causes a redistribution of income from entrepreneurs to rentiers, which may also cause some increase in their consumption. But, on balance, a 'wage reduction may change employment ... but this change is likely to be small ... [and] ... it tends to redistribute income to the disadvantage of the workers.'[7]

Kalecki's conclusion displayed his sense of irony to the full:

> There are certain 'workers' friends' who try to persuade the working class to abandon the fight for wages, of course in its own interest. The usual argument used for this purpose is that the increase of wages causes unemployment, and is thus detrimental to the working class as a whole.
>
> The Keynesian theory undermines the foundation of this argument ... a wage increase may change employment in either direction, but this change is unlikely to be important. A wage increase, however, affects to a certain extent the distribution of income: it tends to reduce the degree of monopoly and thus to raise real wages.
>
> If viewed from this standpoint, strikes must have the full sympathy of the 'workers' friends'. For a rise in wages tends to reduce the degree of monopoly, and thus to bring our imperfect system nearer to the ideal of free competition. On the other hand, it tends to increase the thriftiness of capitalists by causing a relative shift of income from rentiers to corporations. And 'workers' friends' are usually admirers both of free competition and of thrift as a virtue of the capitalist class.[8]

But wages were not the only nor even the most efficient ways to redistribute income: 'It is quite true that the fight for wages is not likely to bring about fundamental changes in the distribution of national income. Income and capital taxation are much more potent weapons to achieve this aim, for these taxes (as opposed to commodity taxes)[9] do not affect prime costs, and thus do not tend to raise prices.'[10]

Kalecki's third original essay was entitled 'The Long-Term Rate of Interest'. This combined elements of his 'Money Market' analysis from the French version of his business cycle theory (see Chapter 7) with a critical assessment of Keynes's finance and the role of the rate of interest in the business cycle. Kalecki wanted to show that investment cannot possibly be constrained by saving. He first put forward a simple case in which every day a bank lends businesses the money to undertake the construction of fixed capital that they do in that day, and each day businesses float a bond to repay the money that they borrowed in the previous day. If there is an increase in investment, then 'since saving is equal to investment [Kalecki might have added that loans have to equal deposits in the banking system], today's additional accumulation of savings on current accounts equals advances taken for additional investment. Tomorrow the flotation of loans to the amount of today's investment will be met out of today's savings. In this way an increase in the rate of investment will directly result in only a negligible addition to the advances and current accounts.'[11] More generally, even allowing for larger advances for longer periods of time, there is still enough finance to satisfy the needs of investment.

Banks will of course need to keep themselves liquid by selling bills and bonds. Who will buy them? Why, the owners of deposits and current accounts, whose deposits have risen as a result of bank advances. The question really is, why does not the combined issuing of new bonds by banks and businesses cause a fall in the price of bonds and a rise in their yields? Kalecki's answer was that the buyers of bonds hold them as reserves and alternatives to holding bank deposits. But the rate of interest on bonds will not change, whereas the rate of interest on deposits changes over the course of the business cycle. 'Thus, the stimulus to keep bonds is the margin between the *present* long-term rate and the anticipated *average* short-term rate over a longer period. Now it is very likely that the change in the present rate on deposits does not greatly affect the expectations of its average over a long period. Thus it is plausible a deposit owner…(of a "non-speculative outlook") may be induced to buy bonds though the rate on deposits has increased much more than the yield of bonds.'[12]

Kalecki went on to examine data on long-term interest rates, using yields on Consols (British government undated stocks) between 1853 and 1932. This shows a remarkable stability; that is, the long-term rate of interest did not change very much. Kalecki drew two important conclusions from this. First of all, the long-term rate of interest could not be a factor in the business cycle.[13] Secondly, since there was 'no appreciable rise' in long-term rate of interest in the boom, 'full employment is approached only in exceptional cases', because interest rates have a strong propensity to rise when price and wage inflation rises. 'In general unemployment (manifest or disguised) is sufficient to permit the boom to develop, and it is not the scarcity of labour which brings it to an end.'[14]

As mentioned above, Kalecki included in his *Essays* the version of his business cycle theory from the *Review of Economic Studies*. He made some significant changes to this version in preparation for publication in his new book. Perhaps the most important one was a rejection of some interpretations of Keynes's theory that in future years came to be known as 'the neoclassical synthesis', because these interpretations combined elements of Keynes's theory with pre-Keynesian general equilibrium ideas. Kalecki mentioned explicitly Meade, Hicks and Lange.[15] These authors highlighted how government policy or market forces could fix a rate of investment that would be stable and maintain full employment. Kalecki argued that this could not happen, because the only stable rate of investment is one where the capital stock is constant and investment is only for the purpose of replacing worn-out equipment. However, once investment deviated from this level, changes in the capital stock would induce business cycle disturbances.[16] Here again were echoes of his earlier reasoning in 'Three Systems'.

Kalecki's *Essays* were largely well received as filling out and clarifying Keynes's arguments. The only exception was Maurice Dobb, who reviewed the book in the *Daily Worker*, the newspaper of the British Communist Party, of which Dobb was a member. Dobb highlighted two key elements of the analysis that, in his view, placed Kalecki firmly in the Marxist camp. Kalecki's approach to both monopoly capital and the problem of realisation of surplus were, in Dobb's view, extensions of Marx's analysis. In more academic reviews, Lange and Simon Kuznets recognized the originality of the analysis but took exception to Kalecki's tendency to draw very broad conclusions from very limited data. Kuznets in particular referred to Kalecki's 'cavalier disregard of available data...the author makes a lightning raid and emerges with a striking conclusion.'[17]

In the summer of 1938, having sent off the manuscript of his book to George Allen and Unwin, the Kaleckis moved back to London, to their first lodgings in Coram Street. As the Cambridge scholarship expired, they travelled back across the Channel to stay with Norman Bay in Paris. By now Kalecki was aware of plans to secure him a position as a statistical assistant at Cambridge. On 27 August, he wrote to Kahn: 'We have decided to stay in Paris until a final decision on my prospective job in Cambridge can be reached.' He asked Kahn if he could keep some of his (Kalecki's) savings in Kahn's bank account.[18] A few days later, on 6 September, Kalecki wrote again to tell Kahn that he had transferred £60 to Kahn's account 'from that of my Paris friend Blanche Bronstein'.[19] The amount was more than two months of the salary that Kalecki was about to secure.

12.2 A job in Cambridge

In the end, the job that Kalecki got was in Cambridge, part of a complex effort to set up some research capacity in the Faculty of Economics, along the lines of those already in existence at the universities of Manchester and Oxford and at the London School of Economics under Beveridge. At Cambridge the eventual outcome was the Department of Applied Economics. But as an interim arrangement, a Cambridge Research Scheme was set up at the end of 1938, with Kalecki as its sole full-time employee. The scheme and its background were complex. It was by no means an attempt to force Dennis Robertson's departure, as has been suggested recently.[20] The origins of the scheme lay in discussions at Cambridge to organise more systematic economic research there.

In fact, much of the initiative appears to have come from Robertson himself, who was on the Council of the National Institute for Economic and Social Research, then financed by a Treasury grant. On 22 May he reported to Keynes that the institute had some £5,000 to distribute for research in projects 'external' to the institute (something like £170,000 in 2012 – JT). Some of this could be directed to Cambridge 'if we show that we can use it'.[21] Keynes immediately saw the possibilities for research on the distribution of goods, the construction industry, statistics on gross and net investment, savings and 'the relation of real and money wages to national income'. 'As to personnel,...the sort of team I have in mind – Champ[ernowne], Austin [Robinson], Dennison, Kalecki and Stone would make a fine team.'[22] The Faculty Board in Cambridge set up a committee to organise the establishment of such research.

The chief problem with setting up the scheme proved to be in reconciling the strongly held opinions on the research that were held by key interested parties, any one of whom may have blocked the scheme. Inevitably, if Kalecki was involved, the research would have a distinctive business cycle flavour. However, Robertson considered the business cycle to be his own specialisation at Cambridge and resented trespass on the subject by Keynes and his associates. As Austin Robinson reported to Keynes, 'D. H. R[obertson] definitely dislikes and distrusts Kalecki, and I think substantially distrusts the rest of us', the 'rest' being Keynes, Austin Robinson, Joan Robinson, Piero Sraffa, who was involved in his capacity of Assistant Director of Research in the Faculty, and Maurice Dobb.[23] An academic appointment required the approval of the Faculty Board, where Robertson, who chaired the board, was in a position to veto any candidate put forward. David Champernowne, who was involved in his capacity as lecturer in statistics, wanted the appointment of Erwin Rothbarth, a German refugee and a much younger man (born in 1913), who had recently graduated from the London School of Economics. Rothbarth had formal training in statistics, which Kalecki lacked. Kalecki and Rothbarth had met at the London School of Economics research seminars and shared a common interest in business cycle analysis.

Then there was Noel Hall, whose support, as director of the National Institute for Economic and Social Research, was crucial. His support for the kind of research represented by Kalecki (and Keynes) was ambiguous. He 'is inclined to be opposed to Trade Cycle research (by which I imagine him to mean deductive thinking) but is not, so far as I can discover, opposed to factual research in relation to this group of problems.'[24]

The summer of 1938 was spent in an elaborate round of discussions and letter writing in efforts to overcome the blocking tactics deployed by interested parties who found the matter moving in directions that they did not like. To avoid bringing in the Faculty Board, it was decided to appoint a statistical assistant. In July a committee of selection considered both Rothbarth and Kalecki. Kahn reported to Keynes on 14 July, 'the sub-Committee (of selection) meet again tomorrow, and I suspect that they will fail to come to any decision, deciding to refer the whole matter to the Board... there is a majority in favour of K. but... under the circumstances, they do not feel able without further instructions from the Board to over-ride the minority of one.'[25]

Austin Robinson, who was on the subcommittee, was able to give more details: 'The Committee appointed to select a statistical assistant has found it almost impossible to make up its mind. I think three of us (M.H.D – P.S – E.A.G.R.) thought Kalecki the best applicant. Champ.

was determined to have Rothbarth, who is unquestionably a very able young man, but a mirror image (intellectually) of Champ. himself – full of bright ideas, rather on the make (at least P.S. feels that) and obviously a person who ought to be considering his own reputation and advancement rather than buying himself loyalty in someone else's work'.[26]

In the event providence intervened once more in Kalecki's favour. In the autumn of 1938, Rothbarth obtained an academic position in the Statistics Department, leaving Kalecki as the only appointable candidate. Approval was obtained from the National Institute for a grant of £600 to be awarded to the Cambridge faculty, effectively as a personal grant to Austin Robinson. This avoided the need to secure formal university and faculty agreement. Of the £600, £350 was allocated as a stipend to Kalecki. This was considerably less than his Rockefeller scholarship. But it was, at least, a salary.

One formality remained, that of obtaining a work permit from the Ministry of Labour: As a Polish citizen, Kalecki had no right to be employed in the United Kingdom and, by the end of 1938, had run out of money. On 12 January 1939, Austin Robinson reported to Keynes that '[o]n my return [to Cambridge after the Christmas recess] I found waiting for me a permit for Kalecki to work in England. Before I went away we arranged with Sraffa to make him a temporary loan to carry him through. I think his financial position is now all cleared up.' Keynes added a note back to Robinson, 'Yes, I learnt this was all right when I saw Hall on Thursday.'[27]

13
Kalecki and His Myrmidons

13.1 Statistical research in Cambridge

As indicated in the previous chapter, the Cambridge Project was not a project of the University of Cambridge nor of its Faculty of Economics but of the National Institute of Economic and Social Research. It was located in Cambridge because that was where Keynes was hoping to establish a permanent economic research unit that was to be the Department of Applied Economics. This, rather than the machinations of a Keynesian faction in the Faculty of Economics, explains the peculiar administration of the project. The actual title of the project was the Cambridge Research Scheme of the National Institute for Economic and Social Research. Its purpose was to study 'the process of Economic Change in the United Kingdom since 1928'.[1] The finance for the project was from the NIESR, managed by a supervisory committee consisting of Arthur Bowley, a retired Professor of Statistics at the London School of Economics; Lionel Robbins, Professor of Economics at the London School of Economics; Noel Hall, Director of the National Institute and Professor of Political Economy at University College, London; as well as Keynes and Austin Robinson.

The finance was to support a Cambridge research group that consisted of Keynes and Austin Robinson (chairman and secretary, respectively), Richard Kahn, Joan Robinson, Piero Sraffa, David Champernowne (the university lecturer in statistics) and Kalecki, who was described as working for the group 'as their Statistician'. Kalecki in fact was the only member of the group who was employed full-time in the research, assisted by two research students, Brian Tew and Yu-Nan Hsu. An initial report on the work of the project referred to the 'functions' of the other members of the group – that is, Kahn,

Austin and Joan Robinson, Sraffa and Champernowne – as 'primarily critical and supervisory.'

The very top-heavy structures established to manage the project were in large part due to the requirements of the NIESR, whose director, Noel Hall, wanted to avoid pressure to use the Institute's funds for 'private and personal investigations'. However, by the late 1930s empirical investigations of the business cycle were widespread.[2] In a letter to Keynes, dated 22 September 1938, Hall had expressed his reservations concerning an earlier version of the research proposal presented by Austin Robinson; Hall thought it was 'very much too wide' and therefore likely to lead to 'overlapping and duplication' of similar work at the institute and in other universities.[3] The initial year of study was subsequently changed to 1924, and the scope of the study was narrowed to examining the relation of prices to costs in different industries; the relationship of employment to output 'in a number of industries...for which statistical information is satisfactorily available and for which the industrial classification under the Census of Production is sufficiently comparable with the employment and unemployment figures of the Ministry of Labour'; consumption and foreign trade; and the relationship between foreign investment and exports.

In the matter of foreign trade, 'The main purpose of these inquiries is to discover the factors influencing the size of "the multiplier" and the limits imposed by international trade upon the power of one country to act independently of others in dealing with a depression.'[4] The project was also to study sources of saving, bringing up to date the estimates given in the Liberal Industrial Inquiry:[5]

> It is hoped to use this approach as a check on estimates of investment made from the industrial data. Important theoretical and logical problems of definition and method are likely to emerge, concerned e.g., with the avoidance of double counting, the keeping of capital intact, the proper allowance for changes in the volume of credit and the part played by financial machinery in converting capital into income and vice versa.[6]

The project was located in the Marshall Library, the library of the Faculty of Economics, that had been established after Marshall's death in 1924 by his widow, Mary Paley Marshall, with his book collection at its core. The library was in a building on Downing Street of a Victorian faux medieval style beloved by university teachers because it lends gravitas to academic scholarship. The Kaleckis moved into lodgings in 42 Garden

Walk, on the other side of Chesterton Road. In the Library Kalecki settled down to gathering data on industrial production by industry and the share of 'prime costs' (labour and raw materials) in the total output of the coal, cotton, steel, tobacco, shipbuilding and electricity supply industries. The result was a series of papers that have not hitherto been published but are deposited in the Keynes and Kahn Papers in King's College, Cambridge. The papers are largely concerned with statistical methods to obtain consistent data series.[7] But they nevertheless are substantial pieces of work, designed to illustrate Kalecki's essential analysis of prime costs and competition. In particular he used them to show that the standard Marshallian upward sloping average or marginal cost curves were not characteristic of production. Instead there was a stable 'prime cost' (the cost of wages and raw materials) that was the basis of industrial price formation.

'A Note on Coal-Mining', for example, gives figures and estimates for employment and unemployment in the industry, for labour productivity and for proceeds (sales). This was followed by Kalecki's much more extensive 'A Supplement to a Note on Coal-Mining', estimating index numbers for profit margins, output and labour inputs during a 'competitive' period and then during a period when the industry was 'cartelised'. Kalecki used the data to argue that competition was a more important factor in industrial pricing than diminishing returns, as would be suggested by a Marshallian approach to costs and pricing (although Kalecki was too diplomatic to refer directly to Marshall's approach).[8]

Hsu, assisted by Kalecki, wrote 'Explanatory Notes' on 'Prime Costs, Proceeds and Output in the Cotton Industry'. Again, this gave figures for output and employment, showing an underestimation in the census of production figures for the industry. Earnings were estimated to have fallen by over 10 per cent in the industry since 1924. However, due to the fall in the price of raw cotton, overall costs had fallen by some 60 per cent since 1924, while the value of sales had fallen by over a half. The ratio of total proceeds to total costs fluctuated but did not go below 95.5 per cent of its 1924 level.[9]

Brian Tew, assisted by Kalecki, contributed a study called 'Proceeds, Prime Costs & Output in the Steel Industry: General Considerations'. This showed that changes in sales proceeds in the iron and steel industry did not coincide with data on output and changes in price indices. Tew argued that there were two possible explanations for this. The first was that during the slump, manufacturers gave secret rebates on official prices. However, the divergences between sales and the sales predicted by output and price indices did not confirm this. The paper therefore suggested a second explanation; namely, that manufacturers moved towards more expensive types of products in the slump. Overall, the ratio of proceeds to prime costs (labour and raw materials) was estimated to have risen by some 20 per cent since 1924.[10]

Kalecki and G. A. Bauer produced the study 'Prime Costs and Proceeds etc. in Shipbuilding, with a Note on Machine Prices'. The paper identified a statistical problem in calculating continuous output from an industry whose products are so lumpy that 'tonnage launched' is poorly related to the actual work done in shipyards during a given period. Kalecki and Bauer got around this by calculating an average construction period in shipbuilding, from which a continuous series for shipbuilding construction is derived. From this they derived prime costs and proceeds for the industry, showing the ratio between the two to have stayed more or less stable between 1924 and 1935. However, the relative share of labour costs (and labour income in the industry) fell by over 20 per cent between 1924 and 1931, rising by some 10 per cent afterwards. This was offset by a fall in raw material costs after 1930.[11]

Kalecki also wrote the study 'Prime Costs and Proceeds etc. in Tobacco'. This showed the ratio of prime costs to proceeds rising from 1924 to 1930 and then falling by some 10 per cent after 1930. This was largely accounted for by the rise and fall of raw material costs, with wage costs staying relatively stable.

There were two more general studies which Kalecki wrote. The first was a summary of the data from the six industries that were the subject of the project's investigations – the coal, pig iron, steel, cotton, shipbuilding and tobacco industries. 'The task of this inquiry is to throw some light on the process of price formation...This seems to show that in the industries considered diminishing returns did *not* play a predominant part in the price formation as compared with the degree of monopoly...we find in some cases a tendency for the proceeds-prime-costs ratio to change in the opposite direction to the (average) money prime costs i.e., certain "stickiness" in prices. (This amounts obviously to the rise of the degree of monopoly when wages and raw material costs fall, and conversely). A typical example is tobacco'.[12] Finally he examined in this study the share of manual labour income in the net output of the six industries and came to a conclusion that qualified, at least, his earlier conclusion, in 'Money and Real Wages', that the relative share of manual labour in national income was more or less constant. 'In the light of this investigation the stability of the relative share of manual labour in the national income during the trade cycle appears to be of a peculiar character. This series does not show such stability in particular industries. But its changes are sufficiently irregular in each industry to give rise to a relative stability in this series computed for a sample of six industries. The stability of the relative share of manual labour in the national income in the long run obviously cannot be explained in this way. And indeed stability does not appear in our sample taken as a whole which renders it perhaps doubtful whether it is as general a phenomenon as such stability in the course of the trade cycle.'[13]

Finally, Kalecki contributed a study entitled 'The General Index of the Proceeds Prime Costs Ratio'. This used data from Colin Clark's *National Income and Outlay* (which Kalecki had already used in his essay on the distribution of national income; see Chapter 10) with cost indices from Phelps-Brown and Shackle's *Statistics of Monetary Circulation in England and Wales 1929–1937* to calculate an aggregate ratio of proceeds to prime costs for the economy as a whole. As an index number (1930 = 100, the ratio being 1.38 in that year) this ratio rose from 94.7 in 1924 to 100.9 in 1935.

13.2 Audacious approximations

Signs of trouble for the research scheme emerged in the summer of 1939. Arthur Bowley, who had retired in 1936 from a chair in statistics at the London School of Economics and was on the supervisory committee of the Cambridge Research Scheme, wrote to Keynes on 12 June on the headed notepaper of the Econometric Society, of which Bowley was president. Bowley had looked again at Kalecki's 1938 article 'Determinants of the Distribution of National Income'. Kalecki had made use of some of Bowley's data, data which Bowley had modified in the study cited by Kalecki, and 'the modification affects Kalecki's numerical work on his p. 109. I think he is wrong in classing all salaries with capitalist income. Great part of this is of the same nature as wages for manual labour... Clark's figures may be approximately correct, but his evidence for salaries since 1924 is quite insufficient... Kalecki should have included Employers contributions [i.e., to employment insurance] with wages... Thus I do not think that any of Kalecki's numerical estimates p. 106, 109–10 are worth anything. As regards the approximate constancy of the proportion of earnings to profits – I should have supposed that the main determinants were the quantity of labour available and the rate of interest in the long run, and that was no à priori reason why there should not be a gradual change... If Kalecki is working at Cambridge it will be well to see that he does not follow Clark in assuming precision which is unwarranted by data.'[14]

Kalecki was not the only butt of Bowley's criticism. So too were Clark and Keynes himself, for his recent article 'Relative Movements of Real Wages and Output'.[15] Keynes wrote back on 22 June suggesting that Bowley write up his remarks as a note for the *Economic Journal*. 'On the main issue, I agree with you that it is most difficult to see any *a priori* reason why there should not be a gradual change in the proportion of earnings to profits...I would definitely expect such a change and am extraordinarily surprised at a stability. If therefore you are able to dispute the "undisputed facts" of page 48 of my Economic Journal article, no one will be better pleased than I shall, for I remain greatly bothered by a stability which I cannot explain. Kalecki has made a brave effort to explain it, but, as I have said in the article, I am not clear that he has been successful in doing so. On the other hand, the revised figures you give on the second page of your letter still produce quite extraordinary stability. So that, for the time being at least, the "undisputed facts" remain undisputed.'

Keynes went on to suggest that rather than the supply of labour and the rate of interest in the long run, as Bowley had proposed, the main determinants of the ratio of labour income to profits should be the skill as well as the quantity of labour supplied and the quantity of capital and 'technical considerations'. The dispute over how to treat 'the small-salaried class' seemed endless, although 'it seems a matter on which we ought to be able to get reasonably agreed figures.' 'Have you any objection to my letting Kalecki see your letter.'[16]

Bowley replied on 25 June to say that he had no objection to letting Kalecki see his letter, provided 'you will exclude the phrase in which I implied that his statistical work needed watching'. He would not write a note for the *Economic Journal* because he was not working on estimates of national income and it would be 'inappropriate' to write anything new on the subject at present'.[17]

Keynes therefore forwarded, on 4 July 1939, to Kalecki the text of Bowley's letter and his own response to Bowley.[18] Kalecki wrote back on 10 July to say that 'my argument shows only that the relative share of wages in the value added *may* be stable even over long periods; but it does not establish the necessity of its being stable in the long run generally.' He gave data from the US census of manufacturing industry to show that the relative share of wages in the value added of American manufacturing varied from 52 per cent in 1849 to 36 per cent in 1935. '[M]y argument does explain why the relative share of wages in the value added changes little in the course of the cycle', because changes in the degree of monopoly and in the prices of raw materials tend to operate in opposite directions.[19]

Keynes wrote back on 17 July to put forward 'two reasons for feeling a little difficulty about accepting your explanation as sufficient.' These were that the relatively stable share of wage income is a 'long period phenomenon' that requires a 'long-period explanation', whereas changes in the degree of monopoly and raw materials prices were 'short-period changes'. Secondly, he thought it implausible that the degree of monopoly and changes in raw materials prices would offset each other. Rather he thought that if prices were falling below long-run average costs, there would tend to be resort to either 'cut-throat' competition or tacit agreements to maintain prices.[20] Kalecki replied on 22 July to deny that he regarded either cut-throat competition or tacit agreements as stable in the short period; just that changes in them would tend to offset changes in raw materials prices to keep variations in the relative share of wages in national income to modest proportions – say, between 5 and 10 per cent.[21]

It is obvious from this correspondence that Bowley and Keynes had in mind a different 'short period' to that of Kalecki. For them, the 'short period' is the analytical or abstract Marshallian short period, in which prices and the capital stock are held constant, whereas for Kalecki it was whatever phase of the business cycle an actual economy happened to be in. The objection to Kalecki's work was to the theoretical conclusions that he drew from the statistics.

The next person to enter his reservations about Kalecki's statistical work was Richard Stone. His objection appears to have been that Kalecki was drawing theoretical conclusions, rather than solely statistical ones, from his analysis. On 7 August 1939, Stone penned a four-page handwritten letter to Austin Robinson devoted largely to criticising Kalecki's methodology, together with notes, now lost, on the estimates from the tobacco industry. In the case of the iron and steel estimates, Kalecki should check a report of the Imperial Economic Committee and the Iron and Steel Federation's figures. More could be done to explain away discrepancies with the figures from the census of production. 'I do not understand why finished steel is less than the total amount given for example in table 22 of the 1936 "Statistics of the Iron & Steel Industries".' There was something wrong with the figures for net sales of semifinished steels. '[T]his item (1,488,000 tons) checks out very well with the 1935 census figure of 1,500,000 tons. I should be most interested to know how the latter is worked out. I may say quite candidly that it defeats me.'

He concluded: 'Have you obtained a reply yet to the two questions I raised when we last met namely – (a) how does M.K. arrive at his figures for hours worked in coal mines & (b) has he been in touch with T. Koopmans on the subject of calculating the period of production of merchant ships, since at first blush their methods do not seem the same, though I have not examined them carefully.'[22]

So much is to be expected of one statistician commenting on the work of another one. However, much more serious doubts had already been expressed privately within the research group at Cambridge. Keynes had already raised the matter with Richard Kahn who, it should be noted, had analysed short-period profits as the difference between total sales proceeds and prime costs in his (still unpublished) fellowship thesis. At the end of May, Keynes expressed to Kahn his strong reservations about Kalecki's work:

> I have now looked through the material you sent me at the end of last term from Kalecki. I confess I am rather dismayed, and do not feel at all happy about it. We must try to get down to what we really think. Meanwhile, the following are the considerations which are prominent in my mind.

First of all, Keynes wanted to know what the aim of Kalecki's gathering of statistics was. It would then be possible to judge the relevance of possible errors in the data. 'I imagine that the proportion of prime costs to sales proceeds is not the ultimate purpose.' Secondly, 'if the next step is to relate this ratio to changes in output, the conclusions so far appear entirely chaotic. There doesn't appear to be any correlation worth bothering about.'[23] Thirdly, 'there are certain profound doubts on the question of method. The way the problem is tackled seems to me as though it was a case of Scotland Yard dealing with the I.R.A. The proportion of prime costs to sales proceeds must be a known figure for any business which keeps the rudiments of cost accounts. Surely it would be better to ask selected firms what the figures actually are rather than, by underground detective work, to arrive at aggregate figures which are almost certainly full of errors'. Fourthly, there was the question of the homogeneity of the output of each industry. The error here was most obvious in the case of cotton but was almost as bad in iron and steel. 'They appear to have amalgamated the American and Egyptian branches of the cotton industry. Now, during the period in question, one was holding its own, while the other was rapidly declining. They were subject to widely different considerations.' Keynes wondered how 'one can get any results of the slightest value, by amalgamating the two branches of the industry.... Moreover, this happens to be a case where the statistics allow you to a great extent, to separate them.'

Keynes concluded: 'I see evidence of great industry, but what may turn out to be a total lack of flair for this kind of enquiry. I may have misunderstood it, and have not read it carefully enough, but this is my first impression. It strikes me, for example, as greatly inferior to what one would expect from, say, Singer.'[24]

Kahn had a discussion with Kalecki about the points raised. Predictably, Kalecki's response was one of barely suppressed outrage. In a letter to Kahn dated 9 June 1939, he thanked him for having spared the time on the previous day to discuss the matter with him. 'After careful consideration of what you told me yesterday I came to the definite conclusion that I should not stay for the next year in Cambridge...I cannot take the risk that *two* years will be considered wasted...fully...I simply think that in a case [where] the results of research are not considered satisfactory one must draw the consequences...the rest of the time of this year I should like to devote to bringing in order the work done and writing a theoretical interpretation of the results.[25]

On 11 July 1939, Kahn wrote to Kalecki 'to deal with the more general questions. In my other letter[26] I have already suggested that it would be very helpful to show in the case of each industry how the actual price and constituents of prime cost had varied per ton. One might perhaps then be able to go some way towards dealing with the question raised by Keynes in his March article of distinguishing between the effect of a change in wages and the effect of a change in output...the real objective should be the supply curve.' Kahn referred to a memorandum, which he had seen, by Joan Robinson, in which '[o]ne of the questions, perhaps the main question to be answered, is whether the price always moves in exact proportion to the cost of raw materials and labour. Mrs. Robinson demonstrates in her memorandum that the ratio of proceeds to prime costs provides only a partial answer to this question. I agree with her that one ought to try to adjust the price for changes in the price of raw materials and labour...I would suggest that it is essential to take account of secular changes and to attempt to measure the variations from the trend. This raises the whole question of whether annual figures are adequate for your purpose. As you know, I have always pleaded for quarterly figures...the cost of labour would have to include the effect of those changes in output per head which are part of the secular trend and not merely the result of short period fluctuations in output. But it is questionable whether the necessity for allowing for them does not imply that you are being carried too far outside the short period for the results to be interesting'.

> I should myself interpret your results for steel as broadly reflecting the big technical changes... the adoption of more capitalistic methods of production. It would be rather formalistic to say that these technical changes can be represented as a change in the degree of monopoly.... At the same time, I would be interested to investigate whether the necessary change in the degree of monopoly which must be the concomitant of such technical changes had been brought about by the reduction in the number of firms.
>
> Changes in the profitability of an industry in the ordinary sense should also be brought into the picture. Is it your contention that the difference between a profitable and an unprofitable industry is purely one of output, and that the ordinary view that it is partly a question of the ratio of output to capacity, is entirely fallacious because price depends only on prime costs? I feel myself that the universal prevalence of surplus capacity can be exaggerated in this connection.
>
> I was very much interested in the 'general index'. I should like myself to feel a little clearer about the assumptions on which it is drawn up. I take it that your assumption of a constant structure of output involves the assumption of a constant ratio of raw materials to finished product. I take it, however, that it does not involve a constant ratio of labour to finished product and that your index of 'wage cost' includes the effect of changes in output.[27]

On 27 July 1939 Kalecki sent back a detailed response, with points concerning iron and steel answered by Tew with Kalecki. In the absence of much of the original detailed criticism of Kalecki's work, it is possible to infer only partially what those detailed criticisms were. Kalecki started off with the heading 'Sources': 'I am rather puzzled by this passage. It is almost always indicated wherefrom a given figure is taken'; 'Presentation of final result: I quite consciously used in it indices and not actual figures to the ratio of proceeds to prime costs in order not to encourage comparison between absolute levels of this ratio in various industries. This is undesirable because they are not comparable for various reasons... I quite agree, however, that it is by no means correct to neglect small changes in the indices, for they may mean a very great change in net profits... Price series may be easily calculated by multiplying the index of average prime costs by the index of our ratio of proceeds to prime costs'.

> It is useful to add that the series of the ratio of proceeds to prime costs has a great advantage over the series of prices and average costs of being independent of the arbitrariness involved in the construction of output index numbers. I do not consider it as serious as Mr. Keynes does but in some cases (e.g., steel industry) it may be quite appreciable.

Under the heading 'General discussion of method', Kalecki wrote:

> I must confess that I do not see very clearly the alternative way of calculation that you propose. Let us take the steel industry as an example. I gather that you suggest to calculate the aggregate proceeds simply by multiplying the various categories of steel products by relevant prices. The categories in question represent, however, by no means a uniform product while the price quotations are given for one of numerous categories included in a category... I should like to add here that we had a preliminary discussion of this method in the meeting of the Committee at the end of the winter term.

Under the heading 'Choice of industry and heterogeneity': 'The industries investigated were chosen by me together with Mr. and Mrs. Stone chiefly as more or less suitable for statistical inquiry. The other "candidates", brewing and wool industry, involve just the same difficulties as tobacco and cotton... To cotton you object owing to heterogeneity. Now it must be first stated that the production Egyptian section of Spinning constituted in 1935 only 15 per cent of the value of the Cotton Industry as a whole (reckoned without duplication). Thus its inclusion could not much affect changes in the ratio of proceeds to prime costs of the Cotton Industry as a whole...'

> 'Cotton': The check suggested by you is wrong. A correct check is given on page 9 (top) and in table XI...
>
> 'Shipbuilding'. It is quite true that the ratio of proceeds to prime costs in intercensal years is less correct than in other industries of our sample... It is probable, however, that this does not matter much for the change in *average* returns of manual labour is not likely to be very important and the wage bill makes only about one-third of the aggregate prime costs... What is the point in comparing the average cost of labour which is affected by the changes in its efficiency with the series based on hourly earnings only?

> 'Tobacco'. The figures you ask for are as follows... The method of interpolation is the same throughout all the inquiry.[28]

No evidence of any further exchange could be found. By this time, in any case, Keynes was in discussion with the Rockefeller Foundation about setting up the Department of Applied Economics at Cambridge.[29]

Six weeks later Germany invaded Poland. Adela Kalecka had travelled there in 1939 and saw Kalecki's mother for the last time. With war the National Institute found itself with new priorities. In the early weeks of the war, it considered a report on the work of the Cambridge Research Scheme that was written earlier that summer, around the time of Kalecki's exchanges with Kahn:

> The services of Mr. Kalecki were secured early in October 1938, and preparatory work was begun. His work, and that of two research students (Mr. Tew and Mr. Hsu) has been mainly directed during the past eight months to the measurement of output per head, the share of labour in the product, and the ratio of total proceeds to raw material and labour costs during the years 1924 to 1935 in coal, cotton, steel, tobacco, shipbuilding and electricity... The extremely laborious calculation for the various industries are now finished. The interpretation of the results, and in particular of the relation of the ratio so obtained to the level of output, has not yet seriously been attempted. Mr. Kalecki is proposing to devote part of the rest of the summer to this analysis, while at the same time the methods, results and conclusions are to receive the careful attention of some of the members of the Committee with, it is hoped, the assistance of Mr. and Mrs. Stone whose experience in this field of work should facilitate a critical appraisal of the reliability of the results. In this way it is proposed by the autumn to submit this portion of the work conducted under the Cambridge scheme in more definitive form than is as yet possible. The committee regret the delay in presenting what forms the major element in their scheme... They would at the same time point out that the work did not commence until after the academic year was under way, and that the preliminary stages were necessarily lengthy.

'It has not yet been possible to start work on Section III [the foreign trade part of the work], though both Mr. Kalecki and Mr. Marrack will during the course of the next year be concerned with certain aspects of these problems. Nor has work yet been started upon section IV or V [the 'measurement of saving' and the 'relation of the condition of Full

Employment to the breakdown of the boom'], but Section V is likely to come within the scope of Mr. Kalecki's proposed work during the course of next year.'

'It is the wish of the Cambridge Committee that Mr. Kalecki, when he has completed the work on which he is now engaged, should undertake a detailed statistical study of the mechanism of post-war trade cycles in Great Britain, partly for constructive purposes and partly to test the validity of other work, including in particular the important studies recently published by Dr. Tinbergen. The fundamental question that faces the investigation of these problems is how far the existence of a statistical correlation throws light on causation, and in particular on the direction of causation. Owing to the inherent difficulty of work of this kind, it does not seem desirable to attempt any precise forecast of the line that it will assume until preliminary investigations have indicated what is, and what is not, likely to prove fruitful. It has been made clear to Mr. Kalecki that in the event of the approval of this programme by the Supervisory Committee, his work must be so organised as to enable him to wind up by September 30, 1940, up to which date it is hoped that the Supervisory Committee will authorise the Cambridge Committee to extend his appointment.'[30]

14
Shared Ideas amid Mutual Incomprehension

> Cambridge is a very isolated place.
>
> (Johnson 1977)

> Having centred his attention on the problem of change, Keynes does not, however, treat it in explicitly dynamic terms. True to the Cambridge tradition, he resorts to the Marshallian substitute for dynamic theory – the 'short-run' analysis.
>
> (Leontief, p. 100)

14.1 The end of the Cambridge project

The breakdown of the Cambridge project, amid mutual incomprehension, was a considerably more complex transition than a mere rejection of Kalecki's methodology. In Cambridge the ending of the project was a precondition for the establishment of a better financed and academically supported Department of Applied Economics under Richard Stone. At the end of 1939, Kalecki left Cambridge for Oxford. But he retained his dependence on Keynes, through whose good offices at the National Institute for Economic and Social Research Kalecki had his salary paid at Oxford. Perhaps even more importantly he retained the support of Keynes, who saw in him some potential to realise Keynes's critique of Tinbergen's attempts to determine the course of inter-war business cycles by statistical means alone.

Nevertheless, discussions about the relationship between Michał Kalecki and John Maynard Keynes have rightly focused upon the compatibility of the ideas of the two men. The emergence at the end of the 1960s of post-Keynesian economic theory out of the reappraisal of Keynesian economics could not avoid inconsistencies between different interpretations of Keynes, usually resulting from a bias towards one aspect of his analysis, as critic of neoclassical theory, monetary reformer or philosopher of uncertainty. Those interpretations have not always found Kalecki to be complementary to Keynes. Joan Robinson famously did.[1] But her close associate in Cambridge, Richard Kahn, who had been detailed to criticise Kalecki's work, did not regard Kalecki as quite so complementary.[2]

Some clash of ideas had occurred, and it is useful to consider what those ideas were and why Kalecki was unable to submit his research to a standard Cambridge method of reasoning – or 'mode of thought', in Sheila Dow's much more vivid phrase. Such a consideration lies at the heart of the relationship between Kalecki and Keynes and their many arguments over method. Yet it is largely missing from the replete literature on the relation between the theories of the two great men, drawn mainly from Joan Robinson's claim of independent discovery of common theoretical positions[3] and Kalecki's own claim to priority in that discovery: In a letter to T. C. Chang dated 17 February 1955, Kalecki wrote of a lecture that he gave in Cambridge in which 'they made a point of it to stress in the introduction my discovery of General Theory before Keynes.'[4] At the end of his life Kalecki was even more convinced of the priority of his 'discovery', referring to his own papers published 'in Polish before Keynes' *General Theory* appeared and containing, I believe, its essentials'.[5]

A recent paper on Keynes's methodological differences with Kalecki concludes correctly that Keynes's analytical methods were 'foreign to [Kalecki]' but does not really explain why.[6] Another paper suggests that the whole Cambridge project was merely an elaborate ruse to remove Dennis Robertson from Cambridge as a way of obtaining the hegemony of Keynesian ideas over economics in that university.[7] The evidence for this is tenuous at best. It does not explain why Robertson was the victim and not Arthur Pigou or Maurice Dobb or even Piero Sraffa, none of whom were Keynesians, and confuses the style of Cambridge for its substance: Just because nothing can happen in Cambridge without a conspiracy does not mean that everything that happens in Cambridge is a conspiracy. There were other factors at work. Even if, as Aslanbeigui and Oakes suggest, Kalecki was dispensable after Robertson had resigned from Cambridge, Keynes certainly did not cease to support Kalecki after the project collapsed. Robertson in any case returned to Cambridge as Professor of Political Economy in 1943, when Pigou retired.

The principles common to both Keynes and Kalecki were, according to Joan Robinson, their common interlocutor, 'that the rate of saving is governed by the rate of investment, that the level of prices is governed by the level of money wage rates, and that the level of interest rates is governed by the supply and demand for money.'[8] Any notion of a common monetary and financial analysis may be dismissed despite serious claims that post-Keynesian monetary principles may be found in Kalecki.[9] Any notion that the originality of Keynes and Kalecki was due to their shared emphasis on the importance of aggregate demand as a determinant of output and employment may also be dismissed. By the 1930s such ideas were hardly original; they could be found, for example, in Ralph Hawtrey's well-known *Good and Bad Trade,* which had been published in 1913.

In his most serious examination of the *General Theory,* Kalecki himself identified 'the proposition that investment determines the global volume of production' as a principle which he had 'proved in a similar way to Keynes's in my *Essay on the Business Cycle Theory.*'[10] However, even among post-Keynesians, such a proposition is hardly common ground. The serious question for Keynesian economics that arises from the preceding chapters of this book is why, if the two men had made common discoveries, did their closest collaboration in Cambridge in 1939 end in such apparent incomprehension? Part of the enigma arises because the question has always been approached from the point of view of Keynes's originality in Cambridge economics, an intellectual project to which Joan Robinson recruited Kalecki, who joined willingly because he agreed with essential elements of Keynes's ideas and had few other professional options. As she put it: 'The interesting thing is that two thinkers, from completely different political and intellectual starting points, should come to the same conclusion. For us in Cambridge it was a great comfort.'[11]

The question of the degree to which Kalecki had 'anticipated' Keynes or held common ground with him is a matter of textual exegesis whose starting point has to be what Keynes really meant. The true meaning of Keynes's theory is not an issue on which his partisans themselves agree. Keynes himself sanctioned a wider discussion of his core ideas in his 1937 article in the *Quarterly Journal of Economics* in which he wrote, 'I am more attached to the comparatively simple fundamental ideas which underlie my theory than to the particular forms in which I have embodied them, and I have no desire that the latter should be crystallised at the present stage of the debate.'[12] His most enthusiastic follower, George Shackle, endorsed this transcendentalist view of Keynes's ideas by referring to 'Keynes's ultimate meaning'.[13] In his last book Alan

Coddington documented the varieties of ostensibly core Keynesian ideas.[14] Specifying the nature and significance of Keynesian ideas is therefore a major task that cannot satisfactorily be concluded in an essay towards an intellectual biography of Kalecki. In relation to the failure of his project in Cambridge, the question 'did Kalecki anticipate Keynes?' should really be 'if Keynes and Kalecki held key ideas in common, why was Kalecki's work at Cambridge terminated?'

Answers to this may be found in the incompatible personal chemistry of the two men, the one an urbane, 'moderately conservative', upper-class Englishman, the other a Polish Jew of pronounced left-wing and Marxist sympathies, who was as socially awkward as he was confident in his views. The financially insecure Kalecki nevertheless yearned for acknowledgement from Keynes of the former's priority in discovering the principles behind the *General Theory* – another misjudgement, since Keynes was least inclined to intellectual modesty.[15] Keynes's failure to understand Kalecki is illustrated, for example, in a remark that Keynes made, in parenthesis, in a letter to Kahn, dated 30 April 1938, referring to the Polish economist's 'appalling method of exposition'. 'His mathematics seems to be largely devoted to covering up the premises and making it extremely difficult to bring one's intuition to bear. If only he would state his premises in the most illuminating possible manner and be perfunctory over his mathematics, instead of the other way around, one would have a better idea of what he is driving at'. Keynes's way of dealing with this, he wrote, was 'to disentangle painfully exactly what the assumptions amount to and then consider whether the conclusion appears to be correct, not bothering much about the proof which, in spite of the appearance to the contrary, obviously contains endless loopholes for introducing fresh assumptions'.[16] The 'appalling method of exposition' was that of Kalecki's *Econometrica* article 'The Determinants of Distribution of National Income'; 'one's intuitions' were obviously Marshallian!

Another answer may be in the plans that Keynes had to replace his project at Cambridge with a full-scale Department of Applied Economics. This too does not provide a satisfactory answer to the question of why Kalecki had to leave Cambridge. With his salary paid by the National Institute for Economic and Social Research, Kalecki would have been able to continue to promote Keynesian economics at Cambridge at no cost to the putative department.

Much of the criticism that Kalecki's research met in Cambridge was methodological. There was no doubt that Kalecki's interest in gathering statistics extended only as far as they illuminated his theoretical preoccupation with the business cycle and the theoretical framework that he had developed to understand changes in economic activity. This provides not only the rationale for his departure but also the clue to the differences that he had already had with Keynes over his publications and which he was to have after leaving Cambridge. While the textual exegetes have pored over the two men's work in search of similarities and complementarities, the fact remains that their differences were rooted in different methodological approaches that went beyond Kalecki's class approach and Keynes's more obvious preference for explaining economic phenomena in terms of individual choices. At the interface between Cambridge (including its most original thinker after Marshall, Keynes) and Kalecki was a much greater, even impersonal, incompatibility between the economic tradition in Cambridge that had formed Keynes and the continental European economics from which Kalecki had emerged.

Kalecki's rendezvous in Cambridge was a part of a limited interchange between continental European and Cambridge economic theory. His arrival in Cambridge may be called the third emergence, or impact, of continental European economic theory in an intellectual community made introverted by its dispersal around a federal university and its common struggles to establish and maintain economics teaching at that university. Some of this introversion is apparent in Robert Skidelsky's generous chapter on what he called 'Cambridge Civilisation'.[17] A somewhat more bilious account is provided by the otherwise judicious and scholarly Terence Hutchison in an extended essay, 'The Philosophy and Politics of the Cambridge School'.[18] Earlier, Harry Johnson had painted a picture of Cambridge economics that took exception, in similar terms to Hutchison's, to the Marxian influence at Cambridge. However, Johnson emphasised explicitly the influence of Kalecki's ideas, through their advocacy by Joan Robinson, in the Cambridge version of Keynesian economics.[19]

However, Kalecki's was not the first confrontation between European economic theory and the tradition established by Marshall in Cambridge.

The first emergence of continental European economics in Cambridge came with the arrival there in the mid-1920s of Piero Sraffa. Sraffa had sent a shot across the bow of Cambridge economics by showing that Marshall's elaborate scheme of partial equilibrium in perfect competition was incompatible with increasing (or even constant) returns to scale, in a paper which his friend Keynes published in the *Economic Journal*.[20] Joan Robinson remarked that

> When I returned to Cambridge in 1929 and began teaching, Mr. Sraffa's lectures were penetrating our insularity. He was calmly committing the sacrilege of pointing out the inconsistencies in Marshall...and at the same time revealing that other schools existed...The elders reacted by defending Marshall as best they could but the younger generation was not convinced by them. The profound inconsistency between the static base and the dynamic superstructure had become too obvious.[21]

However, shortly after her return to Cambridge, Sraffa withdrew from teaching and quietly nurtured his critique of Marshallian economics until the publication of his major reconstruction of Ricardian economics in 1960. While he participated significantly in many of the key discussions between Keynes, Joan Robinson, Kahn and Kalecki, 'it remains a puzzle that the two escape routes from Marshallian orthodoxy – the one associated with Sraffa and imperfect competition, the other with Keynes and effective demand – never converged in Keynes's lifetime, though leading disciples like Kahn and Joan Robinson were heavily involved in both 'revolutions.'[22] Even earlier, Joan Robinson claimed that the two 'revolutions' had converged in Kalecki's work: '[T]he two streams of thought were combined by Michał Kalecki'.[23]

The second emergence of continental European economics at Cambridge came with the arrival, at the beginning of 1931, of Friedrich Hayek at the London School of Economics. He came at the behest of Lionel Robbins, who was then an admirer of Austrian economic theory. Hayek became the chief exponent in Britain of continental European economic ideas. But his first lectures, published as *Prices and Production*, were poorly received in Cambridge. His monetary analysis and capital theory were ferociously criticised by Keynes, Sraffa and subsequently by Hayek's former student Kaldor.[24] Hayek's own aversion to state intervention ensured that, as the Great Depression corroded established economic theory and policy, Hayek and his supporters excluded themselves from mainstream economic discussions until the 1980s. By the 1930s, especially after the publication of his *General Theory*, Keynes, with only fragmentary notions of what was being discussed among economists on the Continent but with editorial control over the *Economic Journal*, was setting the agenda for economic theory in Cambridge.

When Kalecki arrived in Cambridge, he brought with him a version of continental European analysis that was methodologically and philosophically incompatible with the Marshallian tradition. At the root of his difficulties in Cambridge lay the different approaches that had been adopted in Britain and continental Europe in answer to the most fundamental question of the scope and significance of economic analysis.

The question of the extent to which economic systems may create determinable calculations for production, employment income and so on, in isolation from social and political circumstances, had been raised in the third quarter of the nineteenth century by John Stuart Mill, Auguste Comte and Karl Marx. All of them had concluded that the economy is an abstraction from the way in which societies organise production and distribution. There were therefore no universal economic 'laws' that were not conditional upon some associated social arrangements. Economic models, which claimed to represent any real situation, were always going to be underdetermined, because any given real situation would have, among its determinants, social, historic and cultural, as well as economic factors. In other words, economic analysis could not give rise to unambiguous conclusions, because these would always depend upon social, historic and cultural influences upon economic activity. Out of this came the notorious German *Methodenstreit*, which pitched historicism against deductive analysis. But by the early twentieth century, the discussion had moved on in Europe and in Britain to uncover those elements of economic analysis that could be combined into determinate models, self-determinate subsystems of evolving social systems.

14.2 The Cambridge peculiarity

In Britain the major economic systems builder who brought academic economics out of the grasp of social theory was Alfred Marshall (1842–1924). His ingenious solution to the problem of economic underdetermination was established at Cambridge and continues to hold sway throughout the English-speaking world and, increasingly, throughout mainstream economics. Marshall's solution was to divide up economic activity into discrete systems which, he postulated, operated in periods that allowed them to determine particular outcomes. The periods roughly coincide with observed time periods. The basic period is a market 'day', in which the prices that bring the supply of and demand for commodities into equilibrium are fixed. During that period firms supplying goods and individuals buying them are influenced only by prices and therefore can come to an agreement as to the prices that will satisfy them all. During that period, too, productive capabilities do not change. Given those prices, firms then determine how much to supply. In a separate 'short term' period firms decide where production is most profitable and expand into the most profitable markets, eliminating excess profits. In yet a third, 'long-term' period, firms decide on what scale to produce.[25] This – and the associated assumption that all these decisions could be made in a state of perfect competition – was the point that aroused Sraffa's criticism of Marshallian analysis (see above).

One of the difficulties of Marshall's solution to the problem of economic underdetermination is that it results in an overdetermined system capable of multiple equilibria. It is useful on its own terms only if the equilibrium in each period is arrived at one period at a time. Once all things are allowed to change, it is possible to have different general equilibria in the whole system according to, for example, the different scales of production or investment in the system. Moreover, Sraffa's critique had the important methodological implication that developments in one period, such as the increasing returns long-term, may subvert the mechanisms that are assumed to bring equilibrium in other periods. Therefore it may not be possible to move through successive periods, establishing successive equilibria to the satisfaction of the analyst, in the way postulated by Marshall. Nevertheless, the Marshallian method of getting determinate solutions for particular economic subsystems defined by their periods was a way of dealing with the complexity of an economy that was otherwise underdetermined. Hence, when Keynes came to consider the complexity of an economy as a whole in his *General Theory*, it was natural to use this Marshallian method.[26] As Axel Leijonhufvud noted: 'Sequential period analysis is simpler in that it substitutes step-functions for more complicated time-paths of the variables.'[27]

Wassily Leontief was later to describe the Cambridge approach to time and economic dynamics in Keynes's analysis as follows:

> Having centered his attention on the problem of change, Keynes does not, however, treat it in explicitly dynamic terms. True to the Cambridge tradition, he resorts to the Marshallian substitute for dynamic theory – the "short-run" analysis. The short-run analysis is related to a truly dynamic approach in the same way as the, also Marshallian, partial equilibrium theory stands in relation to the Walrasian general equilibrium analysis. In both instances the problem at hand is simplified by selective omission of some of the relevant

> relationships, on the one hand, and treatment as independent of some of the really dependent variables, on the other.[28]

In one of her most insightful comments on the economics derived from her teacher Alfred Marshall, Joan Robinson was later to distinguish 'periods' in which all other factors are held constant but one economic subsystem adjusts to equilibrium, from the more common time periods over which economic activity occurs, by calling the first 'logical' time and the second 'historical' time. She concluded:

> There is much to be learned from *a priori* comparisons of equilibrium positions, but they must be kept in their logical place. They cannot be applied to actual situations...In a model depicting equilibrium positions there is no causation. It consists of a closed circle of simultaneous equations. The value of each element is entailed by the values of the rest. At any moment in logical time the past is determined as much as the future. In an historical model, causal relations have to be specified.[29]

As a result, she might have added, analysis in logical time may be driven by intuitions derived from empirical observation. But such analysis has no empirical content, if only because actual economic events occur in historical time. Kalecki's empirical study of industrial prices, indeed any empirical study, could not fail to challenge the methodological preconceptions of Cambridge economics.

14.3 The German economic determination

By the time he came to be aware of it, continental European economic thought, which Kalecki had not so much been taught as absorbed in the course of his economic journalism and researches at the Institute for Research in Business Cycles and Prices, had resolved the problem of economic underdetermination in a very different way. Instead of dividing up economic decisions into discrete determinate periods, analytical economics in continental Europe identified two key systems of economic variables that were determinate. The first of these was the circular flow of income – that is, the income flows created in the process of production, as firms' expenditure, which returns to them as sales revenue when those who have received incomes spend them. This economic relation may have been rooted in a social process of production, but its outcome in an identity between aggregate output, income and expenditure is obviously a logical and determinate system. Moreover, since flows occur over time, the circular flow of income offers a neat way of linking up economic activity in successive periods, as opposed to a unique equilibrium that, once obtained, disappears from history.

The origins of this analysis went back to Quesnay's *tableau économique*, but it had found its way into Austrian economic theory in large part through the discussions that followed the publication in 1885 of volume II of Marx's *Capital*, subtitled *The Process of Circulation of Capital*. It should be remembered that the 'capital' whose circulation Marx analysed in this volume consisted of the total costs of production (in aggregate total national income) that in the process of production are placed into circulation in the economy by capitalists. Thus, in his first exposé of the history of economic thought and economic methodology, Josef Schumpeter identified the circular flow of income, as enunciated by the physiocrats, as a methodological cornerstone of economics that showed

> [H]ow each economic period becomes the basis for the subsequent one, not only in a technical sense but also in the sense that it produces exactly such results as will induce and enable the members of the economic community to repeat the same process in the same form in the next economic period; how economic production comes about as a social process... As long as economic periods were viewed merely as a technical phenomenon, and the fact of the economic cycle through which they move had not been recognised, the connecting link of economic causality and an insight into the inner necessity and the general character of economics was missing. It was possible to consider the individual acts of exchange, the phenomenon of money, the question of protective tariffs as economic problems, but it was impossible to view with clarity the total process which unfolds itself in a particular economic period.[30]

The circular flow of income eventually found its way into English-language economics as the identities between income output and expenditure that are used in the compilation of national income statistics, in whose development Richard Stone played such an important part. However, this being a branch of applied economics, the circular flow of income was not a part of English economic theory, although the idea that income depends on expenditure is the foundation of Keynes's paradox of thrift and arguably one of the key innovations in his thought following the publication of his *Treatise on Money*. As for Kalecki, the circular flow of income was embedded in his ideas from at least 1931, when he started investigating aggregate income and expenditure. The circular flow of income became the foundation of the 1929 national income statistics for Poland that Kalecki and his colleague Ludwik Landau published in 1934.[31] After his move from Cambridge at the end 1939, Kalecki embraced even more strongly the circular flow of income as a fundamental principle integrating economic phenomena. Using it, he came to his theory of profits, on which basis he elaborated his analysis of capitalist dynamics after his move from Cambridge.

14.4 Kalecki's economic determination

Kalecki's fullest understanding of how the circular flow of income determines economic variables was to come after he arrived in Oxford and started working on his theory of profits. However, even before his arrival in Britain, he had become aware of the methodological problems of trying to isolate economic variables and combine them into determinate systems. His excursion into this methodological territory was in 'Three Systems'. Kalecki's conclusion underlines his methodological rather than analytical concerns:

> [W]e have only examined the formation of equilibrium...within the already existing capital equipment.... Investment activity...(will result in) a continual movement through a series of equilibria...until the final equilibrium is attained.... If we consider the time of construction of new investment goods...it may also turn out that...the position of final equilibrium will never be attained...these are proper business fluctuations.[32]

In other words, there is no actual determinate equilibrium in a capitalist economy but a series of constantly changing variables. Furthermore, there is a clear echo of this conclusion in Kalecki's judgement about Keynes's short-period equilibrium analysis in the *General Theory*: 'Equilibrium', then, is not reached, and the growth of investment will still persist (we are dealing here, as may easily be seen, with a cumulative Wicksellian process).'[33]

Kalecki was here clearly analysing movements in what Joan Robinson had called 'historical' time, as opposed to the 'logical' time in which Keynes had couched his *General Theory*. But Cambridge remained wedded to the Marshallian tradition of treating subsystems of variables in logical time. For Cambridge, 'dynamic' analysis in 'historical' time meant shifting from one closed subsystem of variables (with factors such as the capital stock assumed constant or irrelevant) to another closed subsystem in which the capital stock was allowed to vary but such other factors as relative prices and competition were taken as constant.[34] This provides the clue to the methodological enigma that Keynes, Joan Robinson, Kahn and all those Cambridge sympathizers of Kalecki found in his work. The notion of a circular flow of income integrating prices and economic decisions was as foreign to economists brought up to believe that the complexity of an economy could be made tractable or calculable by having individuals make economic decisions simultaneously in different periods as the German-language economic literature was in Cambridge. Kalecki's refusal to fit price theory into Marshallian methodology condemned his Cambridge research. Keynes, who already in 1937 had sought to disentangle some more familiar presuppositions from Kalecki's theory of taxation, remained uncomprehending of Kalecki's 'assumptions'. But the incomprehension arose because Kalecki was not a Marshallian. The arguments over method were to concentrate Kalecki's thinking even more on the circular flow of income, out of which was to come yet more arguments with Keynes and the centrepiece of Kalecki's economics, his theory of profits.

A surprising aspect of Kalecki's departure from Cambridge is how little both sides learned from each other in the process of their researches, as might be suggested by the standard approach to economic methodology, nicely expressed by Kalecki's friend Oskar Lange in his review of Josef Schumpeter's magisterial *Business Cycles*:

> The choice between Mr. Kalecki's (or Mr. Kaldor's, or any other) theory and that of Professor Schumpeter can be made only on the basis of empirical investigation. It is necessary to find the concrete functions involved parameters, then to investigate what periods, amplitudes, damping, etc. are to be expected from the different theories, and to confront these expected values with empirical data. Only in this way is it possible to choose the 'true' theory from among those theoretically admissible. It is possible, even likely, that the 'true' theory will prove more complex and will have to combine elements of the different *a priori* theories developed'.[35]

Such an approach would have welcomed Kalecki's empirical researches in Cambridge. However, the failure of the Cambridge Research Project was due not only to Keynes's ambitions for a Department of Applied Economics but also to the unreal distinction between a theory that is supposed to emerge innocent of empirical observation and empirical observation that is supposed to be innocent of theory. That theory cannot be entirely free of inductive presuppositions was common knowledge in Cambridge. Alfred Marshall himself had argued that scientific advance commences with generalisations based on induction:

> sciences...aim at precipitating the result of a multitude of observations into provisional statements, which are sufficiently definite to be brought under test by other observations of nature. These statements, when first put forth, seldom claim a high authority. But after they have been tested by many independent observations, and especially after they have been applied successfully in the prediction of coming events, or the results of new experiments, they graduate as *laws*. A science progresses by increasing the number and exactness of its laws; by submitting them to tests of increasing severity; and by enlarging their scope till a single broad law contains and supersedes a number of narrower laws, which have been shown to be special instances if it.[36]

Kalecki's experience showed that there is no 'objective' examination of data. The very choice of the form in which economic data is selected for examination comes from the theory within which the investigation will be conducted. When Kalecki put forward changes in income, expenditure and competition rather than stylised changes in supply and demand to explain shifts in prices and employment, this proved too much for his Cambridge supporters. The differences over the choice of data considered important for business cycle analysis masked even more fundamental differences over three key elements of Keynesian and Kaleckian theory. The first of these elements was the theory of value, or price theory. Kalecki rejected the notion that prices are determined by supply and demand in markets abstracted from each other and abstracted from the process of investment or capital accumulation, an abstraction fixed in the Marshallian distinction between the price setting 'day', the 'short period' in which output and employment decisions are made, and the 'long period' in which investment decisions are made. For Kalecki the price system determines the real wage rate and hence total consumption in the economy (since capitalists' consumption, by and large, is not affected by changes in their income). That same price system also determines the distribution of profits in the economy among individual capitalists or firms. In affecting the distribution of profits, the price system also affects investment and is itself affected by it.

The second key element was the theory of investment. Keynes remained wedded to essentially marginalist principles of determining investment by the margin of the *expected* return over the long-term rate of interest. Kalecki attached much more importance to the rate of profit, capacity utilisation and the extent of businesses' own liquid reserves in relation to their indebtedness. Since debt is fixed in money terms, price changes can affect the real value of debt; that is, its value in relation to current profits. This again was an important reason why, in a credit economy, price adjustments could not be relied upon to bring an economy into equilibrium. Kalecki's distinction between investment *decisions* and actual investment projects which take time to implement makes investment inelastic, so that projects under way feed disequilibrium into the Marshallian long period (see Chapter 10).

Finally, Kalecki and Cambridge, including Keynes, differed over the significance of monetary policy for the business cycle. Keynes, an enthusiast for active monetary policy, believed it could be used to stabilise the economy at high rates of employment. Kalecki, who was more sceptical, saw monetary policy and conditions as endogenous to the business cycle, as affected by that cycle rather than determining its course.

Despite the best efforts of Joan Robinson, Cambridge clung to Marshall's principles of economic analysis. The Second World War brought to an end the rendezvous in Cambridge, financed by the Rockefeller Foundation and the National Institute for Economic and Social Research, before Kalecki and the Keynesians could overcome their mutual incomprehension.

Notes

Preface

1. Sawyer, *The Economics of Michał Kalecki*, 1985; Osiatyński, *Michał Kalecki on a Socialist Economy*, 1988.
2. Julio López and Michaël Assous, *Michal Kalecki*, 2010.
3. Tadeusz Kowalik, 'Biography of Michał Kalecki', 1964.
4. Palgrave Macmillan 2011.

1 Early Years

1. The Kalecki *Collected Works* refers to Kalecki's father's factory as a cotton mill (J. Osiatyński (ed.) *Collected Works of Michał Kalecki*, vol. VII, *Studies in Applied Economics 1940–1967*, 1997, p. 587). In a study of the 1905 revolution in Łódź, the factory is listed as a 'wool-spinning factory' (N. Gąsiorowska (ed.) *Źródła do dziejów Rewolucji 1905–1907 w okręgu Łódzkim*, 1957, p. 700).
2. Transcript of Kalecki's birth certificate, in his private papers at the Polish Academy of Sciences (hereafter PAN) MK file III-319/18. This transcript, in its Polish original, was evidently made after 1918, when the Gregorian calendar replaced the Julian calendar, after which it became necessary to add 12 days to dates recorded before 1918.
3. PAN MK-319/67, p. 15.
4. Ibid.
5. *Książeczka Wojskowa*, in PAN MK-319/18.
6. Interview with Tadeusz Kowalik, PAN III 319/67, p. 15.
7. The Russian market and tariffs, as key factors in Polish industrialisation at the end of the nineteenth century, are analysed in Rosa Luxemburg's doctoral thesis: R. Luxemburg, *Die Industrielle Entwicklung Polens*, 1898.
8. N. Gąsiorowska (ed.) *Źródła do dziejów Rewolucji 1905–1907 w okręgu Łódzkim*, 1957, p. 92.
9. R. E. Blobaum, *Rewolucja Russian Poland, 1904–1907*, 1995, p. 24.
10. PAN7319/67, p. 5.
11. Ibid., p. 11.
12. Ibid., p. 9.
13. Ibid., p. 14.
14. Interview with Tadeusz Kowalik, PAN III 319/67, p. 6.
15. 'on był taki kameralny bardzo człowiek.' Ibid, p. 14.
16. PAN III 319/68.
17. Ibid., p. 6.

2 In the Crucible of the Revolution

1. S. Kalabiński and F. Tych, *Czwarte powstanie czy pierwsza rewolucja, lata 1905–1907 na ziemiach polskich*, 1969, p. 21.

2. Ibid., pp. 28–9.
3. R. E. Blobaum, *Rewolucja Russian Poland,* 1995, pp. 38–9.
4. Ibid. A good account of Bund activity in Łódź is provided by Paweł Samuś in his essay 'The Bund organisation in Łódź', 2001.
5. R. E. Blobaum, *Rewolucja Russian Poland,* 1995, p. 52.
6. Ibid.
7. S. Kalabiński and F. Tych, *Czwarte powstanie,* 1969, pp. 52–3.
8. Ibid., pp. 55–6.
9. Ibid., p. 83.
10. Ibid., pp. 85–6.
11. Ibid., pp. 88–9.
12. Ibid., pp. 170–1.
13. Ibid., pp. 173–5.
14. Ibid., p. 195.
15. Ibid., pp. 207–8.
16. Ibid., p. 219.
17. Ibid., p. 375.
18. Ibid., p. 381.
19. Ibid., pp. 376–8.
20. Ibid., pp. 381–2.
21. Ibid., p. 394.
22. Ibid., pp. 383–92.
23. Ibid., p. 278.
24. In N. Gąsiorowska (ed.), *Źródła do dziejów,* 1957.
25. Interview with Tadeusz Kowalik, PAN III 319/67, p. 14.
26. Maria Koszutska was then in PPS-Lewica. In 1918 she became a founding member of the Polish Communist Party, KPP. She perished in Stalin's purges.
27. M. Koszutska Wera-Kostrzewa, 'Kartele, trusty i związki przedsiębiorców', 1961.
28. M. Koszutska Wera-Kostrzewa, 'Bezrobocie Łódzkie', 1961.
29. J. Osiatyński (ed.), *Collected Works of Michał Kalecki,* vol. VII, 1997, p. 586.
30. In a later autobiographical sketch, Kalecki stated that he attended the Father Ignacy Skorupka *Gimnazjum* ('Życiorys Michała Kaleckiego', in PAN III 319/31). This is reported in biographical notes given in the Polish and English editions of the Kalecki *Collected Works* (*Collected Works of Michał Kalecki,* vol. VII, 1990, p. 586). In fact Kalecki never attended any school that was called the Father Ignacy Skorupka *Gimnazjum.* The Philological Lycée, which he did attend, was renamed the Father Ignacy Skorupka *Gimnazjum* in 1920, after Kalecki had matriculated from it, when the school was given the name of a Catholic army chaplain who died in the defence of Warsaw during the Polish-Soviet War of 1920–1. As an adult, Kalecki never attempted to hide his Jewish origins and enjoyed goading anti-Semites. His suggestion that he was the product of a patriotic, anti-Bolshevik and Catholic education would have goaded well in Poland.

3 Economic Journalism

1. Adela Kalecka's notes, PAN III 319/68; Interview with Tadeusz Kowalik, PAN III 319/67.

2. The Polish term *koniunktura*, or *konjunktura*, derived from the German *konjunktur*, is only loosely translatable as 'business cycle'. It certainly includes the notion of industrial or economic fluctuations. But it also includes the state of business at any one time or the current situation in different markets, with an implication that this situation or state of business is continually shifting. The addiction to general equilibrium in British and American economics means that English language economics has no equivalent to *koniunktura*. See also the discussion of the establishment of the Institute for the Study of Business Cycles and Prices in Chapter 5.
3. Adela Kalecka's notes, PAN III 319/68.
4. Ibid.
5. Interview with Tadeusz Kowalik, PAN III 319/67, tape 2, p. 6.
6. PAN III 319/18.
7. J. Osiatyński (ed.), *Collected Works of Michał Kalecki*, vol. VII, 1997, p. 587.
8. M.I. Tugan-Baranovsky, *Promyshlennye Krizisy v Sovremennoi Anglii*, 1894; J. M. Keynes, *A Treatise on Money*, 2: *The Applied Theory of Money*, 1915, pp. 89–90.
9. J. Osiatyński (ed.) *Collected Works of Michał Kalecki*, vol. I, *Capitalism: Business Cycles and Full Employment*, 1990, p. 425.
10. J.A. Hobson, *The Evolution of Modern Capitalism A Study of Machine Production*, 1926, chs VIII–IX.
11. Interview with Tadeusz Kowalik, PAN III 319/67, p. 20.
12. *Centralny Związek Przemysłu, Górnictwa, Handlu i Finansów*, known commonly as *Lewiatan* or the Leviathan, on account of its apparently limitless reach and influence.
13. M. Kalecki, 'Zbliżenie gospodarcze amerykańsko-rosyjskie a Polska', 1927.
14. M. Kalecki, 'Konsekwencje gospodarcze zatargu angielsko-sowieckiego', 1928a.
15. M. Kalecki, 'Zmierzch Deterding'a' (The fall of Deterding), 1932b.
16. M. Kalecki, 'Ivar Kreuger', 1932a.
17. 'The match king', *The Economist*, 2007.
18. R. Skidelsky, *John Maynard Keynes*, vol. 2: *The Economist as Saviour 1920–1937*, 1992, p. 435.
19. J. M. Keynes *The Collected Writings of John Maynard Keynes*, vol. XXI: *Activities 1931–1939: World Crises and Policies in Britain and America*, 1982, p. 90.
20. J. M. Keynes, *Collected Writings*, vol. XXI, 1982, p. 93.
21. *Metale*, in *Przegląd Gospodarczy*, 1928, nos. 9/17, 9/19, 9/21, 9/23. The notes do not appear in either the Polish or the English editions of the Kalecki *Collected Works*, even though Kalecki continued writing these notes right up to the end of 1934, well after he had begun his career as an economist.
22. It advertised itself as a weekly of the Ministry of Trade and Industry, with the participation of the Ministries of Finance, Agriculture and Communication.
23. M. Kalecki, 'Niemcy: Opanowanie przemysłu przez kapitał zagraniczny' (Control over German industry by foreign capital), 1929b.
24. M. Kalecki, 'W sprawie aktywizacji bilansu handlowego' (On activating the balance of trade), 1929a.
25. J. Osiatyński (ed.), *Collected Works of Michał Kalecki*, vol. I, 1990, editorial notes, p. 424.

4 To Warsaw

1. M. Kalecki, 'Światowy kryzys finansowy', 1931a.
2. Adela Kalecka's notes in PAN III 319/9.
3. Adela Kalecka, Interview with Tadeusz Kowalik, 23 January 1979, PAN III 319/9.
4. Letter of Blanche Bronstein to the author, 11 March 1991.
5. *Mały Rocznik Statystyczny*, 1937, p. 107.
6. J. Osiatyński (ed.), *Collected Works of Michał Kalecki*, vol. VI, *Studies in Applied Economics 1927–1941*, 1996.
7. M. Kalecki, 'Europejski kryzys węglowy', 1929c.
8. At the League of Nations, the institute was referred to simply as the Institute for Economic Research; League of Nations, *The Course and Phases of the World Economic Depression: Report Presented to the Assembly of the League of Nations*, 1931, p. 110.
9. J. Osiatyński (ed.), *Collected Works of Michał Kalecki*, vol. I, 1990, p. 434.
10. R. Górecki *Poland and Her Economic Development*, 1935, p. 111.
11. 'Dnia 21 lutego r.b. ukazało się w Dzienniku Ustaw rozporządzenie o powołaniu przy Ministrze Przemysłu i Handlu Instytutu Badania Konjunktur Gospodarczych i Cen. Zeszyt niniejszy jest pierwszą publikacją tego Instytutu z zakresu konjuktury gospodardzej...w ten sposób zainteresowane sfery otrzymywałyby dostatecznie wcześnie informacje które są nizbędne aby wyrobić sobie pojęcie o siłach działających w zmiennym przebiegu gospodarczej.' *Konjunktura Gospodarcza*, 1928, Rok I, nr. 1.
12. E. Lipiński, 'O badaniu koniunktury gospodarczej' 1926, p. 873.
13. R. Skidelsky, *John Maynard Keynes*, vol. 2, 1992, p. 106.
14. Ibid. See also Jerzy Osiatyński's illuminating notes about business cycle indicators in J. Osiatyński (ed.), *Collected Works of Michał Kalecki*, vol. VI, 1996, pp. 522–4.

5 At the Institute

1. The Commercial Bank in Warsaw, which still operates today.
2. M. Kalecki, T. Kowalik and K. Secomski, 'Ekonomia Edwarda Lipińskiego', 1969.
3. T. Kowalik, *Historia Ekonomii w Polsce 1864–1950*, 1992, chs XI–XII.
4. Ibid., 149. See also J. Nowicki, *Teoria ekonomii II Rzeczypospolitej*, 1988, chs IX–X.
5. M. Kalecki, 'Dynamika spożycia pieczywa pszennego oraz mięsa w Polsce', 1930a.
6. M. Kalecki, 'Marża zarobkowa drewna tartego', 1930b.
7. M. Kalecki, 'The Problem of Effective Demand with Tugan-Baranovski and Rosa Luxemburg', 1967.
8. M. Kalecki, 'Nakręcanie koniunktury światowej', 1933a.
9. M. Kalecki, 'Kwitnące przedsiębiorstwo' (Flourishing enterprise), 1932c.
10. M. Kalecki and J. Wiśniewski, 'Eliminowanie sezonowości w odsetka bezrobocia', 1931.

11. M. Kalecki, 'Konsekwencje dumpingu', 1931b.
12. M. Kalecki, 'Ludwik Landau – ekonomista i statystyk', 1964a, in J. Osiatyński (ed.), *Collected Works of Michał Kalecki*, vol. VII, 1997, 325, 533.
13. M. Kalecki, 'Koniunktury przemysłu włókienniczego', 1929d.
14. M. Kalecki and L. Landau, 'Szacunek rozmiarów ruchu inwestycyjnego', 1931.
15. M. Kalecki and L. Landau, 'Szacunek rozmiarów ruchu inwestycyjnego w Polsce i wskaźnik kwartalny inwestycji', 1932a.
16. M. Kalecki and L. Landau, 'Handel włókienniczy w Polsce: Zarys struktury', 1932b.
17. M. Kalecki and L. Landau, 'Szacunek dochodu społecznego w. R. 1929', 1934.
18. M. Kalecki and L. Landau, 'Dochód społeczny w r. 1933 i podstawy badań periodycznych nad zmianami dochodu', 1935.
19. M. Breit, *Stopa procentowa w Polsce* (The Rate of Interest in Poland), 1933.
20. H. S. Ellis, *German Monetary Theory 1905–1933*, 1934; J. A. Schumpeter, *History of Economic Analysis*, 1954, pt IV, ch. 8.
21. See Chapter 6.
22. F. A. Hayek, *Geldtheorie und Konjunkturtheorie*, 1929.
23. M. Breit, 'Przesunięcie kapitalizacji w Polsce w dobie przesilenia', 1934.
24. M. Breit, 'Problemy rynku pieniężnego i kapitałowego na tle depresji', 1935a.
25. M. Breit, 'Konjunkturalny rozwój kredytu długoterminowego w Polsce', 1935b; the reference is to A.C. Pigou, *The Economics of Welfare*, 1920.
26. See Chapter 6.
27. M. Breit and O. Lange, 'Droga do socjalistycznej gospodarki planowej', 1934.
28. M. Breit, 'Ein Beitrag zur Theorie des Geld- und Kapitalmarktes', 1935c.
29. B. Winawer, 'Wywóz wyrobów przemysłowych w latach 1930 i 1931', 1932.
30. Letter of Blanche Bronstein to the author, 11 March 1991.

6 The Socialist Discussions

1. Kalecki and Landau's calculations in M. Kalecki and L. Landau, *Mały Rocznik Statystyczny 1937* 1937, p. 60.
2. Ibid., p. 247.
3. M. Kalecki, T. Kowalik and K. Secomski 'Ekonomia Edwarda Lipińskiego', 1969.
4. M. Kalecki, 'Światowy kryzys finansowy', 1931a. The article is summarised in Chapter 3.
5. J. Osiatyński (ed.), *Collected Works of Michał Kalecki*, vol. I, 1990, p. 427.
6. T. Kowalik, 'Biography of Oskar Lange', 1964.
7. R. Hilferding, *Finance Capital: A Study of the Latest Phase of Capitalist Development*, 1910, pts III–IV.
8. See in particular Kalecki's 'The Fascism of Our Times', in M. Kalecki, *The Last Phase in the Transformation of Capitalism*, 1972; and R. Luxemburg, *The Accumulation of Capital*, 1951.

9. H. Grossman, *Das Akkumulations-Zusammenbruchsgesetz des kapitalistischen Systems (Zugleich eine Krisentheorie)*, 1929.
10. Grossman had originally been a member of the Bund but joined the Polish Communist Party after the First World War. See T. Kowalik, *Historia Ekonomii*, 1992, pp. 128–32.
11. J. Osiatyński (ed.), *Collected Works of Michał Kalecki*, vol. I, 1990, pp. 427–8, pp. 434–5.
12. M. Kalecki, 'Obniżka płac w czasie kryzysu' (Wage reductions in times of crisis), 1932f.
13. M. Kalecki, 'Wage reductions', 1932f.
14. M. Kalecki, 'Podstawy konfliktu mandżurskiego', 1932g.
15. M. Kalecki, 'Uwagi o hitleryzmie i „sferach gospodarczych"', 1932h.
16. *Zinsknechtschaft*, which Kalecki translated into Polish as 'niewolnictwo procentów', in fact means something broader than the 'interest slavery' into which the German term, popularised by Nazi critics of finance, is translated in the English edition of Kalecki's *Collected Works*. See J. Osiatyński (ed.), *Collected Works of Michał Kalecki*, vol. VI, 1996, p. 162.
17. M. Kalecki, 'Wojna na Wschodzie', 1932i.
18. K. H. Marx, *Capital*, vol. 1, 1957, p. 843. The quotation was itself taken by Marx from the English writer on trade unions, T. J. Dunning.
19. M. Kalecki, 'Przewidywania p. Keynes'a', 1932j.
20. J. M. Keynes, a lecture in the series 'The World's Economic Crisis and the Way of Escape', 1932.
21. J. M. Keynes, 'The World's Economic Crisis', 1932, p. 58; quoted also in M. Kalecki, 'Przewidywania p. Keynes'a', 1932j.
22. M. Kalecki, ibid.
23. M. Kalecki, 'Czy możliwe jest "kapitalistyczne" wyjście z kryzysu', 1932e; J. Osiatyński (ed.), *Collected Works of Michał Kalecki*, vol. I, 1990, pp. 48–53, pp. 75–81.
24. M. Kalecki, 'Czy możliwe jest "kapitalistyczne" wyjście z kryzysu', 1932e.
25. M. Kalecki, 'Inflacja a Wojna', 1932m.
26. M. Kalecki, 'Inflacja a Wojna', 1932m.
27. M. Kalecki, 'Na marginesie wydarzeń niemieckich', 1932n.

7 The Enigma of the Business Cycle

1. D. Laidler, *The Golden Age of the Quantity Theory of Money*, 1991.
2. See F. A. Hayek, 'Note on the Development of the Doctrine of *Forced Saving*', 1932.
3. A printer's error in the English edition of the *Collected Works* refers to this hyperinflation as occurring 'in the early 1930s'.
4. M. Kalecki, 'Koniunktura a zbrojenie' (The business cycle and armaments), 1935a.
5. M. Kalecki, 'Nakręcanie koniunktury światowej', 1933a.
6. M. Kalecki, 'Inflacja a Wojna', 1932m.
7. M. Kalecki, 'Wpływ kartelizacji na koniunkturę', 1932l.
8. R. Hilferding, *Finance Capital*, 1910, chs 15 and 20.

9. It is interesting to consider here where the association of steadier profits and output comes from. Quite clearly it comes from those who operate cartels; they experience stabler business but do not see that it is at the cost of instability in the rest of the economy – hence the belief that were the competitive sector cartelised, the economy would fluctuate less. This has important methodological implications. Businessmen in cartels correctly perceive that competitive businesses are less stable and incorrectly conclude that if those competitive businesses were to be cartelised, like their (the cartel businessmen's) own firms, they too would experience greater stability. Such a conclusion might even be confirmed by econometric evidence comparing the variance of business in competitive markets, as opposed to the variance of business in cartelised markets. This fallacy of composition illustrates how misleading is the Marshallian methodology of relying upon the opinion of men in business for insight into macroeconomics and policy, as opposed to the systematic investigation of the conjunctures from which they draw their experiences and perceptions. It marks one of the fundamental differences between Kalecki and the followers of Marshall, including Keynes.
10. A. Aftalion, *Les Crises périodiques de surproduction*, 1913, p. 401.
11. J. Tinbergen, 'Ein Schiffbauzyklus', 1931.
12. This and the origins of the other elements of Kalecki's theory are extensively discussed by Jerzy Osiatyński in his editorial notes in volume I of the Kalecki *Collected Works*; J. Osiatyński (ed.), *Collected Works*, vol. I, 1990, pp. 437–42.
13. M. Kalecki, *Próba teorii koniunktury*, 1933b, p. 79.
14. Ibid., p. 80.
15. Ibid., pp. 80–1.
16. Ibid., p. 95. According to Tadeusz Kowalik, Kalecki got the idea that investments finance themselves from one of the co-editors of *Przegląd Gospodarczy*, T. Sławiński. Sławiński was a proponent of conservative monetary and financial practices, such as the gold standard and balanced government budgets. But he also argued that changes in the velocity of circulation of banknotes tended to alleviate shortages of credit. J. Osiatyński (ed.), *Collected Works*, vol. I, 1990, p. 473. However, the general idea goes back before the Polish discussions, through German monetary theory to Wicksell.
17. M. Kalecki, *Próba teorii koniunktury*, 1933b, p. 97.
18. R. M. Goodwin 'Kalecki's Economic Dynamics: A Personal View', 1989, p. 249. Geoff Harcourt has pointed out to me that Kaldor was in Leyden for the presentation of Kalecki's paper in French. Kalecki's later interventions in London appear to have made a more notable impression upon Kaldor. N. Kaldor, 'Personal Recollections on Michał Kalecki', 1989, pp. 3–4.
19. E. Varga, *The Great Crisis and Its Political Consequences: Economics and Politics 1928–1934*, 1935.
20. A. Rajchman 'Uwagi krytyczne o jednej z matematycznych teorii koniunktury' 1933.
21. M. Kalecki, 'Odpowiedź na „Uwagi krytyczne o jednej z matematycznych teorii koniunktury" A Rajchmana', 1933c.
22. K. H. Marx, *Capital*, vol. II, 1974, ch. XVII.
23. J. Osiatyński (ed.), *Collected Works*, vol. I, 1990, p. 444.
24. Letter of Blanche Bronstein to Jan Toporowski, 11 March 1991.
25. M. Kalecki, 'A Macrodynamic Theory of Business Cycles', 1935b.

26. J. Osiatyński (ed.), *Collected Works*, vol. I, 1990, pp. 444–6.
27. M. Kalecki, 'Comments on the Macrodynamic Theory of Business Cycles', 1936a.

8 Sweden

1. See S. Chapple, 'Did Kalecki get there first? The race for the general theory', 1991; M. Assous, 'Kalecki's 1934 model vs. the IS-LM model of Hicks and Modigliani', 2007; M. Assous and G. J. López, *Michał Kalecki*, 2010, pp. 60–6. The editor of the Kalecki *Collected Works*, Jerzy Osiatyński, himself expresses puzzlement about Kalecki's apparent use of neoclassical assumptions in this paper (J. Osiatyński (ed.), *Collected Works of Michał Kalecki*, vol. I, 1990, p. 492), but he may well have started off this equilibrium interpretation of Kalecki's paper with the article 'Unemployment Equilibrium: A Note on Kalecki's and Keynes's Approach', 1987.
2. M. Kalecki, 'Three Systems', 1934a, p. 219.
3. A. M. Neuman, 'O „Trzech układach"', 1934.
4. M. Kalecki, 'Odpowiedź', 1934b.
5. M. Kalecki, 'Losy eksperymentów', 1934c.
6. M. Kalecki, 'Losy eksperymentów', 1934c.
7. M. Kalecki, 'Koniunktura a dobrobyt', 1934d.
8. Ibid., pp. 177–8. See also below.
9. M. Kalecki, 'Koniunktura a bilans płatniczy', 1935c; J. Osiatyński (ed.), *Collected Works of Michał Kalecki*, vol. I, 1990.
10. M. Kalecki, 'Eksperyment niemiecki', 1935d; J. Osiatyński (ed.), *Collected Works of Michał Kalecki*, vol. VI, 1996.
11. A. J. Prażmowska, *Poland A Modern History*, 2010, pp. 124–5.
12. J. Osiatyński (ed.), *Collected Works of Michał Kalecki*, vol. I, 1990, p. 496.
13. Rockefeller Archive Center, documents filed under 35041 SS 9.
14. Rockefeller Archive Center, 35041 SS 9.
15. D. Laidler, *The Golden Age of the Quantity Theory of Money*, 1991, ch. 5; H. S. Ellis, *German Monetary Theory 1905–1933*, 1934, pp. 54–8.
16. B. Hansson, *The Stockholm School*, 1982; G. Myrdal, *Monetary Equilibrium*, 1939, pp. 193–5; E. Lindahl, *Studies in the Theory of Money and Capital*, 1939, pt II.
17. Rockefeller Archive Centre, 35041 SS 9.
18. J. Robinson, 'Michał Kalecki on the economics of capitalism', 1977.
19. G. L. S. Shackle, *The Years of High Theory Invention and Tradition in Economic Thought 1926–1939*, 1967, p. 127.
20. G. R. Feiwel, 'Introduction' to M. Kalecki, *The Last Phase in the Transformation of Capitalism*, 1972, p. 13.
21. T. Kowalik, 'Biography of Michał Kalecki', 1964, p. 5
22. See J. Osiatyński's editorial notes to vol. I of the Kalecki *Collected Works* p., 500; J. Osiatyński (ed.), *Collected Works of Michał Kalecki*, vol. I, 1990.
23. According to the biography in vol. VII of the Kalecki *Collected Works*, the Kaleckis moved in March; see J. Osiatyński, 'Main Dates and Facts in Kalecki's Life', 1997, pp. 589–90. However, in November 1936 Kalecki reported to the Rockefeller Foundation that he had been in Stockholm up to 11 April; Rockefeller Archive Center 35041 SS 9.

24. M. Kalecki, 'A Theory of the Business Cycle', 1936–7.

9 London

1. Malinowski was later to be Kalecki's colleague at the United Nations in New York and helped to set up the UN Conference on Trade and Development.
2. Nicholas Kaldor, 'Personal Recollections', 1989, p. 3.
3. Ibid., pp. 3–4.
4. PAN III 319/30.
5. W. Zawadzki, 'Nowa teoria pieniądza Keynesa', 1936.
6. Kalecki, 'Some Remarks on Keynes's Theory', 1936b, p. 118.
7. Ibid., p. 228.
8. At this point, when Joseph Schumpeter queried why Kalecki did not allow the rate of interest to bring saving and investment into equilibrium, he appears to have suffered an unusual lapse of understanding. See Schumpeter, *Business Cycles*, 1939, p. 188.
9. Kalecki, 'Some Remarks on Keynes's Theory', p. 230.
10. Keynes, *General Theory* p., 148.
11. Kalecki, 'Some Remarks on Keynes's Theory', p. 231.
12. More than ten years later, Wassily Leontief argued much the same: 'Having centered his attention on the problem of change Keynes does not, however, treat it in explicitly dynamic terms. True to the Cambridge tradition, he resorts to the Marshallian substitute for dynamic theory – the "short-run" analysis.... For the analytical purpose at hand, this short-run argument is hardly more adequate. The short-run analysis is related to a truly dynamic approach...by selective omission of some of the relevant relationships, on the one hand, and treatment as independent of some of the really dependent variables, on the other.' Leontief, 'Postulates: Keynes's *General Theory* and the Classicists', p. 100.
13. Kalecki, 'Some Remarks on Keynes's Theory', p. 231.
14. Kalecki, 'A Theory of the Business Cycle', 1936–7.
15. J. Osiatyński, *Collected Works of Michał Kalecki*, vol. 1, 1990, p. 524. The correspondence continued, with Kalecki making use of recent data published by Simon Kuznets to show that the prices of new investment goods had fallen relatively since 1929. 'Thus it is clear that the gap between prospective rate of profit and the rate of interest was much lower in the depression than in the prosperity. But then some thing besides the prices of investment goods is required in the formation of "equilibrium".' (Kalecki, letter to J. M. Keynes, 4 April 1937, in *The Collected Writings of John Maynard Keynes*, vol. XII, 1983, pp. 793–6.
16. See Chapter 7.
17. Marx, *Capital*, vol. III, p. 359.
18. The summary description by Kaldor of Keynes and Kalecki, respectively, in Kaldor, 'Personal Recollections', 1989.
19. 'Wstęp', in J. M. Keynes, *Ogólna teoria*, 1956.
20. Keynes, *The Economic Consequences of the Peace*, 1919, p. 273. 'Wstęp', in J. M. Keynes, *Ogólna teoria*, 1956.
21. Ohlin, 'Some Notes on the Stockholm Theory', 1937.

22. Rockefeller Archive Center file. See also correspondence between Keynes and Haberler in the *Collected Writings of John Maynard Keynes*, vol. XXIX, 1979, pp. 269–75.
23. J. Robinson, 'Disguised Unemployment', 1936.
24. *Collected Works of Michał Kalecki*, vol. I, pp. 500–1.
25. Ibid. This is perhaps the first expression of what was to become conventional wisdom among many Post-Keynesians later in the century: that Kalecki's theory complements rather than substitutes more effectively for Keynes's analysis.
26. Marshall, *Principles of Economics*, 1920, pp. 378–80.
27. *Collected Works of Michał Kalecki*, vol. I, p. 503.
28. Kaldor, 'Personal Recollections'.
29. See A. Asimakopoulos, 'Kalecki and Robinson', 1989; G. C. Harcourt, 'Joan Robinson 1903–1983', 1995; and G. C. Harcourt and Prue Kerr *Joan Robinson*, 2009, ch. 12.
30. *Collected Writings of John Maynard Keynes*, vol. XIV, 1973), p. 140.
31. *Koniunktura Gospodarcza*, 1928, no. 1 (see Chapter 4).
32. *Koniunktura Gospodarcza*, 1936, no. 3.
33. Letter of Blanche Bronstein (Blanka Winawer) to the author, 11 March 1991; Kowalik, *Historia Ekonomii w Polsce*, 1992, p. 275.
34. J. Osiatyński (ed.), *M. Kalecki Dzieła*, vol. 1, 1979, p. 503.
35. Rockefeller Archive Center file. N. F. Hall was Noel Hall, the Professor of Political Economy at University College London, who was later to assist in the setting up of the Cambridge Research Project, on which Kalecki was employed in 1939 (see Chapters 10 and 11).
36. Hayek, *Prices and Production*, 1935.
37. Kahn Papers, RFK/13/57/397–9.
38. Kahn Papers, RFK/13/57/393. In later conversations with the author, Adela Kalecka pointed out that a condition of the Rockefeller Foundation fellowships was that the fellows had to return to their country of origin at the end of their fellowship. This condition may have been a factor in Kalecki's assurances about plans for employment in Warsaw on his return.
39. Rockefeller Archive Center file. The 'School of Commerce' was the *Szkoła Główna Handlowa*, where Lipiński worked.

10 From London to Cambridge

1. Breit, 'Ein Beitrag zur Theorie des Geld- und Kapitalmarktes', 1935c; and 'Problemy rynku pieniężnego i kapitałowego na tle depresji', 1935a.
2. See Chilosi, 'Breit, Kalecki and Hicks on the Term Structure of Interest Rates', 1982; Mott, 'Kalecki's Principle of Increasing Risk', 1985–1986; and 'Kalecki's Principle of Increasing Risk', 1982.
3. Buchanan and Calkins, 'A Comment on Mr. Kalecki's "Principle of Increasing Risk"', 1938.
4. Kalecki, 'A Comment on the "Principle of Increasing Risk": A Reply', 1938a.
5. ibid.
6. Lange, 'Review of M. Kalecki *Essays in the Theory of Economic Fluctuations*', 1941b.

7. Steindl, *Random Processes and the Growth of Firms*, 1965.
8. *The Collected Writings of John Maynard Keynes*, vol. XII, 790.
9. Ibid., 790–8. See also Chapter 9.
10. J. Osiatyński (ed.), *Collected Works of Michał Kalecki*, vol. I, 558.
11. The argument is extended in Laramie and Mair, *A Dynamic Theory of Taxation*, 2000.
12. Kalecki's nice quotation at the end from Joan Robinson's review of Roy Harrod's *The Trade Cycle* (in the *Economic Journal*, December 1936, 691–3) was 'excised' from the review when it was published in her *Collected Papers*, vol. 1, 59–61.
13. Rockefeller Archive Center file.
14. Kalecki, 'The Lesson of the Blum Experiment', 1938c.
15. The increase in prices appears to have been first confirmed by Norman Bay, Kalecki's old friend from his Gdańsk studies, in whose construction firm in Warsaw Kalecki had occasionally worked as a designer in the later 1920s. In the 1930s Bay had moved to Paris, where he ran a building company. Kalecki stayed with him while in Paris in 1937. Bay pointed out to his friend that his tender prices were the pre-Blum prices plus 61%. See Osiatyński, *Collected Works of Michał Kalecki*, vol. I, 566.
16. Kalecki, ibid.
17. Despite its label, Keynes had only hinted at this effect in chapter 19 of his *General Theory*, the chapter in which he (Keynes) analysed the effects of changes in money wages, an analysis made overly complicated by Keynes's choice of the 'wage unit' as his unit of analysis (see Chapter 9). The 'Keynes effect' would arise when, with a given money supply, wages and prices go up or down. Such prices changes would cause proportionate increases or decreases in the demand for money for the purpose of transactions in the exchange of goods and services. The draining of additional money from the money market (to service transactions, in the case of an increase in wages and prices) or its redeposit in the money markets (in the case of a fall in prices and wages) was supposed to raise or lower the rate of interest in the money markets.
18. Kalecki, ibid.
19. Marjolin, 'Reflections on the Blum Experiment', 1938.
20. Ibid.
21. Ibid. See also Osiatyński, *Collected Works of Michał Kalecki*, vol. I, 564–5. Employment in France in 1936 was approximately three-quarters of its level in 1930.
22. Osiatyński, *Collected Works of Michał Kalecki*, vol. I, 565.
23. Letter of Mark Liddell Wehle to J. M. Keynes, dated 12 May 1938, in Keynes papers, EJ/1/5/173.
24. Keynes Papers, EJ/1/5/174.
25. Keynes Papers, EJ/1/5/175.
26. Keynes Papers, EJ/1/5/176 and EJ/1/5/177.
27. Keynes Papers, EJ/1/5/88.
28. Singer, 'Price Dispersion in Periods of Change', 1938.
29. Rockefeller Archive Center file.
30. Jewkes, *Wages and labour in the Lancashire cotton spinning industry*, 1935. See also Chapter 11. After the Second World War he became a fierce critic of

government economic interventionism and, from 1962 to 1964, was president of Hayek's Mont Pelerin Society.
31. Lerner, 'The Concept of Monopoly and the Measurement of Monopoly Power', 1934.
32. If marginal costs – that is, the cost of producing the last unit of output – are more or less constant, then the difference between the price and the marginal cost is more exactly equal to the profit margin. Constant marginal costs arise if firms are operating with excess capacity (that is, all factors of production are not being fully utilised), which Kalecki believed was the common situation in capitalism. See Kriesler, *Kalecki's Microanalysis*, 1987, ch. 4; F. S. Lee, *Post-Keynesian Price Theory*, ch. 7.
33. Kalecki, 'The Distribution of National Income', 1938.
34. Harrod, *The Trade Cycle*, 1936, 86–7. See also note 12 above.
35. Cf. Keynes, *Treatise on Money*, vol. 2, 1930, ch. 37.
36. Kriesler, *Kalecki's Microanalysis*, 1987, 3. See also Halevi, 'On the relationship between effective demand and income distribution in a Kaleckian framework', 1978.

11 Seeking Work Again

1. Rockefeller Archive Center file.
2. Alexander Loveday, who had lectured in economics at Cambridge from 1913 to 1915 and worked at the League of Nations in Geneva throughout the interwar period.
3. Kahn Papers, RFK/13/57/391.
4. John Condliffe, a distinguished New Zealand economist who was active in League of Nations discussions on international trade. In 1938 Condliffe was appointed to the London School of Economics as a lecturer in economics.
5. Dennis Robertson, who was assisting with research at the League of Nations in Geneva.
6. Kahn Papers, RFK/13/57/386, RFK/13/57/387.
7. Kahn Papers, RFK/13/57/386 RFK/13/57/387.
8. Kahn Papers, RFK/13/57/388, RFK/13/57/389.
9. Kahn papers, RFK 13/57/385.
10. Kahn Papers, RFK/13/57/383.
11. Kahn Papers, RFK/13/57/383, RFK/13/57/384.
12. This is probably Tinbergen's 'On the Theory of Business-Cycle Control', 1938.
13. Keynes's remarks, in January 1938, on Tinbergen confirm that his notoriously critical 1939 review of Tinbergen's work, 'Professor Tinbergen's Method', was no momentary aberration.
14. Kahn Papers, RFK/13/57/381, RFK/13/57/382. Kalecki's article in the *Economic Journal* was 'The Lesson of the Blum Experiment', 1938c.
15. Kahn Papers, RFK/13/57/380. The British Overseas Bank had been set up in 1919, on the initiative of the Prudential Assurance Company and a number of British banks. In 1920 the bank was involved in the formation of the Anglo-Polish Bank in Warsaw.
16. Ibid. Paul Einzig, a well-known financial journalist and regular contributor to the *Financial News*.

17. Kahn Papers, RFK/13/57/379.
18. Geoffrey Crowther, journalist and deputy editor of the *Economist*. In 1938 he succeeded Walter Layton as editor of the *Economist*.
19. Walter Layton, economic journalist and editor of the *Economist*.
20. Dudley Ward, liberal politician and banker, who had worked at the Treasury with Keynes and previously in naval counter-espionage.
21. Kahn Papers, ibid.
22. Kahn Papers, RFK/13/57/376, RFK/13/57/377.
23. Kahn Papers, RFK/13/57/378.
24. Kahn Papers, RFK/13/57/375.
25. Ibid.
26. Kahn papers, RFK/13/57/373, RFK/13/57/374.
27. Kahn Papers, RFK/13/57/372.
28. Kahn Papers, RFK/13/57/371.
29. Letter to Richard Kahn from Michał Kalecki, dated 6 September, in Kahn Papers, RFK/13/57/339.
30. See Chapter 10.
31. Kahn Papers, RFK/13/57/370.
32. Kahn Papers, RFK/13/57/355.
33. Ibid.
34. Kahn Papers, RFK/13/57/369.
35. Kahn Papers, RFK/13/57/367, RFK/13/57/368.
36. Hubert Henderson was a statistician and fellow of All Souls College. He was active in the Liberal Party and had helped to set up the Oxford Institute of Statistics. He had also established the Economists' Research Group at Oxford with Roy Harrod and James Meade.
37. Kahn Papers, RFK/13/57/357.
38. Now the Council for Assisting Refugee Academics.
39. Kahn Papers, RFK/13/57/358.
40. Kahn Papers, RFK/13/57/360, RFK/13/57/361.
41. Kahn papers, RFK/13/57/359.
42. Kahn Papers, RFK/13/57/357.
43. Kahn Papers, RFK/13/57/353, RFK/13/57/354.
44. 'A bright young economist with the inclination and the capability of teaching, disposed to present his candidature.' Kahn Papers RFK/13/57/350.
45. Ibid.
46. Ibid.
47. Kahn Papers, RFK/13/57/347, RFK/13/57/348.
48. Kahn Papers, ibid. Dennis Robertson was at the time Reader in Economics and Fellow of Trinity College, Cambridge. A student of Alfred Marshall at Cambridge, Robertson had published an early and well-regarded study of business fluctuations, *A Study of Industrial Fluctuation* (1915). He had been close to Keynes but was extremely critical of the latter's analysis in the *General Theory*. In a letter to Keynes, dated 24 August 1938, Austin Robinson observed that Robertson 'definitely dislikes and distrusts Kalecki, and I think distrusts the rest of us.' Keynes Papers, UA/5/4/163.
49. Letter to Richard Kahn from Michał Kalecki, dated 6 September, in Kahn Papers, RFK/13/57/339.
50. Kahn Papers, RFK/13/57/346.

12 The First Synthesis of Theory

1. Stone Papers, Letter to Kalecki, dated 27 November 1937. The letter was sent to Kalecki's former London address in Coram Street.
2. Stone Papers, Letter of Kalecki to Richard Stone, 13 December 1937.
3. Stone Papers, Letter of Richard Stone to Kalecki, 15 December 1937.
4. Brian Tew, who is thanked in a foreword dated June 1938 'for improving the style', told me that Kalecki had not written this dust jacket summary of the scope and significance of his work.
5. Kalecki here refers to volume II of *Capital.*
6. Kalecki, *Essays in the Theory of Economic Fluctuations*, 1939, 45–6. Kalecki was too modest to record his own almost identical solution to the saving 'gap' in *Próba teorii koniunktury* in 1933, and in 'A Macrodynamic Theory of Business Cycles' in 1935.
7. Kalecki, *Essays in the Theory of Economic Fluctuations*, 1939, 88–9.
8. Ibid., 91.
9. Kalecki had in mind sales or value-added taxes. See Chapter 10.
10. Ibid., 92.
11. Ibid., 107–8
12. Ibid., 112–13. The notion that the long-term rate of interest is the average of expected short-term interest rates is called the 'pure expectations' theory of interest rates.
13. Actually, the yields on corporate bonds are rather more volatile. Much of the stability of yields on government bonds is due to a stronger preference for them as 'risk-free' financial assets when business conditions are poor and to the lower issuance of new government bonds during an economic boom. The two factors, in the two different stages of the business cycle, combine to maintain a stable degree of scarcity of government bonds in the markets.
14. Ibid., 115.
15. Meade, 'A Simplified Model of Mr. Keynes's System', 1937; Hicks, 'Mr. Keynes and the Classics'; and Lange, 'The Rate of Interest and the Optimum Propensity to Consume', 1938.
16. Kalecki, ibid., 139.
17. Kuznets, 'Review of M. Kalecki *Essays*', 1939; Osiatyński, 1990, 512.
18. Kahn Papers, RFK/13/57/340.
19. Kahn Papers, RFK/13/57/339. Blanche Bronstein was Blanka Winawer, Kalecki's old friend from the institute (see Chapter 5).
20. Aslanbeigui and Oakes, 'The Theory Arsenal', 2002.
21. Keynes Papers, MM/5/43.
22. Keynes Papers, letter to Dennis Robertson, 22 May 1938, MM/5/41 and MM/5/42.
23. Keynes Papers, UA/5/4/163.
24. Letter of Austin Robinson to Keynes, 9 August 1938, UA/5/4/127.
25. Kahn Papers, RFK/13/57/346.
26. Keynes Papers, letter of Austin Robinson to Keynes, 9 August 1938, UA/5/4/134. M.H.D. is Maurice Dobb, P.S. is Piero Sraffa, E.A.G.R. is Austin Robinson. Kalecki thought highly of Rothbarth and wrote a warm tribute to him after Rothbarth died fighting in the war. Kalecki, 'The Work of Erwin Rothbarth', 1944.

27. Keynes Papers MM/1/4/6. Informal communication between Keynes and Hall was easy and convenient because the National Institute for Economic and Social Research was located at 32 Gordon Square, a short walk from Keynes's house at 46 Gordon Square.

13 Kalecki and His Myrmidons

Keynes's allusion to the Cambridge researchers is in a letter to Austin Robinson written on 10 May 1939; Keynes Papers, MM/1/4/17.

1. Keynes Papers, King's College Cambridge, N15/1/77.
2. The best known of these studies, one still largely underestimated among economists, was Schumpeter's massive *Business Cycles: A Theoretical, Historical and Statistical Analysis of the Capitalist Process*, undertaken at Harvard and published in 1939.
3. Keynes Papers, N15/1/17.
4. Keynes Papers, N15/1/81.
5. Liberal Industrial Enquiry, *Report*, 1928, 109.
6. Keynes Papers, N/15/1/82. The reference to theoretical and logical problems of definition seems to have been inserted by Keynes. In an unpublished note, written some time in 1939 and entitled 'The Process of Capital Formation', Keynes criticised the statistical experts in Geneva, advised by Robertson, for their 'illogical' treatment of saving and investment (Keynes Papers, UA/5/4/464–10). These criticisms were a background to his subsequent attack on Tinbergen in 'Professor Tinbergen's Method', 1939.
7. In addition to the list given by Jerzy Osiatyński in the Kalecki *Collected Works*, derived from documents obtained from Richard Stone (Osiatyński 1991, 525), there is a substantial paper, *Prime Costs and Proceeds etc. in Shipbuilding*, co-authored with G. A. Bauer.
8. Kahn Papers, RFK/5/1/55.
9. Kahn Papers, RFK/5/1/51.
10. Keynes Papers, N15/1/88–N15/1/106.
11. Keynes Papers, N15/1/128.
12. Kahn Papers, RFK/5/1/86.
13. Ibid.
14. Keynes Papers, UA/5/4/294
15. *Economic Journal*, March 1939.
16. Keynes Papers, UA/5/4/296 and UA/5/4/297.
17. Keynes Papers, UA/5/4/300.
18. Keynes Papers, UA/5/4/301, UA/5/4/302, UA/5/4/303.
19. Keynes Papers, UA/5/4/304, UA/5/4/305.
20. Keynes Papers, UA/5/4/306.
21. Keynes Papers, UA/5/4/307.
22. Keynes Papers, MM/1/4/59.
23. This seems to be a reference to the issue of the relationship between real wages and output to which Keynes had so recently devoted an article in the *Economic Journal*, 'Relative Movements of Real Wages and Output', 1939.
24. Kahn Papers, RFK/5/1/142–RFK/5/1/44.
25. Kahn Papers, RFK/5/1/146, RFK/5/1/147.

26. The other letter does not appear to be in the Kahn Papers. However, there is a document among Kahn's papers that is an exposition of Kalecki's degree of monopoly analysis in the form of a Marshallian short-period equilibrium output for a firm, with constant average costs. The explanation, over three and a half pages of single-spaced typing, appears to have been drawn up in an effort to explain to the other members of the research group what Kalecki's 'degree of monopoly' might mean in a Marshallian framework. Kahn Papers, RFK/5/1/138, RFK/5/1/141.
27. Kahn Papers, RFK/5/1/159–62.
28. Kahn Papers, RFK/5/1/164–169.
29. Keynes Papers, letters to Tracy Kittredge, 20 June 1939, UA/5/4/316–7; and to Gerald Shove, 22 July 1939, UA/5/4/443–447.
30. Keynes Papers, NIS/1/77 and NIS/1/79.

14 Shared Ideas amid Mutual Incomprehension

1. Robinson, 'Kalecki and Keynes', 1964.
2. See, e.g., Kahn, 'Some Notes on Liquidity Preference', 1972.
3. Robinson, ibid.
4. Kalecki Papers, PAN III 319/30.
5. Kalecki, *Selected Essays on the Dynamics of the Capitalist Economy 1933–1970*, vii.
6. De Vecchi, 'Keynes on Kalecki's Theory of Taxation', 2008.
7. Aslanbeigui and Oakes, 'The Theory Arsenal', 2002.
8. Robinson, 'Introduction' to M. Kalecki, *Studies in the Theory of the Business Cycle 1933–1939*, 1966.
9. Sawyer, 'Kalecki on Money and Finance', 2001.
10. Kalecki, 'Some Remarks on Mr. Keynes's Theory', 1936.
11. Robinson, 'Kalecki and Keynes', 1964, 337.
12. Keynes, 'The General Theory of Employment', 1937, 111.
13. Shackle, *The Years of High Theory*, 1967, 129.
14. Coddington, *Keynesian Economics*, 1983.
15. Tadeusz Kowalik pointed out to me that even in Keynes's lifetime, Joan Robinson promised to raise the issue of Kalecki's priority with Keynes but procrastinated. Kalecki told Kowalik that he eventually went himself to raise the matter with Keynes. But Keynes, like Joan Robinson later, merely treated this as confirmation of the 'scientific' character of his 'discovery'.
16. Kahn Papers, RFK/13/57/366.
17. Skidelsky, *John Maynard Keynes*, vol. 1, 1983.
18. Hutchison, 'The Philosophy and Politics of the Cambridge School', 1981.
19. Johnson, 'The Shadow of Keynes', 1977.
20. Sraffa, 'The Laws of Returns under Competitive Conditions', 1926.
21. Robinson, 'Introduction' to *Collected Economic Papers*, vol. 1, 1966.
22. Skidelsky, *John Maynard Keynes*, vol. 2, 1992, 290. James Tobin had expressed a similar view in Tobin, 'Review of Patinkin's *Keynes's Monetary Thought*', 1981.
23. Robinson, '"Imperfect Competition" Today', 1958, 241.
24. Keynes, 'The Pure Theory of Money. A Reply to Dr. Hayek', 1931; Sraffa, 'Dr. Hayek on Money and Capital', 1932; Kaldor, 'Professor Hayek and the Concertina-Effect', 1942.

25. Marshall, *Principles of Economics*, 1920, book V.
26. See, e.g., Keynes's definitions of income and saving in chapter 6 of the *General Theory*, 1936.
27. Leijonhufvud, *On Keynesian Economics and the Economics of Keynes*, 1968, 36.
28. Leontief 'Postulates: Keynes's *General Theory* and the classicists', 100.
29. Robinson, *Economic Philosophy*, 1962, 25–6.
30. Schumpeter, *Epochen der Dogmen- und Methodengeschichte*, 1912, 43–4. For Schumpeter, the other key system of determinate relations was of prices. Here he believed that the ultimate breakthrough had been achieved by Léon Walras, with all quantities supplied, and demand brought into general equilibrium by a unique system of prices. Schumpeter concluded that, along with the notion that marginal products determine the shares of 'various factors of production', '[T]he theory of price...really forms the basis for the formation of incomes' (ibid., 197). Although this view fits uneasily with the circular flow of income determination of aggregate incomes, Schumpeter does not seem to have considered the approaches to be incompatible.
31. Landau and Kalecki, 'Szacunek dochodu społecznego w r. 1929', 1934.
32. Kalecki, 'Three Systems', 1934, 218–19.
33. Kalecki, 'Some Remarks on Mr. Keynes's Theory', 1936, 230–1.
34. Notably in Joan Robinson's 'extension of Keynes's short-period analysis to long-run development'; Robinson, *The Accumulation of Capital*, 1956, vi.
35. Lange, 'Review of J. A. Schumpeter *Business Cycles*', 1941.
36. Marshall *Principles of Economics* 1920, 30.

Bibliography

Archives

The surviving papers of Michał Kalecki are held at the Polish Academy of Sciences (*Polska Akademia Nauk*). They are indicated in footnotes by the letters 'PAN' in the file number.
The Keynes Papers are in the Archive Centre of King's College, Cambridge.
The Joan Robinson Papers are in the Archive Centre of King's College, Cambridge.
The Richard Kahn Papers are in the Archive Centre of King's College, Cambridge.
The Nicholas Kaldor Papers are in the Archive Centre of King's College, Cambridge.
The Richard Stone Papers are in the Archive Centre of King's College, Cambridge.
The Austin Robinson Papers are in the Archive Centre of King's College, Cambridge.
The Piero Sraffa Papers are in the Wren Library of Trinity College, Cambridge.
The Maurice Dobb Papers are in the Wren Library of Trinity College, Cambridge.
Summaries of the entries in the Kalecki file of the Rockefeller Foundation are in the Archive Center of the Foundation in Sleepy Hollow, New York; copies in the author's possession.
Federal Bureau of Investigation, U.S. Department of Justice, file on 'Michael Kalecki': file number 65–58960; copy in the author's possession.
Copies of personal correspondence with Adela Kalecka and Blanka Winawer Bronstein are held by the author.

Kalecki's publications

Kalecki, M. (1927) 'Zbliżenie gospodarcze amerykańsko-rosyjskie a Polska'. *Przegląd Gospodarczy* 8/23, 732–4.

Kalecki, M. (1928) 'Konsekwencje gospodarcze zatargu angielsko-sowieckiego'. *Przegląd Gospodarczy* 9/1, 19–20.

Kalecki, M. (1929a) 'W sprawie aktywizacji bilansu handlowego' (On activating the balance of trade). *Przemysł i Handel* 10/30, 1295–7.

Kalecki, M. (1929b) 'Niemcy: opanowanie przemysłu przez kapitał zagraniczny' (Control over German industry by foreign capital). *Przemysł i Handel* 10/40, 1710–11.

Kalecki, M. (1929c) 'Europejski kryzys węglowy'. *Przemysł i Handel* 10/26, 1154–5.

Kalecki, M. (1929d) 'Koniunktury przemysłu włókienniczego'. *Przemysł i Handel* 10/43, 1823–6.

Kalecki, M. (1930a) 'Dynamika spożycia pieczywa pszennego oraz mięsa w Polsce'. *Koniunktura Gospodarcza* 3/6, 181–2.
Kalecki M. (1930b) 'Marża zarobkowa drewna tartego'. *Koniunktura Gospodarcza* 3/5, 157–8.
Kalecki, M. (1931a) 'Światowy kryzys finansowy'. *Przegląd Socjalistyczny* 1/1, 1–3.
Kalecki, M. (1931b) 'Konsekwencje dumpingu'. *Koniunktura Gospodarcza* 4/4, 108–112.
Kalecki, M. (1932a) 'Ivar Kreuger'. *Przegląd Socjalistyczny* 2/9, 5–6.
Kalecki, M. (1932b) 'Zmierzch Deterding'a' (The Fall of Deterding). *Przegląd Socjalistyczny* 2/12, 4–5.
Kalecki, M. (1932c) 'Kwitnące przedsiębiorstwo' (Flourishing enterprise). *Rynek Drzewny* 14/88, 2, initialled 'M.K.'.
Kalecki, M. (1932d) 'Ścianka jako element konstrukcyjny szkieletów żelbetonowych'. *Cement* 3/4, 89–91.
Kalecki, M. (1932e) 'Czy możliwe jest "kapitalistyczne" wyjście z kryzysu'. *Przegląd Socjalistyczny* 2/10, 1–3.
Kalecki, M. (1932f) 'Obniżka płac w czasie kryzysu'. *Przegląd Socjalistyczny* 2/2, 1–2.
Kalecki, M. (1932g) 'Podstawy konfliktu mandżurskiego'. *Przegląd Socjalistyczny* 2/2, 6–8.
Kalecki, M. (1932h) 'Uwagi o hitleryzmie i „sferach gospodarczych"'. *Przegląd Socjalistyczny* 2/3, 5–6.
Kalecki, M. (1932i) 'Wojna na Wschodzie'. *Przegląd Socjalistyczny* 2/5, 1–3.
Kalecki, M. (1932j) 'Przewidywania p. Keynes'a'. *Przegląd Socjalistyczny* 2/6, 4.
Kalecki, M. (1932k) 'Koniunktura a inflacja'. *Polska Gospodarcza* 13/48, 1411–15.
Kalecki, M. (1932l) 'Wpływ kartelizacji na koniunkturę'. *Polska Gospodarcza* 13/32, 932–3.
Kalecki, M. (1932m) 'Inflacja a Wojna'. *Przegląd Socjalistyczny* 2/13, 1–2.
Kalecki, M. (1932n) 'Na marginesie wydarzeń niemieckich'. *Przegląd Socjalistyczny* 2/15, 4–5.
Kalecki, M. (1933a) 'Nakręcanie koniunktury światowej'. *Polska Gospodarcza* 14/37, 1, 111–15.
Kalecki, M. (1933b) *Próba teorii koniunktury*. Warszawa: Instytut Badania Koniunktur Gospodarczych i Cen. In J. Osiatyński (ed.), *Collected Works of Michał Kalecki*, vol. I: *Capitalism: Business Cycles and Full Employment*. Oxford: Clarendon Press, 1990.
Kalecki, M. (1933c) 'Odpowiedź na „Uwagi krytyczne o jednej z matematycznych teorii koniunktury" A Rajchmana'. *Kwartalnik Statystyczny* no. 4.
Kalecki, M. (1934a) 'Trzy Układy'. *Ekonomista* no. 3, 54–70. Translated by Chester Adam Kisiel in J. Osiatyński (ed.), *Collected Works of Michał Kalecki*, vol. I: *Capitalism: Business Cycles and Full Employment*. Oxford: Clarendon Press, 1990.
Kalecki, M. (1934b) 'Odpowiedź'. *Ekonomista* no. 4, 97–100.
Kalecki, M. (1934c) 'Losy eksperymentów'. *Polska Gospodarcza* 15/21, 637–40.
Kalecki, M. (1934d) 'Koniunktura a dobrobyt'. *Polska Gospodarcza* 15/50 1531–4.
Kalecki, M. (1935a) Koniunktura a zbrojenie'. *Polska Gospodarcza* 16/22 701–3.
Kalecki, M. (1935b) 'A Macrodynamic Theory of Business Cycles'. *Econometrica* 3, no. 3, 327–44.

Kalecki, M. (1935c) 'Koniunktura a bilans płatniczy'. *Polska Gospodarcza* 16/45 1385–7.

Kalecki, M. (1935d) 'Eksperyment niemiecki'. *Polska Gospodarcza* 16/49 1574–6.

Kalecki, M. (1936a) 'Comments on the Macrodynamic Theory of Business Cycles'. *Econometrica* 4, no. 4, 356–60.

Kalecki, M. (1936b) 'Some Remarks on Keynes's Theory'. Translated by F. Targetti and B. Kinda-Hass in J. Osiatyński (ed.), *Collected Works of Michał Kalecki*, vol. I: *Capitalism: Business Cycles and Full Employment* Oxford: Clarendon Press, 1990.

Kalecki, M. (1936–7) 'A Theory of the Business Cycle'. *Review of Economic Studies* 4, no. 2. 77–97.

Kalecki, M. (1937a) 'The Principle of Increasing Risk'. *Economica* 4, no. 16, 440–6.

Kalecki, M. (1938a) 'A Comment on the "Principle of Increasing Risk": A Reply'. *Economica* 5, no. 20, 459–60.

Kalecki, M. (1938b) 'The Distribution of National Income'. *Econometrica* 6, 97–112.

Kalecki, M. (1938c) 'The Lesson of the Blum Experiment'. *Economic Journal* 48, no. 1, 26–41.

Kalecki, M. (1939) *Essays in the Theory of Economic Fluctuations*. London: Allen and Unwin.

Kalecki, M. (1944) 'The Work of Erwin Rothbarth'. *Review of Economic Studies* 27, no. 2, 121–2.

Kalecki, M. (1964a) 'Ludwik Landau – ekonomista i statystyk'. *Życie Gospodarcze* 19/11.

Kalecki, M. (1967) 'The Problem of Effective Demand with Tugan-Baranovski and Rosa Luxemburg', in Kalecki (1971).

Kalecki, M. (1971) *Selected Essays on the Dynamics of the Capitalist Economy 1933–1970*. Cambridge: Cambridge University Press.

Kalecki M. (1972) 'The Fascism of Our Times', in M. Kalecki, *The Last Phase in the Transformation of Capitalism*. New York: Monthly Review Press.

Kalecki, M., Kowalik, T., and Secomski, K. (1969) 'Ekonomia Edwarda Lipińskiego'. *Ekonomista* no. 2, 329–65.

Kalecki, M., and Landau, L. (1931) 'Szacunek rozmiarów ruchu inwestycyjnego'. *Koniunktura Gospodarcza* 4/11 276–85.

Kalecki, M., and Landau, L. (1932a) 'Szacunek rozmiarów ruchu inwestycyjnego w Polsce i wskaźnik kwartalny inwestycji'. *Prace Instytutu Badania Koniunktur Gospodarczych i Cen* 1/1, 7–10.

Kalecki, M., and Landau, L. (1932b) 'Handel włókienniczy w Polsce: zarys struktury'. *Prace Instytutu Badania Koniunktur Gospodarczych i Cen* 1/3–4, 30–42.

Kalecki, M., and Landau, L. (1934) 'Szacunek dochodu społecznego w. R. 1929'. Warszawa: Instytut Badania Koniunktur Gospodarczych i Cen.

Kalecki, M., and Landau, L. (1935) 'Dochód społeczny w r. 1933 i podstawy badań periodycznych nad zmianami dochodu'. Warszawa: Instytut Badania Koniunktur Gospodarczych i Cen.

Kalecki and Landau's calculations, in *Mały Rocznik Statystyczny 1937*.

Kalecki, M., and Wiśniewski, J. (1931) 'Eliminowanie sezonowości w odsetka bezrobocia'. *Koniunktura Gospodarcza* 4/3, 62–3.

Landau, L. and Kalecki, M. (1934) 'Szacunek dochodu społecznego w r. 1929'. *Prace Instytutu Badania Koniunktur Gospodarczych i Cen* no. 4, 97–100; published in English as 'An Estimate of Social Income in 1929', in Jerzy Osiatyński (ed.), *Collected Works of Michał Kalecki*, vol. VI: *Studies in Applied Economics 1927–1941*. Oxford: Clarendon Press, 1996.

Secondary sources

Asimakopoulos, A. (1989) 'Kalecki and Robinson', in M. Sebastiani (ed.), *Kalecki's Relevance Today*. New York: St. Martin's Press.

Aslanbeigui, N., and Oakes, G. (2002) 'The Theory Arsenal: Cambridge Circus and the Origins of the Keynesian Revolution'. *Journal of the History of Economic Thought* 24, no. 1, 5–37.

Assous, M. (2007) 'Kalecki's 1934 model vs. the IS-LM model of Hicks (1937) and Modigliani (1944)'. *European Journal of the History of Economic Thought* 14, no. 1, 97–118.

Chapple, S. (1991) 'Did Kalecki get there first? The race for the general theory'. *History of Political Economy* 23, 243–61.

Chilosi, A (1982) 'Breit, Kalecki and Hicks on the Term Structure of Interest Rates, Risk and the Theory of Investment', in M. Baranzini (ed.), *Advances in Economic Theory*. Oxford: Basil Blackwell.

De Vecchi, N. (2008) 'Keynes on Kalecki's Theory of Taxation: Contents Approved, Method Questioned'. *History of Political Economy* 40, no. 1, 163–82.

Feiwel, G. R. (1972) 'Introduction' to M. Kalecki, *The Last Phase in the Transformation of Capitalism*. New York: Monthly Review Press.

Feiwel, G. R. (1975) *The Intellectual Capital of Michał Kalecki: A Study in Economic Theory and Policy*. Knoxville: University of Tennessee Press.

Goodwin, R. M. (1989) 'Kalecki's Economic Dynamics: A Personal View', in M. Sebastiani (ed.), *Kalecki's Relevance Today*. New York: St. Martin's Press.

Kaldor, N. (1989) 'Personal Recollections on Michał Kalecki', in M. Sebastiani (ed.), *Kalecki's Relevance Today*. New York: St. Martin's Press.

Kowalik, T. (1964) 'Biography of Oskar Lange', in *On Political Economy and Econometrics: Essays in Honour of Oskar Lange*. Warszawa: Państwowe Wydawnictwo Naukowe.

Kowalik, T. (1964) 'Biography of Michał Kalecki', in *Problems of Economic Dynamics and Planning Essays in honour of Michał Kalecki*. Warszawa: Państwowe Wydawnictwo Naukowe.

Kowalik, T. (1992) *Historia Ekonomii w Polsce 1864–1950*. Wrocław: Zakład Narodowy Imienia Ossolińskich.

Kowalik, T. (undated) *Michał Kalecki: Kim był, jakim go znałem i podziwiałem*.

Kriesler, P. (1987) *Kalecki's Microanalysis: The Development of Kalecki's Analysis of Pricing and Distribution*. Cambridge: Cambridge University Press.

López, G. J., and Assous, M. (2010) *Michał Kalecki*. Basingstoke: Palgrave Macmillan, 2010.

Mott, T. (1982) 'Kalecki's Principle of Increasing Risk: The Role of Finance in the Post-Keynesian Theory of Investment Fluctuations'. Ph.D. diss., Stanford University, 1982.

Mott, T. (1985–6) 'Kalecki's Principle of Increasing Risk and the Relation among Mark-up Pricing, Investment Fluctuations, and Liquidity Preference'. *Economic Forum* XV, Winter, 65–76.

Nowicki, J. *Teoria Ekonomii II Rzeczypospolitej*. Warszawa: Książka i Wiedza.
Osiatyński, J. (ed.) (1979) *Dzieła*, vol. 1: *Kapitalizm Koniunktura i zatrudnienie*. Warszawa: Państwowe Wydawnictwo Ekonomiczne.
Osiatyński, J. (1987) 'Unemployment Equilibrium. A Note on Kalecki's and Keynes's Approach'. *Oeconomica Polona* no. 2, 259–62.
Osiatyński, J. (1988) *Michał Kalecki on A Socialist Economy*. London: Macmillan.
Osiatyński, J. (ed.) (1990) *Collected Works of Michał Kalecki*, vol. I: *Capitalism: Business Cycles and Full Employment* Oxford: Clarendon Press.
Osiatyński, J. (ed.) (1996) *Collected Works of Michał Kalecki*, vol. VI: *Studies in Applied Economics 1927–1941*. Oxford: Clarendon Press.
Osiatyński, J. (ed.) (1997) *Collected Works of Michał Kalecki*, vol. VII: *Studies in Applied Economics 1940–1967*. Oxford: Clarendon Press.
Sawyer, M.C. (1985) *The Economics of Michał Kalecki*. London: Macmillan
Sawyer, M.C. (2001) 'Kalecki on Money and Finance'. *European Journal of History of Economic Thought* 8, no. 4, 487–508.
Sebastiani, M. (ed.) (1989) *Kalecki's Relevance Today*. New York: St. Martin's Press.

Other sources

Aftalion, A. (1913) *Les Crises périodiques de surproduction*. 2 vols. Paris: Rivière.
Blobaum, R. E. (1995) *Rewolucja Russian Poland, 1904–1907*. Ithaca, NY, and London: Cornell University Press.
Breit, M. (1933) *Stopa procentowa w Polsce*. Kraków: Polska Akademia Umiejętności.
Breit, M. (1934) 'Przesunięcie kapitalizacji w Polsce w dobie przesilenia'. *Prace Instytutu Koniunktur Gospodarczych i Cen* 3/4, 2–13.
Breit, M. (1935a) 'Problemy rynku pieniężnego i kapitałowego na tle depresji'. *Prace Instytutu Koniunktur Gospodarczych i Cen* 4/2, 39–50.
Breit, M. (1935b) 'Konjunkturalny rozwój kredytu długoterminowego w Polsce'. *Prace Instytutu Koniunktur Gospodarczych i Cen* 4/3–4, 94–8.
Breit, M. (1935c) 'Ein Beitrag zur Theorie des Geld- und Kapitalmarktes'. *Zeitschrift für Nationalőkonomie* 6, no. 5, 1935.
Breit, M., and Lange, O. (1934) 'Droga do socjalistycznej gospodarki planowej', in *Gospodarka – polityka – taktyka – organizacja socjalizmu*. Warszawa: Spółdzielnia Wydawnicza Młodzieży Socjalistycznej. English translation: 'The Way to the Socialist Planned Economy'. *History of Economics Review* no. 37, Winter 2003, 51–70.
Buchanan, N. S., and Calkins, R. D. (1938) ''A Comment on Mr. Kalecki's "Principle of Increasing Risk"'. *Economica* 5, no. 20.
Coddington, A. C. (1983) *Keynesian Economics: The Search for First Principles*. London: Allen and Unwin.
Ellis, H. S. (1934) *German Monetary Theory 1905–1933*. Cambridge, MA: Harvard University Press.
Fogelson, S., and Rajchman, A. (1934) 'Jeszcze o jednej z matematycznych teorii koniunktury'. *Kwartalnik Statystyczny* no. 4.
Gąsiorowska, N. (ed.) (1957) *Źródła do dziejów Rewolucji 1905–1907 w okręgu Łódzkim*, vol. I, część 1. Warszawa: Książka i Wiedza.

Górecki, R. (1935) *Poland and Her Economic Development*. London: Allen and Unwin.
Grossman, H. (1929) *Das Akkumulations – Zusammenbruchsgesetz des kapitalistischen Systems (Zugleich eine Krisentheorie)*. Leipzig: C. L. Hirschfeld.
Halevi, J. (1978) 'On the relationship between effective demand and income distribution in a Kaleckian framework'. *Banca Nazionale del Lavoro Quarterly Review* no. 125, 167–90.
Hansson, B. (1982) *The Stockholm School and the Development of the Dynamic Method*. London: Croom Helm.
Harcourt, G. C. (1995) 'Joan Robinson 1903–1983'. *Economic Journal* 105, September, 1228–43.
Harcourt, G. C., and Kerr, P. (2009) *Joan Robinson*. Basingstoke: Palgrave Macmillan.
Harrod, R. (1936) *The Trade Cycle*. Oxford: Oxford University Press.
Hayek, F. A. (1929) *Geldtheorie und Konjunkturtheorie*. Translated into English by N. Kaldor. London: Routledge and Kegan Paul, 1933.
Hayek, F. A. (1932) 'Note on the Development of the Doctrine of *Forced Saving*'. *Quarterly Journal of Economics* 47, 123–33.
Hayek, F. A. (1935) *Prices and Production*. New York: Augustus M. Kelley edition, 1967.
Hicks, J. R. (1937) 'Mr. Keynes and the Classics'. *Econometrica* 5, April, 147–59.
Hilferding, R. (1910) *Finance Capital: A Study of the Latest Phase of Capitalist Development*. London: Routledge and Kegan Paul.
Hobson, J. A. (1926) *The Evolution of Modern Capitalism: A Study of Machine Production*. London: Allen and Unwin.
Hutchison, T. W. (1981) 'The Philosophy and Politics of the Cambridge School', in *The Politics and Philosophy of Economics: Marxians, Keynesians and Austrians*. Oxford: Basil Blackwell.
Jewkes, J. (1935) *Wages and Labour in the Lancashire Cotton Spinning Industry*. Manchester: Manchester University Press.
Johnson, H. G. (1977) 'The Shadow of Keynes'. *Minerva* XV, no. 2, Summer, 201–13. Republished in E. S. Johnson and H. G. Johnson, *The Shadow of Keynes: Understanding Keynes, Cambridge and Keynesian Economics*. Oxford: Basil Blackwell, 1978.
Kahn, R. F. (1972) 'Some Notes on Liquidity Preference', in *Selected Essays on Employment and Growth*. Cambridge: Cambridge University Press, 72–96.
Kalabiński, S., and F. Tych, F. (1969) *Czwarte powstanie czy pierwsza rewolucja, lata 1905–1907 na ziemiach polskich*. Warszawa: Wiedza powszechna.
Kaldor, N. (1942) 'Professor Hayek and the Concertina-Effect'. *Economica* IX, 359–82.
Keynes, J. M. (1919) *The Economic Consequences of the Peace*. London: Macmillan.
Keynes, J. M. (1930) *A Treatise on Money*, 2: *The Applied Theory of Money*, in *The Collected Writings of John Maynard Keynes*, vol. VI. Basingstoke: Macmillan, for the Royal Economic Society, 1971.
Keynes, J. M. (1931) 'The Pure Theory of Money. A Reply to Dr. Hayek'. *Economica* XI, no. 34, November, 389–403. Reprinted in D. Moggridge (ed.), *The Collected Writings of John Maynard Keynes*, vol. XIII: *The General Theory and After*, part I: *Preparation*. London: Macmillan, for the Royal Economic Society, 1973.

Keynes, J. M. (1932) Lecture, in the series 'The World's Economic Crisis and the Way of Escape', in D. Moggridge (ed.), *The Collected Writings of John Maynard Keynes*, vol. XXI: *Activities 1931–1939: World Crises and Policies in Britain and America*. London: Macmillan and Cambridge University Press, for the Royal Economic Society, 1982.

Keynes, J. M. (1936) *The General Theory of Employment, Interest and Money*. London: Macmillan.

Keynes, J. M. (1937) 'The General Theory of Employment'. *Quarterly Journal of Economics* February. Reprinted in *The Collected Writings of John Maynard Keynes*, vol. XIV: *The General Theory and After*, part II: *Defence and Development*, edited by Donald Moggridge. London: Macmillan, for the Royal Economic Society, 1973.

Keynes, J. M. (1939) 'Relative Movements of Real Wages and Output'. *Economic Journal* XXXXIX, March, 34–51.

Keynes, J. M. (1939) 'Professor Tinbergen's Method'. *Economic Journal* XXXXIX, September, 558–68.

Keynes, J. M. (1956) *Ogólna teoria zatrudnienia, procentu i pieniądza*. Warszawa: Państwowe Wydawnictwo Naukowe. Translation by Michał Kalecki and Stanisław Rączkowski of Keynes (1936).

Keynes, J. M. (1979) *The Collected Writings of John Maynard Keynes*, vol. XXIX: *The General Theory and After: A Supplement*, edited by Donald Moggridge. London: Macmillan and Cambridge University Press, for the Royal Economic Society.

Keynes, J. M. (1982) *The Collected Writings of John Maynard Keynes*, vol. XXI: *Activities 1931–1939: World Crises and Policies in Britain and America*, edited by Donald Moggridge. London: Macmillan, for the Royal Economic Society.

Keynes, J. M. (1983) *The Collected Writings of John Maynard Keynes*, vol. XII: *Economic Articles and Correspondence: Investment and Editorial*, edited by Donald Moggridge. London: Macmillan, for the Royal Economic Society.

Koszutska Wera-Kostrzewa, M. (1913a) 'Bezrobocie Łódzkie'. *Z walki i pracy*, June, in *Pisma i Przemówienia*, vol. 1: *1912–1918*. Warszawa: Książka I Wiedza, 1961.

Koszutska Wera-Kostrzewa, M. (1913b) 'Kartele, trusty i związki przedsiębiorców'. *Kuźnia* 26 January, in *Pisma i Przemówienia*, vol. 1: *1912–1918*. Warszawa: Książka i Wiedza, 1961.

Kuznets, S. (1939) 'Review of M. Kalecki, *Essays in the Theory of Economic Fluctuations*'. *American Economic Review* 29, December, 804–6.

Laidler, D. (1991) *The Golden Age of the Quantity Theory of Money*. Princeton NJ: Princeton University Press.

Lange, O. (1938) 'The Rate of Interest and the Optimum Propensity to Consume'. 5, February, 12–32.

Lange, O. (1941a) 'Review of J. A. Schumpeter, *Business Cycles*.' *Review of Economics and Statistics* 23, no. 4, 191.

Lange, O. (1941b) 'Review of M. Kalecki, *Essays in the Theory of Economic Fluctuations*'. *Review of Political Economy* no. 2, 279–85.

Laramie, A. J., and Mair, D. (2000) *A Dynamic Theory of Taxation: Integrating Kalecki into Modern Public Finance*. Cheltenham: Edward Elgar.

League of Nations. (1931) *The Course and Phases of the World Economic Depression: Report Presented to the Assembly of the League of Nations*. Geneva.

Lee, F. S. (2004) *Post-Keynesian Price Theory*. Cambridge: Cambridge University Press.

Leijonhufvud, A. (1968) *On Keynesian Economics and the Economics of Keynes: A Study in Monetary Theory*. New York: Oxford University Press.
Leontief, W. (1948) 'Postulates: Keynes's *General Theory* and the Classicists', in S. Harris (ed.), *The New Economics*. New York: Knopf. In W. Leontief, *Essays in Economics Theories and Theorizing*, vol. 1. Oxford: Basil Blackwell.
Lerner, A. P. (1934) 'The Concept of Monopoly and the Measurement of Monopoly Power'. *Review of Economic Studies* June, 1, 157–75.
Liberal Industrial Inquiry. (1928) *Report: Britain's Industrial Future*. London: Benn, 1928.
Lindahl, E. (1939) *Studies in the Theory of Money and Capital*. London: Allen and Unwin.
Lipiński, E. (1926) 'O badaniu koniunktury gospodarczej'. *Przegląd Gospodarczy* 8/18, 873.
Luxemburg, R. (1898) *Die Industrielle Entwicklung Polens*. Published as *Rozwój przemysłu w Polsce*. Warszawa: Książka i Wiedza, 1957.
Luxemburg, R. (1951) *The Accumulation of Capital*. London: Routledge and Kegan Paul.
Marjolin, R. (1938) 'Reflections on the Blum Experiment'. *Economica* 5, no. 18, May, 177–91.
Marshall, A. (1920) *Principles of Economics*. London: Macmillan.
Marx, K. H. (1957) *Capital*, vol. 1. London: Dent.
Marx, K. H. (1974a) *Capital: A Critique of Political Economy*, vol. 2: *The Process of Circulation of Capital*. London: Lawrence and Wishart.
Marx, K. H. (1974b) *Capital: A Critique of Political Economy*, vol. 3: *The Process of Capitalist Production as a Whole*. London: Lawrence and Wishart.
'The Match King'. (2007) *The Economist* 22 December, 113–15.
Meade, J. E. (1937) 'A Simplified Model of Mr. Keynes's System'. *Review of Economic Studies* 4, February, 98–107.
Myrdal, G. (1939) *Monetary Equilibrium*. London: William Hodge.
Neuman, A. M. (1934) 'O „Trzech Układach"'. *Ekonomista* no. 4, 94–7.
Ohlin, B. (1937) 'Some Notes on the Stockholm Theory of Savings and Investment'. *Economic Journal* XLVII, part I, March, 53–69; part II, June, 221–40.
Pigou, A. C. (1920) *The Economics of Welfare*. London: Macmillan.
Prażmowska, A. J. (2010) *Poland A Modern History*. London I. B. Tauris.
Rajchman, A. (1933) 'Uwagi krytyczne o jednej z matematycznych teorii koniunktury'. *Kwartalnik Statystyczny* no. 203.
Robertson, D. H. (1915) *A Study of Industrial Fluctuations*. London: P. S. King.
Robinson, J. V. R. (1936) 'Disguised Unemployment'. *Economic Journal* June.
Robinson, J. V. R. (1956) *The Accumulation of Capital*. London: Macmillan.
Robinson, J. V. R. (1958) '"Imperfect Competition" today'. *Il Mercurio* December. Reprinted in the original English in *Collected Economic Papers*, vol. 2. Oxford: Basil Blackwell, 1964.
Robinson, J. V. R. (1962) *Economic Philosophy*. London: Watts.
Robinson, J. V. R. (1964) 'Kalecki and Keynes', in T. Kowalik (ed.), *Problems of Economic Dynamics and Planning, Essays in Honour of Michał Kalecki*. Warszawa: Państwowe Wydawnictwo Naukowe.
Robinson, J. V. R. (1966a) 'Introduction' to M. Kalecki, *Studies in the Theory of the Business Cycle 1933–1939*. Oxford: Basil Blackwell.

Robinson, J. V. R. (1966b) *Collected Economic Papers*, vol. 1. Oxford: Basil Blackwell.

Robinson, J. V. R. (1977) 'Michał Kalecki on the Economics of Capitalism'. *Oxford Bulletin of Economics and Statistics* 39, 7–18.

Samuś, P. (2001) 'The Bund Organisation in Łódź', in J. Jacobs (ed.), *Jewish Politics in Eastern Europe: The Bund at 100*. Basingstoke: Palgrave.

Schumpeter, J. A. (1912) *Epochen der Dogmen- und Methodengeschichte*. Tübingen: J. C. B. Mohr (Paul Siebeck) Verlag. English translation by R. Aris, published as *Economic Doctrine and Method: An Historical Sketch*. London: Allen and Unwin, 1954.

Schumpeter, J. A. (1939) *Business Cycles: A Theoretical, Historical, and Statistical Analysis of the Capitalist Process*. New York: McGraw-Hill.

Schumpeter, J. A. (1954) *History of Economic Analysis*. New York: Oxford University Press.

Shackle, G. L. S. (1967) *The Years of High Theory: Invention and Tradition in Economic Thought 1926–1939*. Cambridge: Cambridge University Press.

Singer, H. W. (1938) 'Price Dispersion in Periods of Change'. *Economic Journal* 48, December, 658–73.

Skidelsky, R. (1983) *John Maynard Keynes*, vol. 1: *Hopes Betrayed 1883–1920*. London: Macmillan.

Skidelsky, R. (1992) *John Maynard Keynes*, vol. 2: *The Economist as Saviour 1920–1937*. London: Macmillan.

Sraffa, P. (1926) 'The Laws of Returns under Competitive Conditions'. *Economic Journal* XXVI no. 4, 535–50.

Sraffa, P. (1932) 'Dr. Hayek on Money and Capital'. *Economic Journal* 42, March, 42–53.

Steindl, J. (1965) *Random Processes and the Growth of Firms: A Study of the Pareto Law*. London: Charles Griffin.

Steindl, J. (1989) 'Reflections on Kalecki's Dynamics', in M. Sebastiani (ed.), *Kalecki's Relevance Today*. New York: St. Martin's Press.

Tinbergen, J. (1931) 'Ein Schiffbauzyklus'. *Weltwirtschaftliches Archiv* 34/2, 152–64.

Tinbergen, J. (1938) 'On the Theory of Business-Cycle Control'. *Econometrica* 6, no. 1, 22–39.

Tobin, J. (1981) 'Review of Patinkin's *Keynes's Monetary Thought*'. *Journal of Political Economy* 89, no. 1, 204–7.

Tugan-Baranovsky, M. I. (1894) *Promyshlennye Krizisy v Sovremennoi Anglii*.

Varga, E. (1935) *The Great Crisis and Its Political Consequences: Economics and Politics 1928–1934*. London: Modern Books.

Wicksell, K. (1898) *Interest and Prices*. London: Macmillan, 1936.

Wicksell, K. (1934) *Lectures on Political Economy*, vol. 1: *General Theory*. London: Routledge and Kegan Paul.

Winawer, B. (1932) 'Wywóz wyrobów przemysłowych w latach 1930 i 1931'. *Prace Instytutu Badania Konjunktur Gospodarczych i Cen* zeszyt 2, 25–31.

Zawadzki, W. (1936) 'Nowa teoria pieniądza Keynesa'. *Ekonomista* no. 3.

Index

Lightning Source UK Ltd.
Milton Keynes UK
UKHW021609280120
357745UK00005B/251

9 781349 303229